HARRIETT M. BARTLETT

social work practice in the health field

NATIONAL ASSOCIATION OF SOCIAL WORKERS
2 PARK AVENUE, NEW YORK, NEW YORK 10016

PRICE: $3.50

HV
687
.B35

Library of Congress Catalog Card No.: 61–17630

Copyright 1961
NATIONAL ASSOCIATION OF SOCIAL WORKERS
Printed in the United States of America

foreword

The Committee on Medical Social Work Practice, Medical Social Work Section, National Association of Social Workers, and its counterpart in the predecessor organization have a long history of studying medical social work practice in order to understand it better and continuously improve it. In so doing, the committee has found it useful to examine periodically what medical social work is currently thinking, learning, and doing. The most recent of these examinations, undertaken by Harriett M. Bartlett at the request of the committee, is set forth in the present volume, *Social Work Practice in the Health Field*. It is most fitting that Miss Bartlett was selected for this assignment, since she is the author of two earlier volumes dealing with the content of medical social work practice. These volumes were mainly concerned with casework practice. The present volume, reflecting some changes in philosophy in all social work, presents a many-faceted view of medical social work practice, in which casework takes its proper place. Moreover, the presentation offers a conceptual approach which is applicable and useful for analyzing social work practice in any field.

Thus, the present volume is a valuable contribution to both medical social work and social work as a whole. It describes one field of practice within the framework of a working definition of social work practice and suggests the possibility that other fields may be similarly analyzed, for comparison. From such analyses may come definition of the basic core of all social work practice and identification of the significant and appropriate differences in the practice in the various fields. For these reasons, *Social Work Practice in the Health Field* can be hailed as one more milestone in the professional growth of social work practice.

MARGARET L. SCHUTZ

Chairman, Practice Committee,
Medical Social Work Section, NASW

preface

Studies of the practice of medical social work, initiated in the early twenties, succeeded each other in a steady stream until 1940. Then the momentum ceased. At the time, we thought this was because of war pressures; but as we look back now, we can see that the real explanation was to be found in our conceptual thinking. The casework frame of reference, which had been sufficient to cover hospital practice, could not encompass the wide array of activities into which social workers entered in public health. The dropping of the "specializations" from the generic curriculum left the social workers in the health and other fields without a base, since no equivalent orderly system of thinking had developed in practice. After nearly a decade of groping and confusion, some directions of thinking emerged from the newly united profession that offer an approach for analyzing social work practice. This approach gives promise of enabling us to understand the fields of practice and their particular significance in social work as never before.

In picking up again the study of medical social work practice—now more properly described as social work practice in the health field—I have made a beginning in developing these new ideas, first as they might be used in any field and, second, as they apply in one particular field. The momentum is again established and the stream of studies in medical social work should continue as before.

Many persons inside and outside medical social work have contributed to this monograph and I wish to express appreciation to them all. I owe special appreciation to the members of the Committee on Social Work Practice of the Medical Social Work Section, National Association of Social Workers, who first expressed the need for such a presentation and supported me in its accomplishment. The chairman, Margaret L. Schutz, made a major contribution through review of the manuscript in all its stages and through unswerving encouragement of the writer toward completion of the project. The following persons from the field of medical social work acted as consultants: Dr. Ruth Cooper, School of Social Welfare, University of California (Berkeley); Eleanor E. Cockerill, School of Social Work, University of Pittsburgh; Mary L. Poole, Social Service Department, Hospital of the University of Pennsylvania; Elizabeth P. Rice, Harvard School of Public Health; Margaret L. Schutz, George Warren Brown School of Social Work, Washington University; and Addie Thomas, The National Foundation. All read and commented on the first draft. Dr. Cooper, Miss Rice, and Miss Schutz also commented on sections of the second draft. Ruth D. Abrams, Bess S. Dana, and Theodate H. Soule read and discussed sections of the manuscript involving special problems.

I am indebted to Dr. Stanley Cobb and Dr. James Howard Means, both of Harvard Medical School and the Massachusetts General Hospital, for reading and discussing Chapters VII and VIII, which contain the greatest amount of medical material. Dr. Jean A. Curran, Bingham Associates Fund, Boston, gave counsel regarding the values of medicine and social work. Dr. Stanley H. King, Harvard University Health Service, read materials and discussed the use of social science concepts by the health professions, including medical social workers. I owe a special debt of gratitude to Dr. William E. Gordon, School of Social Work, Washington University, who through our joint participation in several professional committees and through individual conversations has helped me toward better understanding of the nature of professional knowledge and thinking.

Illustrative material and valuable ideas were contributed by Edith S. Alt, Catherine M. Casey, Florence E. Cyr, Dr. Kurt Reichert, Elinor Stevens, and Hyman J. Weiner. I am grateful for permission to use illustrative materials from the practice and

PREFACE

research of the following agencies: Harvard School of Public Health, Los Angeles County Health Department, Massachusetts Department of Public Health, Massachusetts Eye and Ear Infirmary, Massachusetts General Hospital, New York State Department of Health, and University Hospitals of Cleveland.

My conversations with Ida M. Cannon and Kate McMahon during the preparation of the monograph constantly deepened my understanding of medical social work. I am grateful to others, physicians and social workers, who have given help toward clarification of theory and goals through informal discussion. The editorial work of Stella Bloch Hanau, based on sensitive understanding of the material, enabled me to achieve better organization and clearer expression of the essential ideas in the monograph. Finally, I wish to express my great appreciation to Jessie B. MacDonald, who typed both drafts of the manuscript.

HARRIETT M. BARTLETT

Cambridge, Massachusetts
June 1961

contents

    FOREWORD   3
    PREFACE   5

social work practice

1   AN APPROACH TO ANALYZING SOCIAL WORK PRACTICE   13
    Background of medical social work—Underlying concepts—Frames of reference

2   ESSENTIAL ELEMENTS OF SOCIAL WORK PRACTICE   22
    Working definition of social work practice—Implications of the Working Definition

the health field

3   CHARACTERISTICS OF THE HEALTH FIELD   31
    Scope of the health field—Problem of central concern, health and disease—System of organized services—Knowledge, values, and methods—Sociocultural attitudes—Responses and behavior of patients

social work and the health field

4   PLACING SOCIAL WORK IN THE HEALTH FIELD   47
    Responsibility and contribution of social work in the health field—Range of social work activities—Operation of the social service department—Problems of integrating professional services—Medical care programs—New trends in medical care—Implications of new trends

5   SOCIAL WORK IN MULTIDISCIPLINE CARE OF THE PATIENT   72
    Collaboration with the physician—Some characteristics of the social work role

characteristics of social work practice in the health field

6   VALUES IN SOCIAL WORK AND MEDICINE   95

Ultimate values—Problems in defining values—Middle-range values

7   KNOWLEDGE FROM THE HEALTH FIELD   103

Knowledge and concepts relating to health and disease—Preventive approach—Rehabilitation approach—Knowledge and concepts from medical care

8   KNOWLEDGE FROM MEDICAL SOCIAL WORK   130

Early theory in medical social work—Concepts from general social work—Focus of medical social work—Classification of medical-social problems—Concepts derived from practice—Medical-social approach to community health programs—Social worker's own attitudes and responses—Concluding comment

9   SOCIAL WORK METHODS   174

Assessment of medical-social situations—Social casework in the health field—Social work with groups—Program planning as a medical social work activity

10   METHODS CHARACTERISTIC OF THE HEALTH FIELD   225

The teamwork process—Social work in multidiscipline practice—Some aspects of multidiscipline practice in public health—Social work consultation in the health field—Recording as a tool in multidiscipline practice—Participation in teaching of medical students and others—Participation in multidiscipline research

implications for practice

11   IMPLICATIONS AND TRENDS   265

Characteristic activities of social workers in the health field—Significant variations between fields—Implications for ongoing practice—Seeking new ways—A long view

appendix

    AGENCIES IN THE HEALTH FIELD   283

social work practice

1

an approach to analyzing social work practice

There are times when any professional group needs to take a comprehensive view of its practice. Social work in the health field is at such a point. While various facets of its practice have been studied, no inclusive description has been undertaken. What is planned in this first step toward an over-all view is neither a broad survey nor an intensive research study, but an orderly comprehensive analysis that will attempt to get at the essentials of social work practice in the health field.

Some persons hesitate to analyze current practice for fear that such analysis will crystallize concepts in a rigid manner that would limit future growth. Fuller understanding, properly used, leads to greater realization of potentialities and more effective planning of service. We know that our practice is uneven and have been working toward clarification of the less understood parts; but this is a slow process and we cannot wait until work on each separate piece is completed. Furthermore, we find that we need inclusive frames of reference within which the pieces can be placed in clearer relationship to each other. This analysis is, accordingly, an effort to attain a fuller understanding of our practice, to identify what appear to be its strengths and limitations, to note the trends and the promising growing points—in order to assess better its potentialities for the future and what we can do to bring them to fruition.[1]

The primary aim is to attain a *comprehensive view* and to suggest *directions of thinking* through which practice can be better understood. This means the identification of significant characteristics, the use of clarifying concepts, the pointing out of meaningful relationships, and the search for appropriate frameworks for systematizing knowledge about practice. It also means the highlighting of unsolved issues and the pointing out of areas urgently calling for attention.

It is the viewpoint of this discussion that social work is at a transitional stage in which new directions of thought and new perspectives are needed but that the thinking should be left open-ended, not tied into inclusive logical systems. We need to understand a great deal more about the nature of social work through direct examination of its practice, which includes the way social workers think, before we are ready to systematize and solidify our theory. The pattern of thinking in this monograph is, therefore, purposely tentative. It is based upon examination of practice and kept as closely related to practice as possible.

BACKGROUND OF MEDICAL SOCIAL WORK

The current and future practice of social work in the health field must be understood in terms of its past experience.[2] There is a

---

[1] It is recognized that value judgments are involved in such analysis and assessment. They are also present when we drift along without analysis. We make progress by clarifying which of our judgments and actions are based on values and which on knowledge.

[2] The practice under discussion is preferably described as "social work practice in the health field." Because of the length of this phrase, the older term "medical social work" and also the term "medical social worker" are used as needed for readability of the text. No distinction is intended in the use of these terms; all have the same connotation.

rather full literature covering the first half-century of medical social work, since its beginning in 1905. This professional group has been characterized by persistent effort to analyze its functions and improve its practice. The present discussion should be regarded as resting upon the earlier literature and taking its place in it.[3]

The historical growth of social work in the health field can be characterized as a spiraling type of movement, in which periods of uncertainty and fluidity alternated with those of clarity and control. The early developmental period has been described as follows:

> During the first thirty years, medical social work grew slowly but steadily in one direction spreading from one hospital to another over the country, demonstrating its service to medical staffs, exploring the social problems of illness and medical care, and moving toward a definition of its professional role. In the early days, social workers' methods, though undeveloped, were effective because of the relative simplicity of the situations in which they operated. Medicine and nursing were focused on the physical care of the patient —psychiatry had not developed in this country—so that social workers almost alone carried the responsibility for bringing the social viewpoint into the hospital. This was done by demonstrating actual cases to one physician after another. The contrast between the physician's organic focus and the social worker's concern with social factors was so marked that the social worker's role appeared significant and distinctive.
>
> As time went on, the professional status of hospital social work became well established through the formation of a professional organization and through a series of studies and formulations relating to education and practice. With the development of psychiatry and psychoanalysis, psychosomatic medicine was born and social casework became a more refined instrument. Psychiatric social work separated from medical social work and became a new field. Hospital administrators co-operated with medical social workers in active exploration of the social component in "patient management." Thus, just before World War II, it was possible to arrive at a clear definition of social casework as the central function

---

[3] For full understanding of this discussion, the most important studies and reports of the past should be known to the reader. Reference will be made to as many as possible in the text.

of a hospital social service department, to identify the major skills of the competent professional caseworker, and to describe the activities of a department offering such service.[4]

In the late forties and early fifties, following the establishment of the social security program and World War II, the rate of social change accelerated, stimulating a surge of new thinking and activity in social work and medicine. Social and psychiatric concepts were being incorporated into medical education and practice. Psychologists and social scientists appeared in the hospital. Medical social workers were moving out into the expanding public health programs, where they were concerned with large population groups. This changing practice and this activity of many professions in the area in which social work had formerly functioned alone inevitably produced a sense of pressure and uncertainty among medical social workers. New questions arose regarding their professional role both inside and outside the hospital.

By the mid-fifties there was evidence that medical social work was moving into a new phase. The various parts of the practice were emerging with sufficient clarity so that the scope of its potential service in the health field could at last be visualized. Thus the time is now ripe for clarification and redefinition of practice at this new level. Concurrent developments in social work and medicine confirm this judgment. The profession of social work, after a long period of fragmentation, is now becoming united. Concepts regarding basic social work practice are being formulated. Medicine and public health are making remarkable progress, not only in scientific knowledge and effective methodology but also in incorporation of psychosocial concepts and definition of positive health goals.

In order to relate its own activities to present-day social work and medicine, medical social work needs to understand better the knowledge and principles growing out of more than fifty years of experience. Questions are being insistently asked as to how to use knowledge from past and current experience to move toward

---

[4] Harriett M. Bartlett, *Fifty Years of Social Work in the Medical Setting* (New York: National Association of Social Workers, 1957), pp. 15–16.

future goals, how to apply the strengths and competence of this professional group to further more effective service. To make such application intelligently, a view of the whole activity, in its full range and potential, is necessary.

UNDERLYING CONCEPTS

How can one approach the analysis of social work practice in the health field in such a manner as to get beyond the limitations of the past and incorporate the new thinking in the profession? Formerly studies of medical social work and other fields were too separated from one another. The result was fragmentation and overemphasis on "specialization," which was never clearly defined. Now the analysis of social work practice in any field can be better related to a concept of the total profession. Progress in unifying the profession and in identifying its common elements makes it possible to relate the parts to each other and to the whole.

In setting out to analyze social work practice in the health field, the writer found no suitable approaches or methods at hand for accomplishing this task. It was therefore necessary to experiment with new approaches. In thus working on the health field, a series of concepts and a method of applying them developed which are equally applicable to all fields. The reader is referred to *Analyzing Social Work Practice by Fields,* which presents the approach in full and should be read first.[5] The present monograph, which is a comprehensive analysis of social work practice in the health field, is to be regarded as a demonstration and application of the general approach presented in that monograph. Only the main points in the approach are summarized here.

First, the concept of social work and social work practice employed in this discussion should be made clear. Every society meets the major problems of living through developing social institutions that vary from culture to culture. Social work is to be perceived as a social institution in our society, like medicine and

---

[5] Harriett M. Bartlett, *Analyzing Social Work Practice by Fields* (New York: National Association of Social Workers, 1961).

education. Social work is not engaged merely in supplementing the activities of other professions. It makes its own substantive contribution to society, a contribution that is consistent and ongoing even though the specific areas of activity may shift in response to social change. Social work is concerned with the social functioning of individuals and groups in relation to the various problems of living. The wide scope of its concern makes it appear different from other professions, which customarily focus upon one particular area.

Social work is to be distinguished from social welfare. Social work is the profession, while social welfare is the broad system of agencies and programs which meets the welfare needs of society and within which social work operates.

Implicit in this general concept of social work is an assumption of greater self-direction for the profession than has ordinarily been recognized in the past. The profession develops through the action of social forces and increasingly becomes a social force itself, capable of generating its own energy and having significant impact upon society.

Social work services are customarily given within two types of social structure. The agencies in which it functions may be social work agencies, staffed mainly by social workers, or they may be operated under other auspices. Family and child welfare are examples of the first category, and social work in health, education, and corrections are examples of the second. From the social work viewpoint, the two types are usually described as "primary" (social work) and "secondary" (non-social work) settings.

The patterns of practice in social work and its perception of its own practice have gone through several phases in recent decades. Because social work in its middle period grew and expanded through practice in many different fields, there was for a considerable time an emphasis on differences, which led to a confused idea of "specialization." In reaction against this trend, generic principles were emphasized and incorporated in a basic professional curriculum. The next logical step, their application in specific practice, was not, however, carried through. The generic-specific concept was only partially defined. This lag in conceptualization and theory development retarded analysis of practice. Recently there has been recognition that social work actually is practiced in various fields and that this appears to be one of its definite characteristics. In 1957 the Council on Social Work Education requested nine fields of social work practice to undertake a preliminary examination of their practice, as a first step toward determining what content from each field is needed by all social workers and what remains as essential primarily for practitioners in the particular field. Since the concept of a "field of practice" is more comprehensive and useful than the earlier idea of "setting," it is employed here. Its meaning will be clarified as the analysis proceeds.

FRAMES OF REFERENCE

The writer is proposing one approach to the problem of describing social work practice in any particular field. This approach requires three frames of reference. They are set forth in diagrammatic form on page 20, and are fully described in *Analyzing Social Work Practice by Fields*.

The first frame of reference provides for analysis of the *essential elements in social work practice*. These are the foundation of all social work practice. Since the profession has not yet identified or arrived at a consensus regarding the essentials of its practice, at the present stage of development this basic frame of reference should be made explicit as the starting point for any specific analysis. Otherwise the assumptions on which the analysis rests will not be recognized. If there is eventual agreement regarding the essentials, then they can be assumed and such explication will not be necessary.

The second frame of reference provides for analysis of the *general characteristics of the particular field as distinguished from the operations of the professional social worker in that field*. This analysis is important in order to see clearly what social work can contribute and how it is influenced by the environment.

The third frame of reference provides for the *application*

frames of reference for analysis of social work practice in any particular field

1

ESSENTIAL ELEMENTS in Social Work Practice

Value
Purpose
Knowledge
Sanction
Method

(NASW Working Definition of Social Work Practice)*

2

CHARACTERISTICS of the Particular Field
(such as Health or Child Welfare)

Problem (condition) of central concern.
System of organized services.
Body of knowledge, values and methods.
Sociocultural attitudes (in society).
Characteristic responses and behavior of persons served.

3

SOCIAL WORK PRACTICE in any Particular Field

Application of the essentials of social work practice in any particular field. Characteristics of the resulting social work practice.

*Formulated by the Commission on Social Work Practice, National Association of Social Workers.

of the essentials of social work practice in the particular field and the identification of the characteristics of this specific social work practice. This process involves several facets and may eventually come to include subframeworks.[6]

This monograph will make use of these three frames of reference in analyzing social work practice in the health field.[7]

---

[6] *Ibid.,* p. 18.

[7] In 1952 Mary L. Hemmy, Margaret L. Schutz, and the author prepared a comprehensive study outline for the Committee on Medical Social Work Practice, American Association of Medical Social Workers, that had to do with "questions to be answered and assumptions to be tested by study of medical social practice." This outline, which contained over fifty separate propositions, was concerned with the following questions: (1) What needs call medical social work into being; (2) What is its characteristic service; (3) How does it achieve its goals; (4) What are the major components in the ways medical social work achieves its goals; (5) What are the characteristics of the medical setting; (6) What are the characteristic services of other professions in the health team; (7) What are the characteristics of multidiscipline service; (8) Assuming teamwork is a process in that service, what is teamwork, and what is the role of medical social work in teamwork; (9) What are the effects of setting on the social work process?

This study outline had a similar purpose and covered much of the same material as the three frames of reference, but focused directly on medical social work. At that time no general formulation relating to social work practice was available.

2

essential elements of social work practice

The analysis of social work practice in any particular field, such as the health field, rests upon the essential elements in social work practice. These elements are set forth within the first frame of reference, insofar as this is possible at the present time. The analysis is based upon the *Working Definition of Social Work Practice*,[1] developed by the Commission on Social Work Practice of the National Association of Social Workers.[2] When the commission was established within the new professional association in the mid-fifties, it offered a much-needed channel, previously lacking, through which various interests and efforts toward examination of practice could be brought together. A comprehensive view of practice and consistent, cumulative analysis and definition then became possible.

---

[1] Harriett M. Bartlett, "Toward Clarification and Improvement of Social Work Practice," *Social Work*, Vol. 3, No. 2 (April 1958), pp. 3–9.

[2] During the preparation of this monograph the author was chairman of the Commission on Social Work Practice. Great indebtedness is acknowledged to the commission's vigorous and creative thinking, which has influenced this material throughout.

WORKING DEFINITION OF SOCIAL WORK PRACTICE

The *Working Definition* focuses on the operating social worker, who is rendering the characteristic services to people. It describes the practice of the competent professional worker, not the beginning worker right out of school. It is an initial formulation which will be progressively developed. Even in its early form, the *Working Definition* is already demonstrating its value as a set of dimensions by which social work practice can be examined and as an instrument for stimulating further thinking about practice.[3]

Keeping in mind their tentative nature, the *Working Definition* and the thinking which is developing out of it offer the most satisfactory and authoritative formulations available and will be used for this discussion. Readers should refer to and make use of the original 1956 version and subsequent revised versions of the *Working Definition* as they appear. The major ideas in the current thinking are here summarized.

"Social work practice," says the 1956 *Definition,* "like the practice of all professions, is recognized by a constellation of value, purpose, sanction, knowledge, and method. No part alone is characteristic of social work practice nor is any part described here unique to social work. It is the particular content and configuration of this constellation which makes it social work practice and distinguishes it from the practice of other professions." [4] The implication is that some practice will show more extensive use of one or the other components but is only to be regarded as social work practice when all are present to some degree.

Value. As basic values, the *Definition* and the subsequent thinking stress self-realization of the individual and his responsibility to contribute to society and to others. Additional values, which are regarded as derivative from these basic ones, emphasize such concepts as the responsibility of society to provide opportunity for individuals to realize their full potential. In further developing

---

[3] The subsequent discussion of the *Working Definition* and of the essential elements in social work practice is basic to the rationale of both this monograph and *Analyzing Social Work Practice by Fields.* Hence, it appears in both publications.

[4] Bartlett, *op. cit.,* p. 5.

these value formulations the intent is to separate value assumptions as to what is good and desirable from statements that are testable and verifiable, which will be regarded as belonging under knowledge. The social work profession has confused these two types of formulation in the past.

Purpose. The purposes of social work are to implement the values and can be simply expressed as: (1) modification of social conditions that present obstacles to self-realization of individuals and their contribution to others, and (2) creation of conditions that facilitate individual self-realization and contribution. Intermediate goals, characteristic of the social work profession, will have to be identified. As the *Definition* is developed, it will also be necessary to identify the particular focus of social work, which in 1956 was described as being a concern with the equilibrium or disequilibrium between the individual and his environment, but in recent years is more frequently expressed through the concept of *social functioning,* approached from the viewpoint of both the individual and the social system.

Sanction. Sanction denotes the authority for carrying on practice. Social work practice is sponsored by the agencies—governmental and voluntary incorporated agencies—within which social work positions have been established. Sanction is also derived from the organized profession itself, which defines educational and other standards, and the conditions under which practice can be undertaken.

Knowledge. The 1956 *Definition* lists nine areas of social work knowledge which "typically guide" the practice. Subsequent thinking revealed the inadequacy of such an approach. It was agreed that knowledge, although not so recognized at this time, is actually the major definer of social work practice and should be given greater weight in the evolving definition. Concentrated effort will be required to identify the essential nature and components of the body of professional social work knowledge, in order that it may be given its appropriate place in the *Working Definition of Social Work Practice.* The subject of social work knowledge is a large one, which will command considerable attention throughout this monograph.

Method. The section on method in the 1956 *Definition* begins with the following descriptive statement:

> The social work method is the responsible, conscious, disciplined use of self in a relationship with an individual or group. Through this relationship the practitioner facilitates interaction between the individual and his social environment with a continuing awareness of the reciprocal effects of one upon the other. It facilitates change: (1) within the individual in relation to his social environment; (2) of the social environment in its effect upon the individual; (3) of both the individual and the social environment in their interaction.
> Social work method includes systematic observation and assessment of the individual or group in a situation and the formulation of an appropriate plan of action. Implicit in this is a continuing evaluation regarding the nature of the relationship between worker and client or group, and its effect on both the participant individual or group and on the worker himself. This evaluation provides the basis for the professional judgment which the worker must constantly make and which determines the direction of his activities. The method is used predominately in interviews, group sessions, and conferences.[5]

Social casework, social group work, and community organization are regarded as being encompassed by the *Definition* but are not specifically defined in the early formulation.

The concept of *method* has customarily been used in a broad sense and without precise definition in social work. Examination of practice suggests that ordered sequence of actions (in the sense of systematic modes of procedure) is perhaps less characteristic of social work practice than highly flexible action responsive to a wide variety of situations. A new approach, that of professional intervention to bring about change through a variety of techniques, is being explored as possibly more useful and relevant for social work practice than the customary concept of method.

Three basic propositions are stated in this *Working Definition:*

1. Social work practice is recognized by a constellation of value, purpose, sanction, knowledge, and method.

---
[5] *Ibid.,* p. 7.

2. All these components must be present to some degree if the practice is to be considered as professional social work practice.

3. There may be variation in the use of, or emphasis upon, the various components in different areas, segments, or fields of social work practice.

The initial formulation's emphasis on the common elements in social work practice was appropriate, since social work lacked and particularly needed recognition of its common elements. There was definite gain in getting away from an attempt to find any unique characteristic which distinguished social work from other professions and in suggesting rather that it is distinguished by a constellation of factors. There was also value in setting forth a set of criteria that can be tested in practice.

As the *Definition* has continued to develop, steady progress has been made in clarifying the component elements and the relation between them. Steps have been initiated for defining the social work methods and fields within the framework of the over-all definition.[6] Thus, all of social work practice and its parts are being viewed together. Its various groups are contributing to the building of a comprehensive frame of reference, which will facilitate a degree of understanding of practice and communication between practitioners not previously attainable.

Already there is considerable agreement regarding a concept of social work practice focused on the practitioner in action, directed toward some purpose, sanctioned by some auspice, with that action under conscious guidance of knowledge and value and patterned to some extent by method and technique, as set forth in the above formulations. Thus the *Working Definition,* which began as a description of the common elements, is now becoming a definition of the essentials of social work practice. The dynamic

---

[6] At the time this monograph was being written, the Commission on Social Work Practice was preparing criteria for describing fields of practice. At the commission's request the Group Work Section of the National Association of Social Workers was working on a frame of reference for group work and the Committee on Community Organization was preparing a working definition of community organization.

nature of the *Definition* and its capacity to grow have been dramatically demonstrated.[7]

IMPLICATIONS OF THE WORKING DEFINITION

The *Working Definition* provides a concept of the essentials of social work practice as a starting point and foundation for analysis of any segment of practice. It opens the way (although it does not itself follow through) for moving from what is common or "generic" toward specific practice, by indicating that these essentials will be found in the various fields but with varying emphasis. There is the further implication that all of the social work methods will be found in any particular field. Approaching the analysis of social work practice in the health field from such a concept of the essentials of all social work practice eliminates the old problem of separateness and overspecialization. Medical social work is now placed in its proper position in relation to the profession. The part is now related to the whole and the "specific" to the "generic," as they should be related.

The *Working Definition* has further implications. It shows that social work practice is concerned with the following social units: individuals and families, groups (including pairs), communities, mass populations, society; and social agencies, social programs, professions, social institutions.

It can be further seen that social workers are constantly working through two channels to attain their goals. They are: (1) giving direct services to individuals and groups, and (2) collaborating with other persons (professional and lay associates), without direct contact with clients, to improve the services offered to individuals and groups in our society. These ways of working reinforce each other and both are needed.

A review of this discussion of social work practice up to this

---

[7] This summary is based on the following sources: the 1956 version of the *Working Definition of Social Work Practice,* as presented in Bartlett, *op. cit.,* pp. 5–8; and Commission on Social Work Practice, "Report of the Subcommittee on Working Definition of Social Work Practice" (New York: National Association of Social Workers, March 1961). (Mimeographed.)

point will show that the following questions need to be asked and answered in order to understand the various phases of any "piece" of social work activity.

1. Purposes and goals: *Why* are you doing it?
2. Functions and services: *What* are you doing?
3. Methods and processes: *How* are you doing it?
4. Working relationships: *With whom* are you doing it?
5. Sanction: *Under what authority* are you doing it? *Who* gave you the right to do it?
6. Auspice and location: *Where* are you doing it?
7. Point of intervention: *When* are you doing it? [8]

All these questions are significant in analyzing practice. In the course of this monograph all will be considered. Currently there is confusion in social work thinking because clear distinctions are not made between purpose, function, service, method, process, and skill. Consistency in the use of these terms will be attempted.

---

[8] Terms are used with the following meanings:

Purposes are the ends to be attained by consciously directed action.

Function is conceived as action appropriate to achieve professional purposes.

Method is an orderly systematic mode of procedure. In social work it is used to refer to constellations of professional activities customarily employed in dealing with problems and situations, such as social casework method.

Process refers to a series of events involving sequence and time relations not necessarily implied in method. In its broader sense it refers to social interaction between individuals and between groups. In a more particular sense, social work process is conceived as the social worker's intervention and participation in social interaction in the effort to bring about change.

Working relationships encompass both helping relationships with clients, families, and groups, and collaborative relationships with others.

Sanction refers to the sponsorship of the social worker's action by society and its organized groups and by his own profession.

Auspice and location refer to the agency and program, and the actual place in the program, where the social worker is operating.

Point of intervention is that point in the development of the condition or problem (in the ongoing social interaction process) when the social worker comes into direct contact with clients and others to influence the situation.

the health field

3

characteristics of
the health field

We are now ready to consider the characteristics of the particular field of practice under discussion—the health field.[1] In doing this, it should be noted, we are moving from the first frame of reference to the second. In describing these characteristics, five major areas are explored, as shown in the diagram on page 20. These are the: (1) problem (condition) of central concern; (2) system of organized services (programs, agencies, professions); (3) body of knowledge, values, and methods; (4) sociocultural attitudes (in society), and (5) characteristic responses and behavior of persons served.

It should be understood that these areas are interdependent, and may be regarded as forming a constellation. They are used here as the basis for a general description of the health field.

SCOPE OF THE HEALTH FIELD

Health is a basic need of all people and disease is a problem which must be met by all societies. In our American society two major

---
[1] This discussion of the health field is concerned with emotional and bodily reactions in health and disease. It does not, however, cover mental health or psychiatric social work as specific fields of practice.

social institutions—medicine and public health—have developed to meet these needs. Although they interpenetrate, they exhibit separate membership, organization, and method. Together, with the addition of a few smaller groups, they comprise the health field.[2]

Medicine is here understood in its institutional sense, which encompasses more than the medical profession.[3] It covers the activities of physicians and those associated with them in the care of patients and in the related activities of teaching and research. The hospital and other medical care agencies are also included.

The scope of public health is best described in terms of the authoritative definition of Dr. C.-E. A. Winslow: "Public health is the science and the art of preventing disease, prolonging life, and promoting physical and mental health and efficiency through organized community efforts for the sanitation of the environment, the control of community infections, the education of the individual in principles of personal hygiene, the organization of medical and nursing service for the early diagnosis and preventive treatment of disease, and the development of the social machinery which will ensure to every individual in the community a standard of living

---

[2] There are a number of special professional groups, like dentistry, that are practicing in association with medicine and public health. Their activities fall within the health field but will not be specifically discussed in this monograph.

[3] The use of the term "medicine" to describe a whole field of practice has been questioned. Consideration was given to the possibility of using such terms as "the hospital" or "medical care"; but they seem too narrow and do not offer a clear contrast with public health, in which both are included. Actually there is good precedent for the broader use of the term "medicine." In 1947 the New York Academy of Medicine issued a series of comprehensive monographs, in which provision of adequate medical care was one of the basic concerns, under the auspices of a Committee on Medicine and the Changing Order. So also, in the new division of medical sociology that has grown up within the professional discipline of sociology, it is clear that the term "field of medicine" is used to encompass hospitals and medical care, as well as the various types of personnel associated with the medical profession in care of patients. See "The Sociology of Medicine," by George G. Reader and Mary E. W. Goss, in Robert K. Merton et al., eds., Sociology Today (New York: Basic Books, 1959), pp. 229-246.

adequate for the maintenance of health."[4] The focus of public health is here clearly shown to be upon community health (with constant concern for individuals and families), whereas the focus of medicine is primarily upon the individual patient. This can be regarded as a major distinction between them. Working together, they meet the health needs of society as a whole.

PROBLEM OF CENTRAL CONCERN—HEALTH AND DISEASE

The first element to be considered in the analysis of a field is the condition, phenomenon, need, or problem around which the organized services have developed. The basic need explains the existence of the social institution. The purposes of the agencies and professions operating in the field are directed toward meeting some clearly recognized problem. In the health field the focus is upon health and disease, regarded as a continuum. The transition from one to the other cannot be clearly distinguished. In their fullest and most distinct manifestations they are sharply contrasted, however, since health can be defined in terms of ability to function to full capacity in all roles and relationships, whereas illness characteristically produces diminished capacity for social functioning.

Bodily illness is a reality problem with a large social and emotional component. It disturbs the equilibrium of the individual and family. It produces emotional tension in the patient and those around him. In its more severe forms, it brings to the sick person isolation, helplessness, discomfort, dependency on others, uncertainty, and fear. Social and emotional stress are to be regarded not only as results but also as components of illness throughout its course, from the earliest stage of predisposition to the latest stage of chronic invalidism. They are components of medical care in the same manner.

From the viewpoint of society, illness and physical handicap are major social problems. Whether the effects of illness are temporary

---

[4] Quoted in Hugh Rodman Leavell and E. Gurney Clark, *Preventive Medicine for the Doctor in His Community* (New York: McGraw-Hill Book Co., 1958), 2nd ed., p. 10.

or permanent, the socioeconomic costs for the individual, the family, and the community run high, first, because of the medical care itself and, second, because of the immense losses in impaired social functioning. Repeated national surveys over the years have revealed the enormous financial burden of unemployment and economic dependency resulting from illness and handicap. The incidence of medical problems is great in all social welfare programs, particularly in public assistance programs.

While medicine focuses upon disease and public health is primarily concerned with health promotion and prevention of illness, the difference between them is not as large as it formerly was. Medicine has learned that its service is more effective when the curative and preventive approaches are combined; and public health has found that it must take increased responsibility in relation to many diseases and conditions with broad socioeconomic and community implications. Although their activities overlap, we can still identify medicine with pathology and treatment, and public health with positive health and prevention.

SYSTEM OF ORGANIZED SERVICES

In our society a social institution is most readily recognized and described through the organized operations of its programs, agencies, and professions. A few generations ago the family physician was the chief representative of medical practice in the community and hospital practice had only two divisions, medical and surgical. As a result of the rapid advances in scientific knowledge, technology, and service organization, medicine and public health have now become two huge, exceedingly complex social institutions, each composed of many professions, agencies, and programs. Because of the concern for health in American culture and the vast resources invested in health services, this field of activity occupies an outstanding position in our social system.

The enormous growth of knowledge regarding disease and the needs of the sick have produced an elaborate pattern of specialization. In medicine, the physician holds the dominant role and responsibility. He functions increasingly as leader of a medical team composed of members of his own and related professions. Nursing is the major health profession regularly associated with medicine. Other professions frequently found in the team are social work, occupational therapy, physical therapy, and nutrition. Still others are clinical psychology, vocational guidance, and speech therapy, as well as additional professions whose service may be relevant in a particular situation. Public health has from its earliest days seen itself as composed of a group of jointly functioning professions, beginning with the public health physician, the sanitary engineer, and the public health nurse, and now like medicine including a steadily increasing number of other specialists.

The health field is composed of many types of agencies and programs. Hospitals and clinics, general and special, are the major medical agencies with which social work is associated.[5] Hospitals play an important and growing role in the modern community. As yet, social work has had relatively little formal association with private medical practice outside hospitals, although there are signs of change in this area. In public health the typical unit is the program, often consisting of many facets and extending over a wide geographical region. Social work is associated primarily with those sections of the program that have to do with service to people. Physical rehabilitation services, frequently offered within hospitals and public health programs, may be given in independent agencies. Health and welfare councils serve as important auspices for community health planning. National health organizations play an important role, often in relation to one particular disease or condition. Public welfare agencies also have extensive responsibility for medical care. All of these health services and activities are found under both governmental and voluntary auspices, and at national, state, and local levels. Social work has been included in all of them, at all levels, and in all major areas of operation. While the greatest number of social workers has been employed in hospitals, social work is now well represented in the other types of health services. The scope of their work is wide and the tendency is toward increasing spread into new areas.

---

[5] *See* Appendix, "Agencies in the Health Field."

Medical care, particularly in the hospital, is an elaborately organized activity. The number of different kinds of personnel and processes involved in this undertaking makes it one of the most complex in our culture. The efficiency of the modern medical institution is demonstrated by the remarkably high proportion of safe surgical operations and deliveries, as well as the increasing efficiency of medical therapy. The extreme degree of specialization requires that many persons necessarily be involved in the care of one patient. Some of the characteristics of medical care have been described as follows:

> The rendering of modern medical care involves an extremely complex interweaving of personal relationships and impersonal manipulative processes. The administration of a medical institution involves moving large numbers of persons about from one place to another for reasons which are not always clear to them. The tests, examinations, and procedures which are a part of this care seem to many patients mysterious, confusing, and even threatening. How far the impersonality of this process is a necessity is not clear, but there is no question that it is a factor to be taken into account in connection with all forms of organized medical care today.[6]
>
> Another important point is the urgency of illness. A certain degree of tenseness customarily prevails in the atmosphere of a hospital, as a natural consequence of the serious responsibilities undertaken. The physician is accustomed to a quick and precise type of action and expects it from others. Thus the time factor becomes important in connection with work in a medical setting. In relation to acute illness and accident a few hours' delay may be serious. . . . Furthermore, where many expensive services are marshalled together to care for illness, it becomes a matter of practical economy to make these available as rapidly as possible to the largest number of patients. The person working in a medical atmosphere is thus naturally pushed toward some type of objective activity, some plan which will move things forward in the direction of medical care.[7]

---

[6] Harriett M. Bartlett, *Some Aspects of Social Casework in a Medical Setting* (New York: National Association of Social Workers, 1940. 6th printing, 1958), p. 25.

[7] *Ibid.*, p. 24.

Shortage of all types of professional personnel in recent years has increased these pressures.

As the patient moves from step to step in his medical care, he may have increasing difficulty in making the necessary adjustments. Such a situation is particularly likely to occur in clinics, where patients frequently have to consult several physicians and go through multiple tests (each one of which requires a separate visit) before diagnosis and treatment can be established. Thus the public, the press, and the patients are today joining in praise for the miracles of modern medicine but raising many questions as to whether these deficiencies in patient care are necessarily inherent in medical practice. In one study of patients' attitudes toward their care in a moderate-sized metropolitan community offering good medical services, the most serious criticism centered upon the impersonal nature of the medical and nursing care.[8] How to give technical services through an individualized professional relationship is a problem only partially solved by medicine.

KNOWLEDGE, VALUES, AND METHODS

The purposes of all the health professions and agencies are broadly the same—to promote health, prevent and cure illness, and rehabilitate those who cannot be cured.[9] Beginning with the Hippocratic oath, the ethical standards of medicine have been set at a high level, both in terms of the professional practitioner's relation to his patient and the profession's responsibility to society. The obligation to meet the need of the sick person and the confidentiality of the doctor-patient relationship have been consistently emphasized. The responsibility of the profession to maintain and continually improve standards of practice has been recognized and well fulfilled

---

[8] Earl Koos, " 'Metropolis'—What City People Think of Their Medical Services," in E. Gartly Jaco, ed., *Patients, Physicians and Illness* (Glencoe, Ill.: The Free Press, 1958), pp. 113–119.

[9] The attitudes and values discussed in this section are those that are an integral part of the subcultures of medicine and public health. The attitudes and values discussed in the following section are those of the whole society, as directed toward and influencing the health field.

in this country ever since the famous Flexner Report in 1910.[10] The other health professions have followed the leadership of medicine in building a strong foundation of values and standards.

The nature and sources of authority in the health field should be understood. Society delegates legal and social authority to the health agencies and professions to give the services for which they have responsibility. In addition, there is administrative authority essential for operating the services. Medicine particularly and the associated professions also carry a still further type of authority based on knowledge and expertness. Thus the doctor's authoritative position in the health agency in relation to the patient rests on all these types of authority. The social system of the medical institution and the cultural attitudes of society give him high status. Medical knowledge and skill are highly respected. The physician directs patients in matters of greatest importance in their lives. For most patients this is a helpful relationship, which is essential if medical care is to move ahead.

The body of knowledge on which the health professions rest is extensive, extremely technical, and rapidly expanding. It is, in fact, one of the largest bodies of scientific and professional knowledge in the modern world. This knowledge derives from two sources, basic science and professional experience. Some of the most important sciences used in medicine are biology, anatomy, physiology, biochemistry, pathology, bacteriology, and pharmacology. Psychology, psychiatry, and social science appeared later and have not yet gained equal status with the older sciences. Public health requires additional bodies of knowledge concerned with the physical environment, the community, and mass populations, and the administration of large programs. Both the scientific and professional knowledge are continuously tested and extended through comprehensive research.

The care of the patient follows an orderly pattern of study, diagnosis, and treatment. This is the clinical approach, which focuses on the problems of the individual patient. It not only

---

[10] Abraham Flexner, *Medical Education in the United States and Canada* (New York: Carnegie Foundation for the Advancement of Teaching, 1910).

draws on scientific knowledge but itself follows the scientific method, through the steps of examination, collection of data, analysis, assessment, and action based on the findings. The terms "diagnosis" and "treatment," which originated in medicine, have been widely used elsewhere, including social work itself. While the physician's own thinking and skill are the core of this professional method, precision and accuracy in diagnosis and treatment are greatly extended through the use of many instruments and devices for examining, analyzing, testing, and treating. There is a remarkable consistency in medical practice. History-taking and physical examination cover the same essential points regarding body systems and history of illness wherever medicine is adequately practiced. Physicians are taught to think diagnostically from the beginning of a case and to commit themselves to a tentative diagnosis at the patient's first visit. Many laboratory tests are now so exact that almost infinitesimal changes in body balance can be detected as possible signs of incipient disease.

In hospital and clinic practice, physicians learn to record fully the essential steps in the care of the patient, to accept responsibility for their failures as well as their successes, and to evaluate their work regularly in staff meetings and clinico-pathological conferences. In teaching centers, teaching and research are usually carried on concurrently with patient care. Since these activities focus an examining eye upon practice, they tend to improve its quality.

Public health is not so easily described in methodological terms as is clinical medicine. Multiple activities are involved, none of which stands out clearly as central. The general outlines of its methods are, however, beginning to appear. They are perhaps best understood by the social worker through the areas of service that are customarily described as falling under a health department. They can be listed as follows: (1) vital and public health statistics, (2) control of communicable disease, (3) control of environmental sanitation, (4) public health laboratory services, (5) maternal and child health services, and (6) health education. Such special areas of concern as occupational disease, chronic disease, accidents, and alcoholism may also be included. Mental health is part of public health but may be administered by a separate department. Standards for the licensing of hospitals and nursing homes may be among the functions of public health. Industrialization and social change are bringing an ever increasing number of problems within the scope of public health responsibilities and programs.

Multidiscipline practice is becoming a major characteristic of the health field. At its best, the operation of an experienced team in a modern medical center or health agency is a fascinating and beautiful phenomenon. In care of patients the physician is alone responsible for the medical diagnosis, also for recommending medical tests and treatment; but at every step he is assisted by members of the health professions, who work directly with the patient and confer regularly with the physician and each other as they carry out their respective responsibilities. While multidiscipline practice is still a young phenomenon and presents many unsolved problems, it has proceeded far enough to demonstrate its effectiveness as a method.

SOCIOCULTURAL ATTITUDES

From the sociocultural viewpoint, illness and physical handicap can be regarded as social deviations, since ill and handicapped persons are unable to function normally or to carry their usual social responsibilities. This approach is of particular value to the social worker, since it places illness directly within the social work conceptual framework. While illness is a passive type of deviation and thus less harmful to society than destructive types of behavior, it is still of concern because of the social loss resulting from the individual's incapacity, which affects others as well as himself. Since illness is regarded as being largely the result of conditions beyond the patient's control, it is considered an acceptable deviation in our society, with little or no blame or unworthiness imputed to the patient. Sympathy and support are customarily offered to the individual when he becomes ill or is injured. This acceptance is, however, temporary and conditional upon his following the expected behavior, which is to seek medical care and try to get well. During illness the individual, because of his helplessness, is dependent upon others and isolated from his usual social relationships. Therefore, from the viewpoint of society, the goal of treatment is to return the individual to a satisfactory state of independence and social functioning.[11]

If the problems of illness or handicap are not resolved and the situation does not follow the described course, social attitudes can be expected to change. If chronic disease and handicap persist, and the individual becomes increasingly a social burden, the interest of those around him and of the general public tends to slacken, revealing less concern for his welfare and sometimes changing to open rejection. The professions concerned with medical care are becoming increasingly aware that a considerable proportion of illness and disability is related to life problems, representing the individual's response to stress. Thus, in professional terms what is called for in these circumstances is not rejection but increased effort to offer the patient a type of therapy relevant to his interacting medical and psychosocial needs.[12]

In both medicine and public health it is also being recognized that cultural attitudes must be taken into account in offering services to various population groups. Attitudes toward pain, diet and medication, child care, and all phases of living influence the way in which people accept, use, and react to health measures and medical care. An impressive body of experience is developing in the health field in regard to ways of adapting services and programs so that they may be acceptable to the cultural groups to whom they are offered.[13]

Certain social attitudes tend to cluster around specific diseases and conditions because of the image they present and the feelings they arouse. Heart disease becomes associated with "dropping

---

[11] Talcott Parsons, *The Social System* (Glencoe, Ill.: The Free Press, 1951), pp. 436–439, 473–479.

[12] Parsons, "Definitions of Health and Illness in the Light of American Values and Social Structure," in Jaco, *op. cit.*, pp. 165–187.

[13] Benjamin D. Paul, "Social Science in Public Health," *American Journal of Public Health,* Vol. 46, No. 11 (November 1956), pp. 1390–1396.

dead," epilepsy with terrifying seizures, syphilis with moral stigma, and cancer with inevitable progress toward fatal termination. Industry, with its emphasis on efficiency, is unwilling to take the supposed risks in employing older and disabled persons. While gains are being made in the direction of less rigid attitudes, as toward certain diseases like syphilis and toward employment of handicapped persons, these attitudes resist change because they are partly rooted in deep irrational fears that do not respond to direct educational measures.

The concern of society for health is also shown through the services it establishes and supports, such as have been described. Seen as a total program, this American development is impressive. Within any one community or region, however, there exist wide variations in type, quantity, and quality of health services and resources available. These variations are only partially due to economic factors. To a considerable degree they are to be understood in terms of community initiative and values, such as attitudes toward self-help and dependency.

This whole area of the sociocultural aspects of health is one toward which attention has turned recently. Explorations, demonstrations, and discussions in the literature are rapidly increasing. Health practice will improve as the implications and impact of social values are better recognized and understood.

RESPONSES AND BEHAVIOR OF PATIENTS

It is recognized that all the behavior responses possible to man are found in relation to illness or any other basic social problem. It appears, however, that characteristic responses to illness can be identified and that attempts to describe typical behavior are valid and helpful, as long as premature or rigid categorization is avoided. (A clear example of typical behavior from another field is the "acting out" behavior of the delinquent.) Analysis of the health field reveals certain recurrent problems which tend to call forth similar responses in patients and families. As has been pointed out, severe illness produces helplessness, fear, and dependency.

Most patients feel a sense of security and support when cared for by an expert physician who shows strong interest in them as individuals, but the complexity of modern medical care creates confusion in patients and their families.

The responses of the sick person indicated above are to phenomena originating predominantly outside himself. Evidence is mounting that the incidence of illness tends to be higher among individuals and groups required by life circumstances to face social adjustments beyond their integrative capacity. From this viewpoint illness can be regarded as a biopsychosocial process. It is also a form of adjustive behavior, which is harmful rather than helpful to the person and does not solve the original difficulty. These recurrent attitudes, responses, and behavior patterns associated with illness are receiving increasing attention among the health professions. While there are many significant clues and insights, theory adequate for understanding all facets of this complex phenomenon have not yet been developed.

social work and the health field

4

placing social work in the health field

Having discussed separately the essential elements in social work practice (the first frame of reference) and the characteristics of the health field (the second frame of reference), we can now view them together.[1] Before actually applying the social work essentials in the health field, however, an intermediate step must be taken to

---

[1] This discussion covers social work in the whole health field—that is, both medicine and public health—insofar as our present knowledge and the limitations of this monograph permit. There are more likenesses than differences between the two types of social work practice; therefore many things can be said about both. When distinctions are important, they will be indicated. Effort is made to bring out some of the more important characteristics of social work in public health, particularly when it makes a contribution to the whole practice. In considering actual instances of practice, the discussion most frequently starts with the individual patient and his family. This may be regarded as a logical starting point because it is always an individual who is healthy or ill. Furthermore, this phase of medical social work is older and we have more understanding of its nature. We do not yet have knowledge of our practice in public health that will permit us to discuss it as fully as we would wish to do.

consider certain principles that guide this operation and problems involved in its accomplishment. We need to look at certain factors and influences that come into play when social work seeks to establish its place and combine its activities with those of other professions in a non-social work setting. This chapter, therefore, will be devoted to placing social work in the health field; the following chapter focuses directly on some key aspects of the social worker's activity as it appears in this particular environment.

First, it is important to identify the principles that guide the effective inclusion and operation of social work within any particular field. How does it become integrated so as to make its appropriate contribution?[2] An initial group of such principles, which have been developed out of past experience (particularly in medical social work), is stated in *Analyzing Social Work Practice by Fields,* as follows:

> 1. If social work is to play its appropriate role in any field of practice, there must be recognition in that field of the psychosocial aspects of the human need or condition which the program is designed to meet. Social work cannot appropriately function as just a facilitating service "to make the wheels go around" in the agency or to supplement the activities of the other professions. It brings a substantive contribution based on the social nature of the problem and program. This is illustrated in the health field by the scientific recognition of the psychosocial component in illness and medical care and the emphasis on comprehensive care of the patient.
> 2. Social work shares the general objectives and the focus on the needs which the agency or program is set up to meet.[3]

---

[2] Integration means to unify, to form into a whole. It seems clear that if several professions are to work together toward a common objective, there must be unification not only of purposes but of activities. However, from the viewpoint of social work, integration can be—and has been—used in the past to mean giving up too much in order to be included. It cannot be used as a sole, or isolated, principle. All the principles must operate together if integration is to be soundly achieved. Above all, integration does not mean being swallowed up by the larger field so that the very identity of social work is destroyed.

[3] The focus of a profession, such as medicine or social work, may be regarded as encompassing those central elements that characterize

3. Social work also retains its own goals; it cannot function effectively in an environment which does not permit it to retain its own identity.

4. Social work services focus upon the psychosocial aspects of the problems of central concern and of the services characteristic of the particular field.

5. Social work services are offered to individuals and groups under the care of the agency or included within its program in other ways.

6. Social workers collaborate with the administrative and professional staff of the agency in all major phases of social work activity.

These general principles are the same for all fields of practice. They are concerned with the safeguarding of the separate focus and identity of social work, while enabling it to function positively and effectively within the field.[4]

RESPONSIBILITY AND CONTRIBUTION OF SOCIAL WORK IN THE HEALTH FIELD

In describing the practice of medical social work, we have been accustomed to start with care of the individual patient. But when social work, medicine, and public health are viewed together as social institutions, it becomes important to define the social work contribution in the particular field in broad terms. There is evidence that social work in the health field has not yet provided itself such a framework of thinking. Some professional committees engaged in analyzing its practice came to the conclusion that it

---

the profession at any one time. The term "core" has sometimes been used to convey the same idea. To draw boundaries between fluid and constantly changing activities, which show a great deal of overlapping and interpenetration, is difficult, if not impossible. It is easier to identify a professional focus than professional boundaries. A professional focus may be comprised of a constellation of elements, no one of which is unique but which together do distinguish a profession from others. Even in its early stage of formulation, the *Working Definition of Social Work Practice* gives promise of becoming an instrument to distinguish the social work profession in this way.

[4] Harriett M. Bartlett, *Analyzing Social Work Practice by Fields* (New York: National Association of Social Workers, 1961), pp. 45–46.

had been too tied to the conceptual framework of social casework in the hospital, that is, working with the individual in one particular setting. This cluster of concepts has been, and still is, valuable and important for one major segment of practice but cannot be extended to cover its whole scope.

Developments in both social work and public health are calling for a wider and more flexible approach. Public health is showing that the clinical approach is no longer sufficient by itself. Elizabeth P. Rice points out that the time has gone by when medical social work can proceed only on a patient-by-patient basis. She says:

> Until we lift into our practice a broader understanding of the group we serve, until we contribute our thinking and our facts to the programing and planning in the particular agency in which we practice, until we widen our understanding of the individual to see him as he affects and is affected by his family and the community, and until we have a greater understanding both of the dynamics of the family and the dynamics of the community—until this time, we will neglect the potentialities that exist for the more comprehensive practice of social work.[5]

In other words, whatever the particular emphasis in their jobs, all medical social workers must operate within the same comprehensive framework of thinking, which encompasses the interrelated needs of individuals, groups, and communities.

This comprehensive approach means thinking first of the long-range contribution of the whole group of social workers functioning in the field. The over-all social work concern is with improved social functioning of individuals and groups, with particular reference to the problem, condition, or phenomenon central in the field, such as health, illness, and medical care. The major contributions can be described as two related activities:

1. To develop awareness of the significance, and understanding of the nature of the psychosocial components—the social needs—which are a constant element in the central problem or condition;

---

[5] Elizabeth P. Rice, "Social Work in Public Health," *Social Work*, Vol. 4, No. 1 (January 1959), p. 88.

2. To participate actively in the provision of adequate services to meet these social needs, either by giving direct services or by influencing the development of specific programs and of social policy as a basis for future programs.

The social worker in the health field has a special responsibility to make the psychosocial approach truly operative. Although other workers in the health field are, of course, concerned with psychosocial factors, the social worker is the only one in the field with a consistent and central focus on social functioning. Thus, the development of awareness and understanding of psychosocial factors must be the first contribution because the services rest upon this foundation. While physicians and members of the other health professions give general recognition to psychosocial factors in illness, they do not act upon this recognition until they see the implications for their own practice. In working in a scientifically oriented field such as health, social workers must have sufficient command of concepts and theory to be able to convey the essential content to their associates. This may be done through working together on a case or other problem, or through more formal educational channels. The social worker who has helped a young intern or nurse to greater awareness of the social stress in the situation of one of their patients, to better understanding of its nature, and to acceptance of responsibility for doing something about it has done a service as important as rendering a casework service directly to that patient.

RANGE OF SOCIAL WORK ACTIVITIES

The professional practice of social work consists of a number of different kinds of activities, which have not yet been clearly described and classified. Consensus as to the nature of these activities has proceeded far enough so that communication between members of the profession can take place with a good degree of understanding. Some of the activities have been defined in the social work literature by individual authors and by official groups representing segments of the profession. The medical social work group, for example, has from time to time prepared definitions and lists of activities as part of various official statements regarding practice and education.[6] However, comprehensive and authoritative definitions have not been developed by the profession, even in relation to the well-recognized methods of social casework, group work, and community organization. The profession is just at the point of formulating working definitions of its major methods and activities, definitions that will require testing in practice before they acquire validity.

Some phases of social work practice are much better understood and conceptualized than others. In any current list, social casework will stand out with greater clarity than any other because so much more progress has been made in identifying its essentials. Since some way must be found to show the range of social work activities in practice, even at the risk of putting unlike entities together, the following outline is offered:

Professional Activities in Medical Social Work Practice

1. *Administration of the social work program*

The social work administrator is primarily responsible but all staff members participate.

2. *Services to individuals, families, and groups*
   a. Social casework
   b. Social group work
3. *Planning services in agency programs and communities*
   a. Participation in program planning in the agency
   b. Participation in community planning

Both activities are concerned with policy, standards, and services. Both make use of administrative and community organization principles. Within the agency, the social worker's position and responsibility are constant; but in the community he may function under various auspices.

4. *Educational activities*

Carried on within social work practice; with social work students and students of other professions.

---

[6] *Definition of a Medical Social Work Position* (New York: National Association of Social Workers, 1956).

5. *Research activities*
Multidiscipline or independent social work study and research, formal or informal.

6. *Consultation*
Can take place in relation to any of the above activities, with other social workers and other professions. In consultation the social worker does not accept responsibility for action in relation to the problem.

The manner in which the better known social work methods fit into this inclusive list and into a social work program in a health agency is discussed in later sections of the monograph.

OPERATION OF THE SOCIAL SERVICE DEPARTMENT

The practice of social work in the health field now encompasses all social work methods. There is, therefore, a growing problem in selecting appropriate methods for any specific program and in maintaining proper balance between them. This requires knowledge of criteria and planning based on foresight and evaluation of results. Social work administrators carry major responsibility for program development. All staff members share in this responsibility in relation to both the content of their own jobs and the broader program. At the level of the total professional group, the problem of deciding where emphasis should be placed involves leadership of a high order.

A program consists of a number of interrelated services and activities. The effectiveness of each service or activity depends on its relation to the others within the over-all program. Since medical social work is part of a larger program, it has two administrative tasks, the operation of its own professional unit and the integration of its professional services with those of the health agency.

Medical social work most often functions within a formally organized department or unit in the health agency. The number of individuals in such units is not large. In nearly one thousand hospitals with social service departments studied in 1954–1955, the average number of workers was just under four and a considerable proportion of the staffs (44 percent) had less than two workers. Among general short-term hospitals, the largest group with social service staff, there were only six with forty or more social workers.[7]

Administration in medical social work includes responsibility for organization and structure of the social service unit; for planning, directing, and co-ordinating program; for establishing personnel policies and staffing; for providing facilities; for preparing budgets and reports; and for evaluating the service. In the early days of medical social work, administrative planning and principles emerged out of the wisdom of the experienced administrators, through a long course of trial and error. Under the stimulus of several official bodies responsible for standard-setting in hospitals, particularly the American Hospital Association, administrative criteria were formulated in a series of official statements on standards issued by the American Association of Medical Social Workers, beginning in 1936.[8] Some of the principles and criteria enunciated are as follows:

1. Social work should be organized as a definite part of the agency.

2. All social workers in the health agency—whether in regular staff positions or carrying special temporary assignments—should be members of one department.

3. The social service budget should be part of the health agency's budget.

4. All social workers should meet the established professional qualifications, both in terms of educational preparation and competence.

5. Facilities (offices, telephones, interviewing and conference

---

[7] American Hospital Association, National Association of Social Workers, and U. S. Public Health Service, *Social Work in Hospitals* (Washington, D. C.: U. S. Public Health Service, 1956), pp. 8–9.

[8] *A Statement of Standards To Be Met by Social Service Departments in Hospitals, Clinics and Sanatoria* (Chicago: American Association of Medical Social Workers, 1949). Following the formation of the National Association of Social Workers, its Medical and Psychiatric Social Work Sections have worked together on standards for social work practice in hospitals.

rooms) should be adequate for carrying out the professional functions, with proper regard for the confidential nature of the work.

The medical social work literature reveals relatively few papers dealing with the administrative aspects of practice. Those which have been published seem more concerned with problems than principles. A general statement on personnel practices was issued by the professional group in 1941 and revised ten years later.[9] The group did not arrive at the point of exploring administration as an expert professional process until the early fifties. The first study, one of the final publications of the American Association of Medical Social Workers, was concerned with the administration of a hospital social service department.[10] This report analyzed the administrative process in terms of concepts from business administration, focusing mainly on the social work administrator and giving numerous illustrations of the various activities. From this beginning, thinking needs to be extended to cover the full range of administrative activities in the expanding medical-social programs.

John C. Kidneigh defines social work administration as "the process of transforming social policy into social services" and says it requires three interrelated bodies of knowledge, as follows:

> 1. An understanding of relationship principles applying to individuals and groups.
> 2. An understanding of the totality of the process of social work administration.
> 3. An understanding of the various kinds of program characteristic of social work agencies, together with an understanding of the impact of setting upon the process of transforming social policy into social services.[11]

In connection with the first item, relationship principles, it can be said that all social work administration emphasizes the same

---

[9] *A Statement of Personnel Practices* (Chicago: American Association of Medical Social Workers, 1941). Revised 1951.

[10] Celia R. Moss, *Administering a Hospital Social Service Department* (Washington, D. C.: American Association of Medical Social Workers, 1955).

[11] John C. Kidneigh, "Social Work Administration," *Social Work Journal,* Vol. 31, No. 2 (April 1950), pp. 58–60.

general goals for its workers as for its clients, namely, the fullest possible participation and growth. Staff development and supervision are important activities that fall in this area. Understanding of the administrative process, the second item, has lagged in medical social work. With the growing complexity of services and shortage of qualified personnel, it is obvious that greater sophistication in administrative knowledge and skills is needed. Understanding of program characteristics and of the impact of the health environment has been of major importance in medical social work. Much attention has been devoted to this aspect of practice, with considerable success in identification of problems and principles.

Some characteristics of social work practice in a hospital, under favorable circumstances, can be described as follows: Social service is offered all through the program. It is accepted and used by the hospital administration and a varying proportion of the medical staff, including chiefs of service, visiting and resident physicians. Working relations with nurses and other professional groups are soundly developed. Social workers are assigned to various medical services in such a way that teamwork may develop. Regular multidiscipline conferences are in use for planning patient care on a number of the services. Social work reports are included as part of the medical record. The social workers, who are professionally qualified, use the best modern theory (medical and psychosocial) in their practice. Caseloads are moderate and good supervision is available. Patients are referred mainly by physicians, individually or in multidiscipline conferences. By medical request all patients in certain selected diagnostic groups may be seen by social workers, but only if their numbers are sufficiently limited to permit genuine casework. In departments where social work is most effectively practiced, social workers carry no direct hospital administrative duties, as in relation to admitting patients, but are alert to make their contribution to improved social policy and procedures.[12] Good personnel policies prevail, including a staff

---

[12] Activities concerned with determining eligibility and admitting patients to clinics and hospitals are regarded as administrative, not social work, functions. They should be carried out under administrative auspices. Experience shows that admitting and social work functions should be clearly distinguished and carried on separately.

development program and regular staff meetings, some of which are devoted to case discussion. Social workers who have more than one year of experience carry increasing responsibilities in relation to the educational, research, and community activities of the department. Thus the social worker's job includes more than direct service to patients and involves a considerable component of other types of professional activity, varying with the situation and the particular interest or competence of the individual worker.

In public health the proportion of direct service is less, except when the traditional casework service is being given in hospitals under public health auspices. Data for general comparison of the characteristics of social work activities in hospitals and public health programs are not available.

PROBLEMS OF INTEGRATING PROFESSIONAL SERVICES

According to the principles of integration, social work—when part of a larger service—shares the objectives, problem focus, administrative structure, and clients of the agency, all from its characteristic approach. Social work operates through two major channels: (1) giving direct services to individuals and groups, and (2) working with and through the agency staff and community to develop and improve the total service. In entering another field, social work should not take anything away from the other professions practicing there (as has sometimes happened) but should aid them to enlarge their responsibility and service.

When social work is part of a larger institution, one important goal is to create a climate within which it can function at its optimal level. As part of the health agency, medical social work must prepare the way for its own effort by developing a readiness to use what it contributes. All staff members share this responsibility with the social service administrator. Mary L. Hemmy says:

> The dynamic interaction of the professional disciplines requires in a quite literal sense not only that the case worker in a hospital be able to do case work but that she must carry on a continuous process of creating within this interaction an operational setting in which her skills can be used to max-

imum effect. In part this comes about because of the fairly constant change in personnel, especially among the resident medical staff. More particularly, however, it is the result of a continuing and growing process of integration of the efforts of various disciplines working together, out of which work emerge new horizons for, and new methods of carrying on, the co-operative enterprise of medical care. Successful and responsible participation in this dynamic process of the growth of the total service is an essential skill of the case worker in the hospital. It must be learned and developed as consciously as is case work skill. Without it, the most highly skilled technical case work services can be relatively ineffective. As an entity in professional knowledge and skill, it has never been properly named or adequately analyzed and studied.[13]

In other words, the individual social worker must have skill in teamwork and program building to function effectively in a multi-discipline health setting.

Most of the other disciplines in the health setting, such as medicine, nursing, nutrition, physiotherapy, and occupational therapy, can be described as health professions. Their major focus is upon health and illness, and their activities fall mainly within the health field. Social work, on the other hand, is found in many fields and in each instance, as has been shown, must deliberately relate its practice to that of the particular field. This is a complex undertaking, involving many issues, whatever the field. There has been considerable discussion of these problems in the literature of medical social work.

Even though the function of social work in hospitals and health agencies is recognized, its establishment in a new institution or program requires special planning and always involves some problems. Social workers are a small group in a complex multi-discipline setting, where status and role are often rigidly defined. The structure of the medical setting presents barriers to under-

---

[13] Mary L. Hemmy, "Case Work Services in a Hospital Setting," in Dora Goldstine, ed., *Readings in the Theory and Practice of Medical Social Work* (Chicago: University of Chicago Press, 1954), p. 110.

standing and integration.[14] Individual members of the administrative, medical, and nursing staff may lack readiness to accept and collaborate with social workers. Because of these difficulties, some social workers have felt it necessary to find a place by making themselves useful in any way requested by physicians or administrators. This is not an effective way, however, to demonstrate the true contribution of social work and has led to confusion.

Because there is just one administrative department in a hospital in contrast to many medical departments, social workers have sometimes been more successful in developing policies and working closely with the administration than with the heads of the many medical services. There are further problems, not fully solved as yet, as to how to combine administrative and service aspects in social service departments with only one professional worker, of which there are many in the health field. The general principles seem to require modification in this particular situation. Adjustments must also be made when the policies and standards of the social work profession are not fully in accord with those in the agency, as in some personnel procedures. In general, it is clear that the social work administrative policies and procedures should either be the same as, or in consonance with, those prevailing throughout the agency and should operate to promote integration, not separation.

Other problems arise because of the nature and tempo of medical care. Doctors and nurses are accustomed to more direct action than is usual, or even possible, in social work practice. Illness creates urgent situations that call for rapid responses. Many of the methods of the health professions, particularly when instruments are employed, are extremely precise. Doctors and nurses often expect the same type of direct action from social workers and have difficulty in understanding the nature of social work activity.

The reality of the needs associated with illness is steadily impressed upon the social worker in the hospital, who is surrounded by them constantly. Although serving only a portion of the patient

[14] Otto Pollak, "The Culture of Medical Social Work," *Medical Social Work,* Vol. 3, No. 3 (July 1954), pp. 81–89.

group, the worker is conscious of the crowded clinic benches and ward beds full of sick patients. The inner pressure of anxiety over unmet needs may push social workers to undertake more than they can accomplish. There are so many potential avenues of service that choices are difficult. In the past, social workers tried to meet all social problems through their own effort; but now, they are learning to work through the other members of the team.

Some of the most serious problems of integrating services undoubtedly have arisen because of the social work profession's stage of development and lack of clarity as to the nature of its own potential contribution. Social workers lack security because they do not grasp firmly and broadly enough what they have to offer. A focus on casework skill may be too limiting. Social work's own perception of its role requires re-examination in the light of new concepts of social work and expanding health services. Social work must be ever vigilant to avoid being pulled off its own focus by the pressure of the rapidly moving, high-powered medical environment. It must also be ready to respond to the multiple opportunities with a clarity and quality of professional service appropriate to the setting.

MEDICAL CARE PROGRAMS

When social work functions as part of clearly defined programs as is true of medical social work, it becomes important to consider how the goals, structure, and operation of these programs influence the role and performance of the social worker. In his discussion of administrative principles Kidneigh points out that there must be understanding of the various kinds of characteristic programs together with an understanding of the impact of setting upon the process of transforming social policy into social services.[15] Up to this point programs have been discussed mainly in terms of the two major settings in the health field—the hospital and the public health program. Within these larger divisions there are certain subcategories of programs which call for consideration.

---

[15] Kidneigh, *op. cit.*, pp. 60–61.

First should be noted the manner in which essentials and standards of medical care for the masses of people served by these programs are defined by authoritative professional and governmental bodies. The federal agencies and professional organizations (particularly the American Public Health Association, American Medical Association, American Hospital Association, and American Public Welfare Association), working separately or together, are continuously promulgating standards for medical care services offered to the general public and the medically needy. In addition, national voluntary agencies and groups, as well as special conferences to consider specific health problems—such as cardiovascular disease and the health needs of children, of mothers, and of the aged—have issued statements of standards. Thus a succession of authoritative statements regarding the quality and administration of medical care has appeared in recent years.[16] As consultants in health programs and on staffs of agencies, medical social workers have had the opportunity and responsibility to participate in many of these projects. Medical social workers have also participated, and sometimes taken leadership, in the formulation of the medical care standards developed by such federal agencies as the United States Public Health Service, Children's Bureau, and Bureau of Public Assistance for grants-in-aid to states under the social security program. Medical-social consultants in federal programs made a major contribution to the formation of the Commission on Chronic Illness and contributed significantly toward its successful results.

The exact nature of this social contribution to the planning of

---

[16] Joint Committee of the American Hospital Association and American Public Welfare Association, "Hospital Care for the Needy," *Hospitals,* Vol. 13, No. 1 (January 1939), pp. 22–29; *The Quality of Medical Care in a National Health Program* (New York: American Public Health Association, 1949); "The National Conference on the Care of the Long-Term Patient," *Chronic Illness,* Vol. 6, No. 6 (June 1955), pp. 1–11; American Public Health Association and the American Public Welfare Association, *Strengthening Tax-Supported Health and Welfare Services: An Official Statement on Recommended Agency Practices* (Chicago: American Public Welfare Association, 1957).

medical care standards and services has not been documented and would make a good subject for a professional study, perhaps at the doctorate level. This can be regarded as an important function, since these national standards affect the care of millions of persons. As members of government agency staffs and standard-setting professional bodies, these social workers are in a strategic position to direct attention to social factors wherever relevant in planning medical care.

In the traditional hospital setting one program has been outstanding in its influence on the practice of medical social work, that of the United States Veterans Administration. This nationwide hospital program has been built on a broad concept of comprehensive care of high quality, offered by a medical team in which social workers are regularly included. The recognition of the professional nature of social work, with clear civil service definition of positions and adequate remuneration, has strengthened all social work practice. The emphasis on research as a social service responsibility, with regular positions and budgeted funds, has been a further source of strength and is resulting in significant studies. More medical and psychiatric social workers are employed under the Veterans Administration than under any other single auspice. The term "clinical social work" is used to describe their joint practice in these hospitals, in recognition that there are more likenesses than differences in their work.

Beyond the hospital setting, the specific medical care programs in which medical social workers have participated are broadly of three types, those in the areas of public health, public welfare, and rehabilitation. In considering the particular role and contribution of social work it is necessary to take into account the goals, auspices, personnel, and individual characteristics of each medical care program.

In medical care under public health auspices there have been two major programs. One of these was developed through the Health Services Division of the United States Children's Bureau. Under the leadership of Dr. Martha M. Eliot, social work participated in this program from its inception. Standards for a well-rounded program, involving the approach to the "whole child," were established in the Children's Bureau with the assistance of a professional advisory committee. Multidiscipline teams at the federal level—composed of physicians, public health nurses, nutritionists, and medical social workers—implemented these standards through offering regular consultation to the states. Programs for maternal and child health, and for care of crippled children (including a number of smaller programs, as for rheumatic fever or the deafened) were established in all the states. Social workers were included in these state programs throughout the country and found that they could function well within this framework. This Children's Bureau program can be regarded as offering the most complete development of medical social work participation in a country-wide medical care program under public health auspices.

The other major public health program falls under the auspices of the United States Public Health Service. For some time the administration of this agency was divided into sections based on disease categories. Social workers functioning as parts of these various units were able to make some specific contributions, as in relation to tuberculosis and cardiac disease, but found themselves limited by the administrative setup. In recent years the formation of more comprehensive administrative units, as in relation to chronic disease, has offered broader scope for the social work contribution. The activities of social workers at the state and local level have shown considerable diversity, since programs established through Public Health Service grants have not been required to conform to an over-all pattern as the Children's Bureau programs do.

Another important development in the public health field is the employment of medical social workers by voluntary health agencies operating at the national, state, and local level. These programs usually focus on some specific medical condition such as heart disease, cancer, tuberculosis, poliomyelitis, and multiple sclerosis. They are characteristically conditions of a chronic and disabling nature, with a large social component. The social work positions, which are increasing steadily, are consultant in nature and require broad experience in the health field.

Medical care under public welfare auspices represents a different type of program from those described under public health. In this instance, the agency does not itself give the medical services, but has responsibility to see that the clients receive the needed care and to provide the funds to cover the costs. All medical social work is at the consultant and administrative level, so that social workers must have a background of medical-social practice in other programs. In a statement by the American Public Welfare Association the content of the medical social work job is described:

> The medical social worker is concerned with that part of the agency's responsibility which has to do with determining the medical aspects of eligibility; making medical services available; strengthening the agency's policies and procedures so that medical care can be used effectively; and helping staff understand the meaning of illness in their work with the persons served.[17]

Medical social workers have assisted in developing standards and administrative procedures in relation to general medical care and also in relation to the health needs of special groups of clients, such as the blind, the physically disabled parent and the child under Aid to Dependent Children, and pregnant mothers. While it is considered desirable that medical care programs in public welfare should be directed by physicians, the needed number of doctors have not entered the field, so that medical-social consultants have been called upon to assume many administrative functions. Thus they have not been able to develop fully a major social work function, that of helping agency staff to recognize and deal with the psychosocial problems of illness, disability, and medical care to be found in their caseloads. In the most recently developed public welfare program, that of Aid to the Disabled, multidiscipline practice occurs regularly as medical-social consultants work with physicians on review teams to assess the eligibility of disabled applicants for aid. The rehabilitation opportunities in this and

---

[17] *The Medical Social Worker in the Public Welfare Agency* (Chicago: American Public Welfare Association, 1955), p. 3.

other public welfare programs are being increasingly emphasized.

What might be regarded as a third major program area, that of rehabilitation, is less well defined than the others. Rehabilitation can be regarded as both a social concept and a professional process. Out of the concept has grown a social movement which has greatly broadened concepts of medical care and has stimulated extension of resources and services. In program terms, rehabilitation can best be viewed in two parts: (1) the federal vocational rehabilitation program, and (2) the specific rehabilitation services offered under community auspices. When the federal program was given its first major extension in wartime, under the Office of Vocational Rehabilitation, medical social work was offered an unusual opportunity to participate in the formulation of standards for the medical care program—known as Physical Restoration Services—through direct conferences with the medical director and participation in the professional advisory committee established for the new program. Medical social concepts and an appropriate role for medical social work were integrated with the planning from the beginning. Because of shortage of professional personnel and other factors, the program did not develop as visualized and relatively few medical social workers entered this practice during the first phase.

When the services were again expanded by federal legislation about a decade later, medical social work responded to the new stimulus. This time the expansion took place mainly through educational institutions offering preparation for the personnel engaged in the program. The additional sources of funds enabled schools of social work to add faculty in order to develop teaching content and field work opportunities in the area of rehabilitation. The thinking and activity thus engendered spread from education into practice. Meanwhile there was a rapid increase in medical services focused on rehabilitation. Some were definitely called "rehabilitation clinics, wards, and centers." In other instances the rehabilitation emphasis on ongoing services was strengthened and emphasized. Some of these resources were developed by grants from the federal Office of Vocational Rehabilitation and others resulted from the growing concern for rehabilitation throughout health and welfare field. Medical social workers are participating in many such rehabilitation teams and services.

Medical social workers are still in the process of defining their functions in these public health, public welfare, and rehabilitation programs and lack adequate data to evaluate their experience with a long perspective. It was pointed out earlier that social workers function most effectively in agencies and programs based on goals and concepts in consonance with those of social work. Thus medical social workers have functioned best in programs where the concept of medical care is sufficiently comprehensive to permit the inclusion and spread of social concepts and where there is an abiding concern for making medical care of good quality available to all persons who need it. The programs showing these characteristics have been those carried on under health auspices, with medical leadership. Programs administered under nonmedical auspices have for various reasons placed less emphasis on the importance of getting health services to people and on improving the quality of medical care. All of the programs, however, whatever their auspices, have important medical-social implications. The welfare of millions of persons is involved. At an appropriate time the professional group would do well to explore in some consistent manner the opportunities and limitations in working under these various auspices. Attention should be directed toward increasing the effectiveness of medical social work in all these areas.

NEW TRENDS IN MEDICAL CARE

Rapid technological and social change in our society continually produces new approaches to the problems of medical care and new patterns of organizing services. Social workers in the health field are being offered many promising opportunities for participation and service outside the traditional health settings. Flexibility, readiness to function in new ways, and creative use of social work knowledge and skill are called for. Two examples of such trends in medical social work are briefly noted, as illustrations of what is actually happening in practice.

Hospital Home-Care Programs

One manifestation of the recent increasing recognition that the hospital is a part of the community is the expansion of hospital home-care programs. There is already a considerable literature on home care, including several descriptive studies.[18] In all these programs, social workers have been given a significant role, both in the planning and the rendering of the service.

The major purpose of the home-care programs is to extend the hospital's services into the community so that long-term patients can have the necessary care within their own home and family, whenever their condition and the situation make this feasible.[19] The programs can be regarded as good examples of comprehensive medical care. The basic home-care team usually consists of physicians, nurses, and medical social workers. All important decisions are made jointly and the care of the patient is carried on as a team operation. In each case, careful decision must be made as to whether home care is indicated and likely to be successful. Customarily the social worker makes a home visit as a part of the social study of the family situation.

As can readily be perceived, these programs have a salutary effect in stimulating and rounding out the practice of medical social work in certain directions. The patient is clearly placed within his family. The social worker is stimulated to observe and to think constantly about the role of the family in illness and in rehabilitative effort. The necessity for a visit to the home in connection with planning medical care re-emphasizes the home visit as a social work tool. It is now again emphasized and dignified as a method appropriate and necessary for a profession which is primarily concerned with social relationships.

The fact that the home-care team regularly includes the nurse and social worker and recognizes their contribution to medicine

---

[18] *A Study of Selected Home-Care Programs* (Washington, D. C.: United States Public Health Service, 1955).

[19] *The Place of the Medical Social Worker in the Home Care of the Long-Term Patient* (New York: National Foundation for Infantile Paralysis, 1953).

has increased the social worker's security. In the words of Dr. George A. Silver, "... it seemed advisable to lend the scientific internist and pediatrician the skills of social work and public health nursing. These two professions were coming to grips with the increasingly complex social aspects of medical care just as the medical profession was yielding responsibility." [20] There is an added spur to social work performance in the fact that in every case a definite decision and recommendation must be made as to whether, from the social work viewpoint, home care is justified. The social worker must stand up and be counted along with the other professions. There must be readiness to make a social judgment, with the implied prediction as to whether this particular patient and family—in view of the personal, social, and economic factors—can collaborate effectively in a home-care plan. Observation of such home-care teams in action shows that medical social workers have been stimulated to improve their capacity for orderly arrangement of their data, communication to other professions, and capacity for decision-making, as a result of the special opportunities and demands of these service programs.

Social Work in a Prepaid Group Medical Care Plan

Another way in which new trends are appearing is that medical social work is finding a place in other than the traditional settings. One such new auspice is the health insurance program, which serves the average, self-supporting family. The Health Insurance Plan of Greater New York is a community-sponsored organization offering comprehensive medical services, including psychiatric consultation and health education, provided through over thirty separate medical groups. There are more than half a million subscribers and nearly a thousand doctors. From the beginning, the HIP founders believed that social work consultation had a place in a comprehensive health plan. In 1953 Edith Alt began to explore and demonstrate a social work service. This was a dif-

---

[20] George A. Silver, "Social Medicine at the Montefiore Hospital—A Practical Approach to Community Health Problems," *American Journal of Public Health,* Vol. 48, No. 6 (June 1958), p. 730.

ficult undertaking, since no precedent for this type of activity was known. By the end of 1958, four experienced social workers, known as "Consultants in Community Resources," were functioning in four boroughs of Greater New York.[21]

The social work program was defined as offering: (1) direct service, in the nature of brief counseling service to subscribers, (2) consultation service on community resources and social services to HIP doctors and other personnel, also to community agencies, hospitals, and unions, and (3) educational activities, including preparation of written materials. In the process of developing the program, extensive conferences were held with community agencies and hospitals, based on actual problems found among HIP subscribers. Since physicians were to be encouraged to use community resources directly, a *Guide for Community Resources* was prepared and has been reprinted annually.

Social workers employed for this ground-breaking service had to be well-trained, seasoned persons with a medical and psychiatric background, able to work independently and with ability in the broader public health and community approach. Capacity to work in this new kind of setting calls for persons with knowledge, conviction, and flexibility. The wide range of services expected of them requires technical competence in casework, consultation, and education.

The direct service program is planned not only to help with social and psychological needs of referred individuals but also to help referring doctors learn more about the subscriber's problems and feel themselves a part of the effort to improve the situation. Analysis of the first referrals showed that behavior difficulties, including diagnosed psychiatric illness and marital and parent-child problems, ranked highest. Also important were obstacles to arranging care, including high costs for certain items, along with a smaller number of rehabilitation and terminal care problems.

Some results of this social work contribution are already apparent. HIP subscribers are receiving service which otherwise would

---

[21] Edith S. Alt, *Newer Challenges to Social Work in the Prevention of Illness*. Paper presented at National Conference on Social Welfare, Chicago, Ill., May 15, 1958; also other materials on the HIP program.

never reach them. The long search that many people make before they obtain the care they need is evident. Some activities are truly preventive. HIP doctors have been using the social service departments of hospitals in which they work more effectively than in the past. As a result of social work recognition of the problem presented to families by the high cost of prescription drugs, an outstanding city-wide study was carried out and published by a citizens' group, with the participation of the New York Academy of Medicine. Attention was also directed to the economic difficulty of obtaining ambulatory psychiatric treatment for persons of low and middle income. Other unmet needs are being observed and brought to public notice.

Alt points out that participation in this new type of setting, a health insurance program, has stimulated a wide range of activities that might not develop in a more traditional setting. Certain implications for medical social work are of special interest. This clientele differs from that in most hospitals and social agencies in that it is a working population, composed largely of highly motivated, self-directing people, able to use help productively. The relationship of the social worker to the subscriber differs from that in traditional settings in that the latter has contractual rights—an asset for social work through establishing a more independent climate for treatment and requiring greater precision in focus.[22] Questions have been raised whether social workers feel less secure in working with private physicians and subscriber families under conditions of such a program. Obviously this type of experience must be developed, since many trends point in this direction. Medical social workers are working with union groups. They are operating in their own private offices, offering service to private physicians and patients. They are increasingly concerned with insurance patients and self-supporting families. It is already being suggested that a unit covering social work consultation might well be included as a regular part of private group medical practice. As Alt indicates, high competence combined with flexibility is necessary to move with

---

[22] Edith S. Alt, "Social Work Consultation in a Prepayment Medical Care Plan," *American Journal of Public Health,* Vol. 49, No. 3 (March 1959), p. 353.

these rapidly changing patterns of care and the new opportunities which they offer.

IMPLICATIONS OF NEW TRENDS

These developments—the participation of social workers in rapidly developing programs of home care and in prepaid medical care—show the great importance of creativity and perspective. There must be readiness to move and experiment in new directions without throwing over what was learned in the past. How can the social work contribution be at the same time valid and more effective? Whatever changes in the old pattern are made, they should not be seen as adjustments to immediate emergencies, such as shortage of personnel, but in terms of long-range planning and defined social goals.

5

social work in multidiscipline care of the patient

As a further means of placing social work in the health field, it will be helpful to observe the practicing social worker using the social work essentials in a basic service in this field—the care of the patient. To this end, some of the significant aspects of social work participation in the care of the patient are discussed. The aim is to show how social work appears in the constant interchange of multidiscipline practice in the health field.

Multidiscipline practice is becoming a major characteristic of the health field; nevertheless, it still remains a vague concept. Although a considerable literature on the subject has developed both inside and outside social work, a comprehensive and authoritative analysis of basic principles relating to this practice has not yet been produced.

Because of the trend toward multidiscipline practice, there has been great interest in "teamwork" in social work and in the health field. The term is loosely used to describe any and all types of co-operation and collaboration—inside and outside of agencies, between all sorts of personnel, and in all kinds of activities. A distinction is made in this monograph between interagency co-operation and multidiscipline practice, the latter referring to interprofessional collaboration under the auspices of a single agency—in the present instance, a health agency. Multidiscipline practice is the over-all term used to cover all such practice.

Multidiscipline practice is not necessarily a highly organized kind of teamwork. It exists wherever members of two or more professions are working together on the same assignment in one agency. A medical social worker may, for instance, be co-operating with several physicians, nurses, and members of other professions in the care of an individual patient. The social worker will meet them at different times and places to confer about the patient. Many important conferences are held in hospital corridors. The whole group may never meet all together during the course of the case. Yet because each knows his own role and competence, and because the medical social worker asks each the pertinent questions, shares the relevant social data, and in moving along on the plan integrates each segment of such activity into the total planning, this kind of collaboration is successful. This rather informal and fluid pattern is actually one by which the greater part of patient care is now carried on and is likely to be carried on in future. In public health programs, where there are fewer clinicians and the public health nurse is the major practitioner, similar one-to-one working relationships are an important method of collaboration, particularly between medical social workers and nurses.

Multidiscipline practice rests upon two basic requirements: (1) unity of purpose, and (2) difference in knowledge and function. Since it grows out of specialization, each member must make his own expert contribution, distinct from that of others and appropriate to his particular focus. These different contributions must be integrated through common objectives. Multidiscipline practice is a way of thinking, of keeping ideas related; a way of feeling, of readiness to share; and a way of doing, of adding one's contribution to that of others so that something larger emerges from the combination. It is a constant interweaving of all these phases of professional activity.

Persons who have not participated regularly in such practice seem to have difficulty in appreciating its significance. They tend to emphasize its negative and limiting aspects. Actually, in our scientifically and technically oriented economy, which is dependent upon ever increasing specialization, multidiscipline practice is the characteristic and essential work method. When disciplines work together, the contribution of each is enlarged. Furthermore, interprofessional collaboration is in its nature dynamic and may be able to offset some of the limitations of the bureaucratic method, which is another, more rigid way of combining differing contributions. Thus multidiscipline practice is to be visualized as an opportunity, a basic way of bringing service to society. The health field is an outstanding example of such practice at its best.

COLLABORATION WITH THE PHYSICIAN

What is involved for the social worker in being a part of multidiscipline patient care in a meaningful and responsible manner? In attempting to answer this question, the social worker's relation to the medical problem and the physician are emphasized. These relationships are major components of social work practice in the health field. Moreover, although it would be desirable to describe and analyze the social worker's relationship with other team members than the physician and in other activities than patient care, the limitations of our present knowledge and of this discussion require that the situation be simplified for purposes of analysis.

The essential nature of this practice can be identified through such a description. Some of the requirements of collaboration while maintaining social work identity will be observable. A typical instance, covering the care of a patient in a hospital ward, is discussed. The practice as presented is found where medical social work is effectively practiced. It may sound "ideal" because it has been freed from the reality pressures and interruptions that occur in regular practice. At a later stage of analysis it will be possible to consider how the self-image of physicians and social workers, the problems of status, the demands of the daily job, and similar factors affect the actual carrying through of patient care.

The core of medical social work is the situation in which a physician and medical social worker are working together to help an individual patient. The broader services, the preventive emphasis, all other aspects of medical social work have grown out of this patient-focused activity and are still related to it. The subtleties of the process by which doctor, social worker, and patient function together are not fully understood. These professional skills of physicians and social workers have not been described in any comprehensive way in the literature or in social case records. An effort is made here to capture some important facets of the situation not customarily formulated.

A Hypothetical Case

> The situation starts with the referral of a patient to the social worker by the resident ward physician in a hospital. This doctor and this social worker are both regularly assigned to this ward and accustomed to work together. He tells the social worker that the patient is a young man who was admitted to the ward as an emergency five days ago with myocardial infarction (a form of acute heart disease). The patient is making slow progress, has some atypical symptoms, and is excessively anxious. The medical staff would like the help of social service in determining whether the patient's home situation and worries may be affecting his condition. They also think that he may need assistance with his later readjustment, as he has never been seriously ill before. They have seen his wife, who seems distraught and of little help to her husband. The physician indicates that the patient is able to begin talking with the social worker. He is expected to remain in the hospital for about a month. There may be permanent cardiac damage.

The social worker in the medical setting is concerned, like any other social worker, with understanding the client as a person and his definition of the problem. The individual must be understood in relation to his illness, his family, his other social relationships, and his sociocultural milieu. Interviews with the patient (or someone close to him) are the major source for such understanding. The medical social worker, however, regularly derives understanding from other sources, such as the medical staff and record, observation of the patient in ward and clinic, and contacts with relatives and friends who accompany and visit the patient. Thus the social worker must review the total relevant situation and place the patient's problem within this framework.

From the opening conference with the physician, the social worker's next step is a careful review of the patient's medical record. Those not familiar with the medical setting may ask why the medical record is reviewed before seeing the patient. The answer is that the social worker has responsibility, as part of the medical institution, to know and understand the medical situation. In order to help the patient, the social worker must know its implications for him and his family, the problems it presents to them, and the potential stresses. This knowledge is, furthermore, essential for functioning as a social worker in the medical team, which means assisting the team to recognize the psychosocial aspects of the illness in planning the patient's care.

The social worker comes to this situation with a good general knowledge regarding the etiology, treatment, and prognosis of the various forms of heart disease. The worker knows that myocardial infarction frequently strikes suddenly, that all patients are anxious at first, that recurrent attacks and angina occur in some patients, that emotional and social stress can affect the prognosis, and that the convalescent period is of vital importance in recovery and social adjustment.[1] The worker knows further that most patients follow a strict medical regime in the hospital, beginning with complete bed care, and then require additional weeks of convalescence at home, the whole recovery period encompassing two months or more. Some patients are placed on special medication requiring constant medical supervision and frequent laboratory tests after they leave the hospital. The worker must now obtain adequate understanding of this particular patient's medical situation. It will be important not to get lost in the mass of medical details but to push through to the knowledge that is essential for the effective rendering of an appropriate social casework service, included as one part of this man's medical care.

The analysis of a medical record for social work purposes involves a skill that must be learned through practice. The structure

---

[1] Herman K. Hellerstein and Elaine Goldston, "Rehabilitation of Patients with Heart Disease," *Postgraduate Medicine,* Vol. 15, No. 3 (March 1954), pp. 265–278.

of the medical record and the technical aspects of medical reporting must be grasped in order to identify the key elements, including pertinent aspects of past medical history, the diagnosis, the treatment recommendations, and any other features peculiar to the individual case. There may be nursing notes that reveal important facts about the patient's reaction to his illness. The worker is approaching the material from a social work viewpoint. Thus from the beginning the implications of the medical situation for the patient and family are being considered. How clear or confused is the medical picture? Is there disagreement among the doctors (and thus resultant anxiety for the patient) regarding diagnosis and treatment? What evidence is there that the doctors have understood and related understandingly to this person as an individual? These and many similar questions must be considered.

Some of the medical information the social worker needs is not customarily recorded in the record by physicians in the form needed for social work. It is important to know how well the patient will be able to function, what his physical limitations and treatment regime will demand of him, and what his general prognosis appears to be. This information will be sought directly from the physician. Other questions must be answered from the social worker's own evaluation of the total medical-social situation. Two points should be noted. At the start, and throughout the case, the social worker has the opportunity of basing social work practice on an analysis of the situation by another profession—a highly disciplined and scientific type of analysis, which is of great reliability. Furthermore, from the beginning and usually throughout the case, the social worker has greater knowledge than the patient regarding one aspect of his problem, the medical aspect, often thus knowing what stresses lie ahead for him, which he cannot know.

Since this man with myocardial infarction, whom the social worker is about to see, is still acutely ill, the worker will proceed carefully. Before seeing him a conference with the ward nurse will be helpful. In this conference the worker obtains valuable information about the patient as an individual, particularly his attitude and behavior on the ward. The nurse is also in a good position to observe the patient's relation to the various members of his family, as they come to visit him. In seeing the patient, the social worker is taking the initiative in reaching out to him. At once a major characteristic of medical social work appears, namely, that the patient customarily does not himself apply for social work service. The patient comes to the health agency seeking medical care. He often does not know that social work is a part of the medical service or perceive how it could help him. He is most frequently referred by the doctor, or some other professional person, who is aware of problems in the situation. The problems may be large or small, predominantly medical or predominantly social, but they are always concerned with interaction of medical and psychosocial factors. The social worker is thus keenly aware of the need to establish a relationship that will enable the patient to respond to, and make use of, social casework service, if this seems relevant to his needs. The social worker is ready to move slowly and to return for several interviews, since the patient requires time to develop sufficient awareness of his problem and confidence in the worker to decide whether he wishes social work intervention in his situation. Because this is an ill person, the worker is also observing carefully whether illness has produced temporary regression, depression, or other emotional reactions not necessarily characteristic of this individual's normal personality. Under such circumstances lessened self-direction and lessened maturity of attitude are anticipated, while greater dependency is expected as a phenomenon of illness. Continuing with the hypothetical cardiac case:

> The social worker listens to the patient as he makes a beginning in giving his own picture of his situation, his feelings about his illness, his hopes and fears for the future. The worker also talks with his wife to learn her reactions. In this interchange, which may involve a number of interviews, the social worker gains understanding of their strengths and problems, and of their way of handling past stressful experiences, while they gain some initial sense of clarification and support.
>
> The social worker now returns to confer more fully with the physician. These are two responsible professional people planning together for this patient's best care. Out of the considerable knowledge now gained regarding the patient, the social worker has selected and organized those facts most relevant for the physician's medical understanding. The aspects reported and the questions asked are keyed to engage his best medical intelligence. How do these psychosocial

findings affect the medical picture of this particular case? This patient, his illness, and his social situation must be carefully assessed, as important decisions affecting his welfare are being made. Together the physician and social worker evaluate the problem and decide what each will do in forwarding this patient's treatment.

The manner in which the thinking of physician and social worker interweave in progressive forward movement in a case is suggested in the diagram on page 80.

In actual practice the medical and social study and treatment overlap and each stimulates the other. The back-and-forth pattern of interaction within the larger onward flow of movement in the case is the major characteristic to be emphasized.

Having completed this type of evaluation with the physician, the social worker returns to the patient and thus the process continues throughout the case. The orderly method described in the *Working Definition of Social Work Practice* as basic in social work is followed in a general way, although necessarily adapted to each situation. In casework the phases are customarily described as study, diagnosis, and treatment. Social treatment begins with the first contact. Because of the rapid tempo of medical care, considerable social treatment may be needed early in a case to meet immediate problems. Under these circumstances social study and diagnosis move along concurrently with social treatment, at their own pace.

In order to define the focus of social treatment, the social worker must identify the key elements and persons in the situation. Work is frequently done with family members, in terms of their relation to the patient and also in terms of the impact of illness upon them as individuals or upon the family as a unit. In some instances, when the patient is too ill to be able to deal with reality, major work is done with a family member. Sometimes the home is visited. Because the hospital is such a complex environment, much can be done to influence the patient's care through planning with the hospital personnel, not only physicians but administrators, nurses, and other members of the medical team, and also nonprofessional personnel. Sometimes the key figure is a school teacher or worker in a social agency. Much additional work is done through commu-

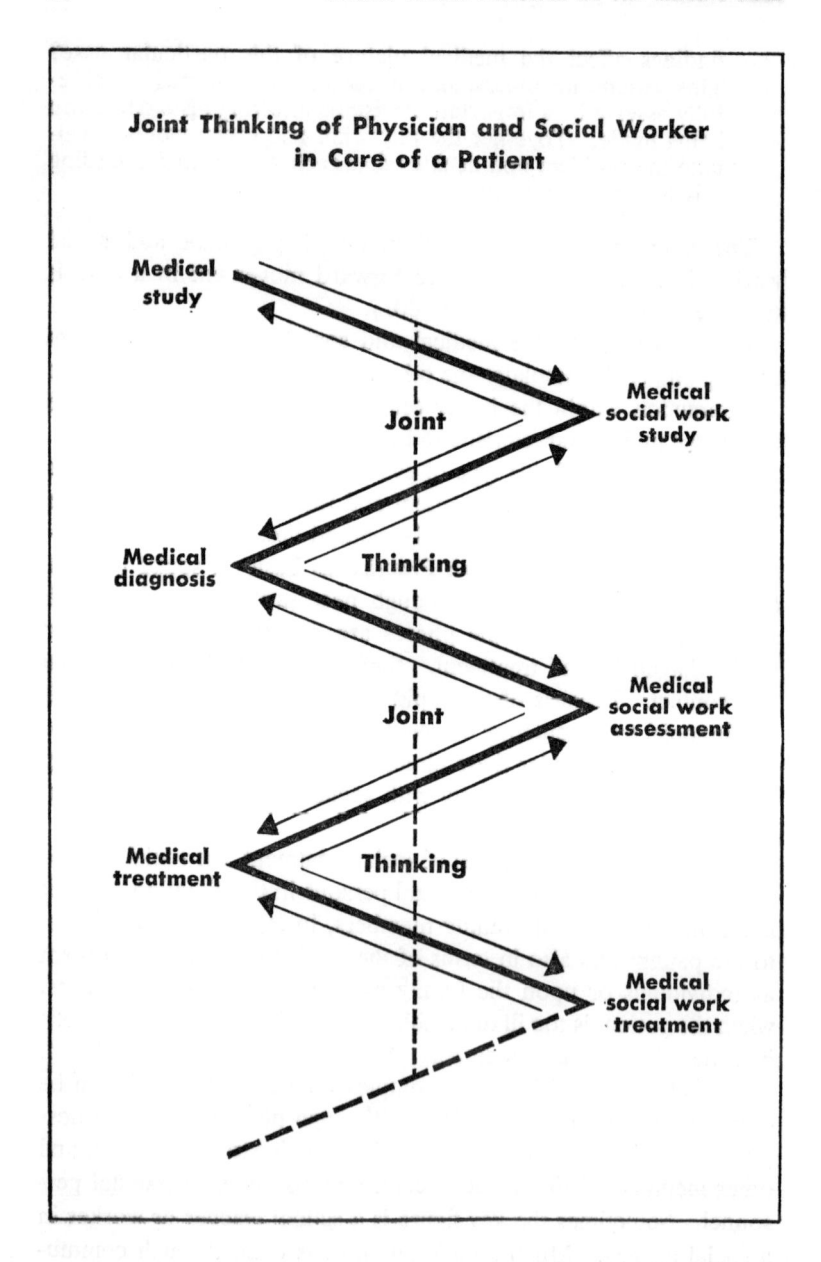

Joint Thinking of Physician and Social Worker in Care of a Patient

- Medical study
- Medical social work study

Joint Thinking

- Medical diagnosis
- Medical social work assessment

Joint Thinking

- Medical treatment
- Medical social work treatment

nity health and welfare agencies, both in learning to understand the patient and family better and in offering needed services.

In moving through the process of study, assessment, and treatment, the social worker keeps closely in touch with the physicians and nurses caring for the patient and the developing history on the medical record; the worker also keeps tying in the new developments with the social work thinking. Poor social work too often results from failure to keep the medical and psychosocial aspects soundly related as a situation progresses. The social worker's basic role can hardly be carried out unless this is done. There have been instances of social workers who came into the hospital from a nonmedical background and who carried on their own interviews with the patient in their offices, following a treatment plan based on their "casework diagnosis," relatively unrelated to the medical team and the ongoing medical situation. The risks of such procedure are only too clear. The patient's medical condition or the medical treatment may change without the worker's being aware of the shift. The casework relationship, under such circumstances, competes with and may undermine the medical team's relation with the patient. The results are likely to be not only disturbing but even hazardous for the patient. It is obvious that a medical institution does not welcome, and cannot afford to sponsor, any professional worker who is not responsibly relating his contribution with that of other team members. This does not mean blind agreement, since many questions may and should be raised by the social worker, but it does mean a kind of integration of all professional efforts which works for the patient's best welfare.

The central element of the medical-social case is the medical-social problem as defined by patient and social worker together in the context of the casework relationship, and integrated with the medical planning through the worker's conferences with the physicians. Each starts with his own perception of the problem. Through discussion and interaction they tend to come together as the case moves. Many cases start from perception of a minor difficulty which proves to be only a symptom of a deeper problem, such as initial need for a diet which opens up all the problems of life adjustment to diabetes. Because of a constant social orientation and special sensitivity, the social worker usually perceives more psychosocial problems early in a situation than the others do. Patient and physician tend to move toward greater awareness and recognition as they discuss the problem back and forth. At present we have only general impressions of this process from experience and need to know how it actually takes place.

> This patient with heart disease proves to be one whose problems are more severe than the average. The first attack leaves him with a damaged heart, which requires adjustment to less strenuous work. Not having built up sufficient security and flexibility in his past life to deal with such a crisis, he is overfearful. Following convalescence, he is afraid to leave the protection of his home to enter retraining directed toward rehabilitation at his place of employment. His wife is not sufficiently mature to give the help he particularly needs at this time. The social worker moves along with the patient as the course of his illness and his own attitudes change, with ups and downs of physical and emotional progression and regression. Gradually he is able to talk more freely to the social worker about his feelings, with some relief and increase in security. The wife, also, makes some gains in learning to help him find a new level of living. The social worker continues working with them both until they can cope with the problems which this illness and its after-effects brought so suddenly and stressfully into their lives.

Casework As Part of Medical Care

This description covers the integration of what is usually known as "medical teamwork" with social casework. From this approach, it becomes clear that the casework process with the patient cannot —and should not—be isolated from the total ongoing medical care, of which it is a part. Two aspects not usually emphasized should be particularly noted.

The social worker is continuously concerned with all the significant working relationships that are involved in care of the patient, that is, the worker-patient relationship, the patient's relationship with physicians and other team members who are closest to him, and the worker's own relationship with them in turn. The social worker consciously assesses the influence of these various relationships upon the progress of the case and endeavors to strengthen the positive aspects of all of them.

The other aspect to be emphasized is that of joint thinking and planning by the professions. In the discussion of "teamwork" there has been so much emphasis on personality interaction (emotional aspects) and joint activity (doing things together) that the importance of the intellectual aspect (thinking together) is sometimes forgotten. In the process here described, there is first communication and interchange of information and knowledge between doctors, nurses, and social workers, leading to some type of professional judgment or decision, on the basis of which there is effective division of labor in rendering service to each individual patient.

Further consideration of multidiscipline practice is presented later. This preliminary discussion is designed to highlight some of the outstanding characteristics of social work when practiced as part of medical care.

SOME CHARACTERISTICS OF THE SOCIAL WORK ROLE

In the preceding instance of multidiscipline practice it is evident that the social worker had to be constantly aware of two orientations: (1) toward the patient and his family, and (2) toward the medical team. This necessity to be constantly oriented in these two directions, toward the persons being served and toward the professional staff of the agency, is a characteristic of social work in non-social work programs. The knowledge, values, and methods required for these two orientations have important differences. The implications of carrying these two orientations together, without serious imbalance or conflict, have not been sufficiently examined.[2] This problem is so important that some review of basic social work concepts will be undertaken at this point in order to clarify this aspect of multidiscipline practice in the health field.

---

[2] The idea of dual identification and dual responsibility also applies here. The concept of orientation is used because it has fewer secondary meanings and because it suggests the changes in the social worker's position and direction of thinking and activity which must actually take place if the identifications are to be maintained and the responsibilities are to be fulfilled.

Social work is recognized as a helping profession, concerned with the improved social functioning of people and whatever promotes or interferes with that social functioning. When social workers give direct service in situations where problems are present, as in casework, the activity can be described as therapeutic, in the original broad sense of the term. It aims to "cure" or alleviate the problem. When the social work activity involves no direct contact with clients, as in community organization, it can no longer be regarded as therapeutic, but it does retain many of the same characteristics.

Social work values emphasize the importance of the individual's self-fulfillment and growth. The social worker starts where the individual is, tries to see the situation through his eyes and endeavors to understand why he behaves as he does. The social work relationship offered to the client is accepting and initially permissive.[3] The client senses that the usual social controls on his behavior have been lessened. He is freed to "be himself" and to express his real feelings. The social worker thus gains understanding of the individual's motivations and hopes to lessen some of the barriers and inhibitions that have blocked him from using his full strengths. When the individual is under emotional stress, the relationship offers support, as needed. The goal is to help the individual to recognize and deal with reality, without evasion, so far as possible through his own strengths and with whatever outside help is needed, as from his family, the social worker, and the resources of the community. Measures to deal with the psychic and social aspects are variously combined according to the social worker's assessment of the situation.

Successful social functioning, free of excessive stress and conflict, demands a reasonable degree of compliance with the prevailing pattern of social relationships and social norms. As the case proceeds, therefore, the social worker necessarily moves away from

---

[3] Elliot Studt shows that the social worker in the correctional field cannot safely offer such a permissive relationship because of the risk that the delinquent might act in a manner harmful to himself and others. The relationship offered to the delinquent aims to help him maintain and strengthen adaptive patterns. *See* Elliot Studt, *Education for Social Workers in the Correctional Field* (New York: Council on Social Work Education, 1959), pp. 23–24.

the initial permissive attitude and directs the client's attention toward the realities of the social environment. The social worker recognizes that the client may not be able to deal with the situation at once and shows that help will be given in taking the necessary steps, but does indicate clearly the social reality that they both must face together. This movement toward a temporarily permissive attitude and then back toward a recognition of social reality is an essential element in the helping process in social work, since the aim is to help toward improved social functioning.[4]

When the social worker has no direct relation with the individual or group, this therapeutic relation cannot operate. But it should be noted that the same basic focus and values continue to prevail. In group planning, in policy determination, in community organization the social worker consistently identifies with the persons being served, starts his thinking where they are, sees the situation from their viewpoint. He seeks not only the outer facts but the meaning of the situation, its particular stressfulness, to individuals and groups. This value orientation and the methodology which accompanies it are of basic importance when social work is functioning in a regular relationship with other professions. When certain aspects of the social system or certain prevailing social norms are found to be stressful and harmful to many people, social work endeavors to modify these elements through the processes of social change. As is often pointed out, the helping role must be understood at two levels, in relation to the individual and in relation to society. It does not aim toward rigid social conformity but toward bringing about change in both the individual and the social environment.

Thus the dynamics of the helping role rest on a certain way of viewing social functioning in terms of its meaning to the people in the situation, identifying with and relating to them, understanding the nature of the problem, and using methods to bring about change in the individual and/or the environment so as to decrease stress and improve the situation. Also, since social work is concurrently active in interpreting to representatives of the social institutions

---

[4] Helen Harris Perlman, "Social Components of Casework Practice," in *The Social Welfare Forum* (New York: Columbia University Press, 1953), pp. 124–136.

and the social order the nature of social stress and the inadequacies of the social system, social work acts as an integrating influence. It helps people to make better use of society's services and helps the social institutions to be more responsive to people's needs.

Orientation Toward the Patient

The social worker shares the aura of authority in the medical institution, which encourages the patient to have confidence in the social worker's understanding of the medical problems and social expertness. The social worker does not, however, carry responsibility for the medical aspects of care and does not make medical recommendations. The physician's position is based on a scientific and professional analysis of the situation which enables him to recommend to the patient what can be regarded as the "best" action to be taken, in the light of medical knowledge. The social worker focuses on the individual's particular life situation and its meaning for him. These positions of the physician and social worker are complementary in contributing toward a more inclusive understanding and handling of the problem than if each were meeting the patient's needs alone.

The social worker's role in multidiscipline practice, as oriented toward individual care, can be better understood by examining its two contrasting manifestations. Let us first assume a medical team in which the members are all working comfortably together as in the cardiac case discussed in the preceding section. The physicians and nurses are interested in the social aspects of patient care, accept the social worker's expertness in this area, and delegate responsibility in appropriate cases. In the greater number of instances the patients can be expected to move along with the team with confidence, as the various members bring their particular expertness to the study and diagnosis of the medical problem and the carrying through of the treatment. The social worker's role is to individualize the patient in relation to the psychosocial aspects of his situation. From the patient's viewpoint, here is someone who listens to him and is primarily interested in what concerns *him*. This person does not push or hurry him toward any plan. He is permitted to say what he needs to say in regard to his illness and the hospital, without being regarded as weak because of his fears or unco-operative because of his criticism. The worker does not necessarily approve what he says but accepts his feelings as important. Furthermore, the social worker helps him to clarify some of his difficulties, to disentangle his confusions, to get his life situation related to his illness so that he can do something about it in his own way. Because of the fact that social workers are trained to accept irrational behavior and to understand the nature of the professional relationship with the patient, the social work role probably appears in rather sharp contrast to the medical role for many patients, under the above circumstances. This difference is a positive factor in its effect upon the patient's care. The patient is enabled to understand and deal with his problem more effectively. The understanding of the psychosocial aspects, gained by the social worker, is conveyed to the medical team, to further the comprehensive care of the patient. This is the traditional positive role of the social worker on the medical team, as repeatedly described in the literature, as understood and accepted by many physicians.

But there are some situations where the patient and the medical team do not move along smoothly together. The causes of the difficulty may be on either or both sides. The patient may not be able to play his part in the relationship, which implies following the physician's guidance and conforming with the expected pattern of behavior in the medical institution. He may find his medical situation extremely stressful and may not be receiving from the medical team the acceptance and help that he particularly needs at this time. Some patients have difficulty in working with authority. Some medical groups make excessively heavy demands and show little flexibility or capacity to accept negative and "unco-operative" patients. If the member of the health profession is authoritative in manner and attitude, the problem is still further compounded. Thus a gap may open between the patient and the members of the medical team.

What does this mean for the medical social worker? The characteristic social work approach, that of identifying with the patient and seeking to understand what the situation means to him, enables the worker to play an appropriate and particularly helpful role.

Without social work intervention such a situation is likely to lead to breakdown of medical care and possibly to "discharge against advice." Before this can happen, however, the social worker reaches out to the patient and moves with him in whatever direction he needs to go in coming to grips with his problem in his own way. The theoretical explanation of this role has been set forth by Dr. James S. Plant. He points out that there are always individuals who cannot fit into the general social pattern, like the truant child in school. Because of various psychosocial problems, these persons are blocked in working successfully with the social institution. They need someone who is a part of the setting yet separate enough so that they can talk freely of their troubles in working with the institution. Then this professional person helps in getting the individual and the institution together again in a more effective working relationship. This is an important role of social work when it is part of a larger institution.[5]

While listening to the patient, the social worker appears to move toward him and away from the medical team. This is not only because the patient is having difficulty over his medical care. It is also because of the difference in the way medicine and social work view him. The physician sees him primarily in his patient role, as an individual who is ill and needs medical care. The social worker sees him as a social being, a member of a family and other social groups, under stress from his illness and concerned with its effect upon his life situation. He must be understood and accepted first from this approach, before he can be helped to deal with the realities of his medical problem. In this process, however, the social worker must make sure that his relationship with the hospital is safeguarded. He must not be allowed to go so far in his negative attitudes that he puts himself beyond the bounds of help. He needs the reassurance that he can resume his patient role, when he is better able to participate in his medical care. The social worker is careful not to relinquish identification with the medical team and makes this position clear to the patient. The worker supports the validity of the medical recommendations but has no need to enforce them.

---

[5] James S. Plant, *Personality and the Cultural Pattern* (New York: The Commonwealth Fund, 1937).

An example can better illustrate this complex situation.

> A self-supporting widow in her late fifties, employed in an office and living alone, was examined in a gynecological clinic and advised to enter the hospital because of a mass in her abdomen, thought to be malignant. She did not return. In their concern over her delay the clinic staff (resident physician and nurse) followed up the patient with several letters and telephone calls, urging her to return at once. When these measures failed, the social worker was asked to help. She arranged to see the patient in her home by appointment and listened for over an hour while the patient first criticized the hospital and then told the many reasons why she had not returned—about her brother who died of rectal cancer which his doctors could not cure, her doubt of the doctors who examined her and seemed "so young," her fears about anesthesia, and her need to get all her affairs at work and at home in order before she went to the hospital. The social worker showed that she respected the patient's viewpoint and, at her request, described in detail just what would happen when she was admitted to the ward (thus giving reassurance that the situation would not get beyond her control). This was obviously a person who had to feel that she was in control of her situation and who had only been driven further away by the pressure exerted upon her by the medical staff. Although at the end of the interview the patient said she would come to the hospital, there was a still further period of delay, during which the social worker maintained contact with her. When the patient finally did enter the ward, the social worker made a special effort to alert the admitting office and ward personnel to her feelings about the hospital and her illness. The surgery was successfully performed. The patient told the social worker, "You were my connecting link with the hospital."

The general outline of this situation is familiar. It shows the characteristic permissive approach of social work (which is the one most helpful to the patient) as contrasted with the authoritative approach of the medical staff. When such a case is in progress the negative and divisive elements may appear so conspicuous as to raise questions about whether the social worker really is functioning as a team member. Such situations place considerable strain on all involved and may result in confusion unless the social worker understands what is going on.

What is required here is an understanding of an important and dynamic *social role*. The social worker must be equipped with certain professional skills but these alone do not determine the role, which grows out of the social worker's goals, focus, and particular position in the medical team and the health agency. It is important to note that the physician and nurse cannot carry this particular helping role, as maintained by the social worker. As Dr. Plant so clearly points out, the physician or nurse is in the patient's eyes the representative of the institution with which he is having difficulty and he cannot talk so freely with them. In this instance, it is the specific social role which determines the relation with the client.[6]

Orientation Toward the Medical Team

As the social worker changes from orientation toward the patient to orientation toward the medical team, the worker's role also changes. Instead of being in a helping role with the patient, the social worker is now in a collaborative role with members of one or more other professions. The goal is no longer treatment, but sharing of data about the situation, interchange of professional knowledge, and arrival at a decision regarding appropriate joint action.

Elliot Studt points out that it is important to know the responsibilities of the social worker in decision-making in each field of practice.[7] What responsibility and authority has the social worker in making decisions in the health field? A case is referred by a physician, who may indicate what step seems desirable, such as convalescent home care. This recommendation does not, however, have the implication of a medical prescription or order. The social worker explores the situation with the patient and family and returns to the physician with a report and recommendation, which may result in a different manner of working out the aftercare plan, perhaps in the patient's home. The social worker does not make a medical diagnosis or determine the medical treatment plan but does influence changes in both. Because of the recognition of the

---

[6] *Ibid.*, p. 60.
[7] Elliot Studt, "Worker-Client Authority Relationships in Social Work," *Social Work*, Vol. 4, No. 1 (January 1959), pp. 18–28.

importance of psychosocial factors in disease, data and interpretation brought by social work result in modification of diagnosis and treatment in many cases where these elements are recognized as significant. The physician may request such a contribution or the social worker may take initiative in bringing it to him. From the earliest days it has been recognized that a particularly "good" case of this kind, well analyzed and presented, may be a turning point in convincing a physician of the importance of the psychosocial component in illness. Now that medicine itself is increasingly receptive to such thinking and channels for regular discussion are developed, opportunity to influence decisions regarding diagnosis and treatment are greatly enlarged and can result in major changes in medical thinking.

The social worker must of course carry full responsibility for decisions regarding the social work phase of action in the situation. It is the decisions regarding the medical aspects that are always shared. There is a constant responsibility to participate with others and to be ready to alert them to the urgency of making certain decisions important for the patient's welfare.

The effectiveness of the social work contribution depends upon capacity for communication with other team members and arriving at clear, sound social work judgments. The member of any profession, facing a new problem, must ask himself, "Taking everything into consideration, what should be done?"[8] Medicine expects professional workers to take such responsibility for decision and action. Several steps are involved, as follows:

1. Each profession starts by studying and analyzing the problem first for its own purposes. Thus the medical social worker first makes a psychosocial assessment relevant for social work.

2. This analysis must then be refocused for the use of the physician and multidiscipline team. What is relevant to the medical purpose is selected, put in order, and synthesized in a concise formulation.

3. The social worker must then be ready to indicate the implications of this analysis in the form of a judgment as to what should

---

[8] Elliott Dunlap Smith, "Education and the Task of Making Social Work Professional," *Social Service Review*, Vol. 31, No. 1 (March 1957), pp. 1–10.

be done, from the social work viewpoint. Doctors expect each expert to make a definite recommendation, on the basis of which a joint decision can be reached.

Requirements of the Two Roles

Some of the differences between the social work role with the patient and with the medical team now stand out even more clearly. With the patient there is major concern for his feelings, with the team an emphasis on intellectual interchange. The flexibility of the social work role with the patient contrasts with the greater directness of the role in the medical team. Other differences will emerge later in the discussion.

There is a certain strain upon the social worker in attempting to meet the requirements of these two roles—with the patient and with the medical team—so that they do not conflict. Jurgen Ruesch has pointed out that human beings cannot be in two positions at once and so, in a situation of this kind, will oscillate from one to the other.[9] Thus the medical social worker moves back and forth, constantly identifying with both patient and team. While interviewing the patient, the social worker moves with him in the direction he needs to go, even if he must express hostility toward the hospital. The social worker's position as part of the hospital and medical team is, however, never relinquished, either in the patient's or the worker's eyes. So also, while working with the physician, the social worker stands firmly as a member of the team, but is constantly presenting the patient's viewpoint. The worker moves from role to role, but whichever is dominant, never gives up the other identification, which is always there in the background. As the dynamics of these roles are better understood, two points become clear—their peculiar appropriateness for social work and the fact that they can only be carried by a worker who is a part of the institution. Thus the social worker helps the patient to work better with the institution, and helps the institution to work better with its patients.

---

[9] Jurgen Ruesch, "The Observer and the Observed: Human Communication Theory," in Roy R. Grinker, ed., *Toward a Unified Theory of Human Behavior* (New York: Basic Books, 1956), Chapter IV.

characteristics of social work practice in the health field

6

values in social work and medicine

We have placed social work in the health field and considered some of its key aspects as they appear in this environment. Thus we are prepared to move directly into the third frame of reference. This deals with the application of the *essential elements of social work practice* (the first frame of reference) in the *health field* (the second frame of reference). This process will lead to full identification and description of the characteristics of social work practice in this particular field.

In this and the following four chapters, we turn our attention to the essential elements as set forth in Chapter II, and consider them in the following order: (1) value and purpose, (2) knowledge, and (3) method. Thus value and knowledge are placed in their proper position as coming before method. It will be noted that value and purpose are considered together and that sanction is not discussed separately. Sanction is given consideration at various points throughout the monograph where the profession's knowledge and expertness, and its relation to society and to the social institutions of medicine and public health are discussed.

ULTIMATE VALUES

If social work is to function appropriately and effectively within any field of practice, its purposes and values must be consistent with those prevalent in the field. In this discussion values are regarded as formulations of preferred behavior that are not verifiable. They are accepted as desirable without proof. Social work is a profession in which values are strongly emphasized and affect every phase of practice.

A while ago a rather clear distinction could be made between the value orientations of medicine and social work. In that earlier period, the physician's major effort was directed toward saving life and curing disease. The social worker's effort was directed toward helping people to meet problems of social living, among which physical health was only one of several important elements. Thus it seemed possible to make a relatively clear distinction between the major concerns of the two professions. However, as medicine has moved toward increasing concern for the patient as a person and has emphasized such objectives as prevention of disease and rehabilitation of the handicapped, the distinction has become blurred.

Examination of the current situation in medicine and social work, as well as in the other professions in the health field, leads to the conclusion that any definitive analysis or comparison of values is impossible at this time because of the overlapping, fluidity, and lack of clarity in this phase of practice. Following the general purpose of this monograph, certain significant issues and directions of thinking can be pointed out. To simplify the problem, the discussion is limited to the professions of medicine and social work.

What, then, can be said as a beginning about the values of medicine and social work in relation to each other? First, it can be perceived that these professions share the same ultimate values, that is, what should be sought as ideal, as desirable and excellent. Medicine as well as social work is deeply concerned with the worth of the individual and the furthering of his most effective social functioning. This implies respect for the patient and concern for his social situation as it impinges upon him.

When social work practices in the health field, it accepts the major purposes and focus of the health professions and agencies, integrating them with its own. Thus, while health objectives and problems of illness and medical care are the concern of all social workers, they move into the central focus for medical social workers. The emphasis is always on their psychosocial aspects.

A formulation of medical values that is useful for social workers is to be found in a statement of the objectives of medical education by the Association of American Medical Colleges. This stresses that the student should not only acquire the necessary knowledge and skill but also "develop those basic intellectual attitudes and ethical or moral principles which are essential if he is to gain and maintain the confidence and trust of those whom he treats, the respect of those with whom he works and the support of the community in which he lives." [1] The statement is permeated with concern for the patient as a person. Both medicine and social work through their professional organizations, the American Medical Association and the National Association of Social Workers, issue codes of ethics, which are revised from time to time in accordance with changing emphases in practice.

PROBLEMS IN DEFINING VALUES

In daily practice the professional worker's decisions have to be made at the level of operational or middle-range values, which define the objectives leading toward ultimate values. At this intermediate level, difficulties arise in further definition and comparison. Social change is creating new issues so rapidly that their value implications cannot be identified or consensus attained. Multidiscipline practice is spreading widely but has been only partially accepted and integrated within the value system of medicine. There are radical differences within the medical profession relating to provision of medical care for the population as a whole.

---

[1] Executive Council of the Association of American Medical Colleges, "The Objectives of Undergraduate Medical Education," *Journal of Medical Education,* Vol. 28, No. 3 (March 1953), pp. 57–59.

Medicine, public health, and nursing, as well as other health professions, are reaching out to include more concern for social factors in their practice and teaching. Social workers are the only members of the health team who have a central focus on psychosocial conditions and problems. What adjustment will eventually be made between these appropriate but overlapping sets of interests is not yet clear.

Further difficulties in analysis of values arise because of the complexities and conflicts of responsibilities within practice itself. In medicine and public health, services to patients and communities, teaching, and research are carried on by the same individuals and within the same program more often than is generally true of social work practice today. Sometimes the purposes of teaching and research operate in such a way as to conflict with those of service. When a clinical teacher brings a group of medical students into an examining room to observe the physical examination of a sensitive young woman or when a research physician prolongs the expensive hospital stay of a patient for tests and examinations mainly needed to clarify a research problem, these physicians do not always recognize how stressful such experiences may be for the individual patient. In changing his role, the physician may not be aware how the changed purpose may affect the patient.

In addition, population growth and expanding scientific knowledge are compounding the pressures upon physicians. Even when they recognize the importance of individualizing patients, staff physicians in clinics and hospitals and private physicians in their offices too frequently cannot find the necessary time and energy to carry their work as they might wish. They are now further removed from the patient's social environment than in the days when in direct contact with him in his home, family, and community. Furthermore, since the practice of any profession encompasses a wide range of individual practitioners with varying backgrounds, personalities, competence, and attitudes, the performance of some physicians will reflect less fully than that of others the medical profession's values in regard to patient care as set forth by its teachers and leaders. Sometimes the difference seems mainly due to the individual doctor's approach. Sometimes the urge to seek reward, power, and status—all of which are important elements in medical practice today—interferes with the ideal of treating the patient as a person. Under these circumstances medical practice becomes less sensitive to the needs of patients and families. The physician concentrates upon the medical essentials, what is necessary for immediate treatment of the medical condition. Patients feel lack of interest in them as individuals, that they are regarded as cases of disease rather than persons. They may feel unduly pressed to conform to the hospital's code of behavior. Under such conditions too many patients are likely to be precipitated into situations involving basic changes in their lives—such as colostomy operations—without being given sufficient opportunity to understand and participate in the decisions so seriously affecting their future.

The pressures and problems that bear upon medicine and tend to divert daily practice from its long range higher purposes operate also within social work. In the younger profession, which is not so firmly established in society and whose professional content and method are less clearly defined, there is the additional problem that values have not yet been formulated with sufficient clarity or integrated with knowledge and method. Social work has left its values at too abstract a level. In a report on the teaching of values and ethics in social work education, Muriel W. Pumphrey shows that the profession has not identified and conceptualized its values in such a manner that they can be taught effectively or readily recognized in practice.[2] Although self-awareness has been emphasized, assumptions underlying values are not clarified. The use of values in decision-making and the conscious choice between values have not received the attention they deserve. An examination of the literature of medical social work reveals that social workers tend to write and think in terms of what *should* be, with constant emphasis on what social workers should do but without

---

[2] Muriel W. Pumphrey, *The Teaching of Values and Ethics in Social Work Education* (New York: Council on Social Work Education, 1959).

clarifying how far the imperatives for such action rest on values, knowledge, or experience.[3] There is thus great unevenness in performance. Social work as a profession has swung from an emphasis on social reform early in its history to an excessively limited focus on the individual in later decades. Medical social workers are only slowly awakening to their responsibility to move beyond the casework focus and to contribute to social policy in the hospital and to social planning in the community.

MIDDLE-RANGE VALUES

It is the middle-range values, rather than the ultimate values, that most often guide specific decisions in professional practice.[4] It is these intermediate values that particularly call for clearer definition and application. They may differ markedly within a profession and between individual members, as has been pointed out. One such analysis of medicine presents a set of paired values regarding the physician's self-image and relation to his patients, colleagues, and the community. It shows that the physician must be emotionally detached in his attitudes toward patients but must avoid becoming callous and should have compassionate concern for the patient. He must provide adequate and unhurried medical care for each patient but should not allow any one patient to usurp so much of his limited time that he does so at the expense of other patients. And so the analysis continues. The demands of blending these more or less conflicting norms into a functionally consistent professional role are obviously very great.[5] All professions, including social work, face similar demands in varying degrees.

When we examine the practice of medicine and social work together, we find that the two professions share not only ultimate

---

[3] William E. Gordon and Harriett M. Bartlett, "Generalizations in Medical Social Work: Preliminary Findings," *Social Work,* Vol. 4, No. 3 (July 1959), p. 75.

[4] Pumphrey, *op. cit.,* pp. 40–49.

[5] Robert K. Merton, George G. Reader, and Patricia L. Kendall, eds., *The Student-Physician* (Cambridge, Mass.: Harvard University Press, 1957), pp. 72–75.

values but also many middle-range values, when their practice is viewed at its best. Both are concerned with prevention of illness and disability, alleviation of physical and emotional stress, and rehabilitation, each approaching these goals from its own particular orientation. Both are concerned with family and community welfare, as well as with patient needs. Often it seems that the difference is more one of degree than of kind; but even variations in emphasis can produce marked differences in practice.

In the medical curriculum, in clinical practice, and in medical research there has been for decades and continues to be an overwhelming emphasis on scientific knowledge. In medicine, "scientific" means predominantly the physical and organic aspects of disease and the laboratory method of study. Psychic and social concepts and theory are being only slowly included. Their acceptance and inclusion are not progressing as rapidly as might have been anticipated because of the remarkable and continuing acceleration of the physical sciences. In social work, on the other hand, the opposite has been true. Primary emphasis has been placed on value and skill rather than knowledge. Only fragmentary bodies of theory have been developed. Generalizations from social work experience have not been formulated to any great extent and the field has not developed its own "professional science." Actually, each profession has interest and concern for the other's area, but the difference between them in valuing and seeking scientific knowledge is large. This difference results partly from the greater relevance of physical science to medicine, since physical science is further developed than social science, is more precise in its generalizations, and thus is more immediately useful in practice. As social work develops its own knowledge and medicine incorporates more social concepts, this difference between the professions will be lessened.

Social work places great emphasis on the importance of understanding the meaning of the situation (such as illness and medical care) to the individual, on obtaining his participation, and on helping him to carry out a plan or deal with a problem in his own way. This emphasis stems from the constant and primary identification with the individual which is characteristic of social work. While the physician will seek to know the patient's interests, he is accustomed to a more authoritative approach, as a medical expert who knows the medical diagnosis and treatment in a manner impossible for the patient and who has been trained to recommend a definite line of action to him. Even though increasing knowledge regarding psychosocial phenomena will enable social workers to attain better understanding of human behavior and social situations, they are not likely to assume an authoritative role similar to that of the physician because of the value they place upon the individual's own goals and definition of his situation.

Thus it is possible to perceive how differing value orientations may influence the relation of physicians and social workers to patients and to each other. The emphasis on scientific knowledge increases the authoritative role of the physician and enables him to move more quickly in working with patients, as he often must do because of the urgency of illness. The social worker's emphasis on the patient's viewpoint requires the development of a professional relationship which will permit the individual to express his feelings and a tempo generally keyed to the individual's readiness.

As shown earlier in the discussion of social work roles in patient care, these varying orientations can supplement each other to further the patient's welfare, if used with proper understanding. Lack of understanding, however, can create problems and confusion for both patients and professional workers. Eventually it will be possible to define and compare the major value orientations in these professions. While the patterns may change with time, some differences are likely to persist because they are so fundamental to each profession. Even a preliminary analysis such as has been presented here confirms the importance of values in social work. It further raises the question whether they may be operational in the practice of social work in a manner which distinguishes it from other professions. This is a question that must be postponed until the characteristics of social work have been more firmly identified.

7

knowledge from the health field

Each field of practice has its own special body of knowledge.[1] Hence, the social worker, in order to function effectively as a member of the professional team in the health field, must master a considerable body of technical medical and related knowledge; the basic concepts and principles relating to health, disease, and medical care must be thoroughly grasped; selected knowledge regarding the major conditions and diseases is necessary; and the needs, attitudes, and behavior of the sick person must be understood. Specific information regarding the current programs and

---

[1] *Knowledge* includes theory, concepts, and generalizations. *Theories* state the relationship between facts (and their component concepts). As a profession grows, theories are brought together into a body of theory. *Concepts* are abstractions, logical constructs, which can be used (and are needed) in any area of thinking. *Generalizations* express what is generally thought to be so, *i.e.*, verified and verifiable propositions. *Principles,* as used in social work, represent guides to action, composed of knowledge and values in combination. See Harriett M. Bartlett, "The Generic-Specific Concept in Social Work Education and Practice," in Alfred J. Kahn, ed., *Issues in American Social Work* (New York: Columbia University Press, 1959), p. 178, *footnote;* and Alfred J. Kahn, "The Nature of Social Work Knowledge," in Cora Kasius, ed., *New Directions in Social Work* (New York: Harper, 1954), pp. 204–205.

the professions active in the health field is another requirement. The social worker must select and adapt all this knowledge for social work use and, at the same time, must know how the other health professions employ it and be aware of the range of their additional knowledge.

KNOWLEDGE AND CONCEPTS RELATING TO HEALTH AND DISEASE

Concepts of health and disease are in a fluid state. In spite of numerous attempts, no satisfactory formulation has been achieved. Some are too restricted and some are all-encompassing. An example of the latter is the frequently used definition in the constitution of the World Health Organization that health is a state of complete physical, mental, and social well-being. A statement covering both health and disease, which has been useful for social workers, is as follows:

> Just as the decisive factor in the maintenance of well-being —of health—is *adequate adaptation* of the individual to *all* factors in his external and internal environment with maintenance of equilibrium or physiologic poise, so the decisive element in illness is the loss of capacity of the organism to regain its normal physiologic equilibrium when the latter is seriously threatened.[2]

The formulation of the health-disease concept in terms of adaptive capacity brings it within the same general framework that is used by social work.

The approach to health is through understanding of normal growth and development, an approach that is shared by public health and social work. In schools of social work the teaching regarding human behavior is now placed within this framework, moving through the various life phases from conception of the child through old age. While social work instruction eventually hopes to encompass the whole person, it has been strong in relation to the emotional aspects of personality and weak in other facets of

---

[2] H. M. Margolis, "The Biodynamic Point of View in Medicine," *Journal of Social Casework,* Vol. 30, No. 1 (January 1949), p. 4.

growth. It does, however, prepare the social worker to think in growth terms.

All social workers should command a solid body of knowledge regarding normal physical growth and development, as a foundation for understanding human needs and working with health and disease. The basic idea to be grasped is that human growth is orderly, that it has continuity and sequence, and that within the general pattern each individual has his own individual growth pattern. Thus individuals with rather widely varying characteristics and growth patterns can all fall within the normal range. Within this general framework, medical social workers find that they need, for effective practice, selected knowledge regarding the range in each phase of growth from infancy through old age. This knowledge is used to assess the individual's potentials in relation to his social functioning, taking into account the particular life phase in which he is. Knowledge of the characteristics of each growth phase permits the social worker to know the specific needs, strengths, and vulnerability of the individual as he faces his life tasks at each period.[3] If he is ill, or threatened with illness, its impact can be so much the better understood. The awareness that some kinds of growth can only occur at a certain period in life (and never again if the opportunity is lost), causes social workers to consider with concern what prolonged illness can do to a child at crucial phases of his growth. Medical social workers require fuller knowledge of physical growth and development than other social workers because their interest centers upon health.

If the individual is well, knowledge of growth and development is used in promoting health. In our culture much distress is caused to parents and children through their expectation that each child should conform closely to the general norms, often as exemplified by other children in the school or neighborhood. When a child has been examined in a medical or health clinic and found to be within normal range, social workers can work with physicians and nurses in giving the child and his parents security and easing their anxiety by helping them to understand and accept the validity

---

[3] Ruth M. Butler, *An Orientation to Knowledge of Human Growth and Behavior in Social Work Education* (New York: Council on Social Work Education, 1959).

of the child's own pattern of growth, no matter how he differs from his playmates.

Turning now from health to illness, the understanding of such a complex phenomenon as a disease requires the use of knowledge from a number of theory systems. Much of this knowledge is too technical for social workers. Over the years medical social workers have learned how to select the basic concepts and supporting data most relevant to their purposes. These are drawn mainly from biology (particularly physiology) and medicine, including psychiatry. The concepts of biochemistry and other medical sciences, while of basic importance for clinical medicine, are less immediately relevant for social work, although the social worker must always be aware of their place in the total picture.

The teaching regarding health and disease in the social work curriculum is only a beginning. Constantly over the years the medical social worker's fund of medical knowledge is being enlarged through a number of channels, such as reference books and journals in medical libraries, conferences with physicians, and attendance at medical rounds and conferences. This process must be continuous, not only because new problems of illness keep arising in the worker's experience but also because medical concepts and knowledge are so rapidly changing. Medical social workers learn how to select what they can use from technical medical writings and are, of course, aided in this process by the admirable summaries customarily included in all medical material. When working on a specialized medical service, a social worker must often gain command of extremely technical concepts in order to function effectively as a member of that particular medical team. As a part of this acquisition of knowledge, the social worker also becomes familiar with the disciplined orderly pattern of medical thinking and feels comfortable in working with it.

Some grounding in physiology is necessary for understanding health and disease. A basic physiological concept is that of homeostasis, developed by Walter B. Cannon.[4] This refers to the maintenance of a steady state in the internal environment of the

---

[4] Walter B. Cannon, *The Wisdom of the Body* (New York: W. W. Norton and Co., 1939), 2nd ed.

body, through automatic adjustment to the various stresses that threaten the equilibrium. Cannon describes the mechanisms by which noxious stimuli produce acute changes in the organism. As a part of this phenomenon of "emergency responses," as Cannon calls them, social workers need to understand the physiological aspects of emotion and the manner in which emotion reverberates through the whole body through the action of the endocrine and central nervous systems. This physiological knowledge is of particular importance because, following the conquest of the major communicable diseases, the pattern of disease is increasingly that of physiological disturbance. Another investigator, Hans Selye, has continued Cannon's work on the "alarm reaction" of the body and is further examining bodily responses under prolonged stress of various types.[5]

Natural History of Disease

In approaching specific diseases, how does the social worker know what to select from the mass of medical detail? The social worker is concerned with how the illness affects the social functioning of the individual and his family, and vice versa. Detailed technical knowledge regarding symptoms, differential diagnosis, and the techniques of treatment is not necessary. What is most useful is a knowledge of the general course of the disease—what is known in public health as the "natural history of the disease"—*i.e.,* its major causes, manner of progression, and prognosis.[6] Through statistical analysis of enormous numbers of cases, medicine can now predict and describe with accuracy the general course of most diseases. Treatment can often be known as soon as diagnosis has been determined and follows directly from it. While individual cases differ, the general pattern is the same. Thus those caring for patients can know and predict what problems lie ahead with

---

[5] Hans Selye, *The Stress of Life* (New York: McGraw-Hill Book Co., 1956).

[6] Hugh Rodman Leavell and E. Gurney Clark, *Preventive Medicine for the Doctor in His Community* (New York: McGraw-Hill Book Co., 1958), 2nd ed., pp. 14–20.

considerable accuracy; such foreknowledge and prediction are not possible in many other professions.

Diseases differ markedly in their psychosocial implications, according to the nature of their course and treatment.[7] Some conditions are reversible but many are not. Some chronic diseases may be static and controllable if the individual carefully follows a certain regime all his life, such as diet and insulin in diabetes. Other conditions are progressive, sometimes slowly with remissions and sometimes rapidly with fatal termination. One not infrequent pattern is that of recurrent illness—such as tuberculosis and heart disease—which leaves the patient more disabled after each exacerbation. Much has been written about the psychosocial implications of various medical conditions but these findings are scattered and require better organization.

Social Aspects of Illness

Beginning with William Osler, Adolf Meyer, and Richard C. Cabot at the turn of the century, there has been a steady stream of medical thinking stressing the importance of social factors in health and disease.[8] Sensitive and thoughtful clinical teachers observed the manner in which the life situations and the illnesses of their patients were intertwined and called this to the attention of their medical associates and students. The thinking of Francis W. Peabody, George R. Minot, and Henry B. Richardson, who wrote in the thirties and forties, has been particularly useful to medical social workers.[9] Teachers of preventive medicine and public

---

[7] Harriett M. Bartlett, *Medical Social Work* (Chicago: American Association of Medical Social Workers, 1934), pp. 87–88.

[8] Richard C. Cabot, *Social Service and the Art of Healing* (New York: Moffat Yard and Co., 1917).

[9] Francis W. Peabody, "The Care of the Patient," *Journal of the American Medical Association*, Vol. 88, No. 12 (March 19, 1927), pp. 877–882; George R. Minot, "Investigation and Teaching in the Field of the Social Component of Medicine," *American Association of Medical Social Workers Bulletin*, Vol. 10, No. 2 (April 1937), pp. 9–18; Henry B. Richardson, *Patients Have Families* (New York: The Commonwealth Fund, 1945).

health reinforced this approach, with greater emphasis on the family and community, as would be expected. With the exception of a few formal studies, this thinking rested on careful observation and rich clinical experience. The fact that the exponents of this social viewpoint were leading medical scientists and diagnosticians added weight to their words. This medical concern for social aspects did not advance far toward conceptualization. It was, however, orderly, continuous, and increasingly forceful. Since most of its exponents were teachers, the effect was most strongly felt in medical schools, which by the mid-forties were showing marked response. These physicians were largely the ones who supported medical social work. It was not, however, until the thinking about social aspects began to find a place in scientific theory about disease that it became fully operative in the diagnosis and treatment of individual patients.

The first effect of scientific discovery in medicine was to focus interest upon the impersonal aspects of health and disease, such as the germ theory and physical and laboratory examination. Disease was regarded as a physical entity and treated as such. Enormous gains were made and are still being made through this approach. The most radical advance was in relation to communicable disease. Through the use of antibiotics, immunization, environmental sanitation, and similar measures, clinicians and public health personnel working together succeeded in bringing under control in this country the major communicable diseases. However, as time went on, it became evident that all health problems could not be solved through a single approach. Many remained that could only be met by working directly with the people themselves. Patients kept coming to physicians with symptoms and complaints that could not be adequately diagnosed or treated through what was regarded as proper scientific method. Furthermore, new problems were appearing. With the longer span of life, chronic degenerative diseases and the disabilities of old age were increasing rapidly. Such conditions do not respond to the "laboratory" approach. People are more than physical organisms and illness can only be understood within a broader frame of reference. Thus there developed the growing emphasis upon the psychosocial aspects of health and disease, which is a current feature although it is still only partially incorporated within the practice of the health field.

Psychosomatic Approach and Stress Concept

The concept of disease has been greatly extended in recent decades through the contribution of psychiatry. During World War I many physicians who had to deal with patients with psychogenic symptoms became convinced of the importance of the emotions in relation to illness. Since that time psychiatry has been slowly but steadily permeating medicine, emphasizing particularly the significance of psychic factors in illness and the recognition of the patient as having a unique personality. Medical social workers welcomed this approach, which reinforced their own.

Psychiatry, particularly psychoanalysis, moved beyond the field of mental disease to direct concern with bodily disease when psychosomatic medicine emerged in the thirties. This has been a field prolific for developing hypotheses and for theory-building. While there has been considerable research, it has often been limited to small numbers of cases because of the intensive nature of psychiatric interviewing. The major hypothesis, of great significance for social work, is that there is a psychic component in all illness and that emotional factors can be of etiological significance in bodily disease.

Medical social workers have watched the rapid development of hypotheses and findings, trying to keep abreast of them. At first most of the work on psychosomatic illness was done from the psychoanalytic approach. Emotional conflicts were hypothesized as the major etiological factor in certain diseases. There was great interest in the problem of "specificity," *i.e.,* why a particular individual develops a particular type of disease. Gradually the sphere of interest broadened. The files of *Psychosomatic Medicine* reveal a trend from a predominantly psychoanalytic emphasis toward increasing concern with physiological aspects. As long as the emphasis was on unconscious emotional conflicts as etiological factors in disease, the social work contribution was necessarily limited. Recent trends are toward areas increasingly relevant to social work. An illustration is a body of hypotheses and findings which is developing around the relation between "life stress and bodily disease." In these medical studies, physiological tests are carried on at the same time that the patient is being interviewed regarding his life problems, and the correlation of physiological and emotional equilibrium or disturbance is closely watched. It should be said that this method was used to some degree in psychosomatic investigations from the beginning but is particularly a feature of current studies. Already a large literature covering the relations between "life situations," emotion, and all the major body systems and diseases has developed.

According to Dr. Harold G. Wolff, a leading exponent of this approach, many life situations are threatening to individuals, thus causing the organism to mobilize its protective reactions, as in an emergency. He states his main thesis as follows:

> The stress accruing from a situation is based in large part on the way the affected subject perceives it: perception depends upon a multiplicity of factors including the genetic equipment, basic individual needs and longings, earlier conditioning influences, and a host of life experiences and cultural pressures. No one of these can be singled out for exclusive emphasis. The common denominator of stress disorders is reaction to circumstances of threatening significance to the organism.[10]

Since the protective reactions of the body are primitive and limited, they often do not relieve the stress when it is of a complex psychosocial nature.[11] Thus they can be described as inept and unsuccessful methods of solving the problem, since chronic abnormal physiological function may produce lesions and eventually irreversible disease. The organism, however, "knows no other

---

[10] Harold G. Wolff, *Stress and Disease* (Springfield, Ill.: Charles C Thomas, 1953), p. 10.

[11] It should be recognized that in medicine the concept of *stress* applies, not to the problems, forces, and pressures, but to the condition they evoke in the individual organism. These etiological factors are thus more correctly described as stress-evoking factors. They can be anything which threatens the organism, from temperature change to deep emotional conflict.

way" and its responses must be understood as a protective device.[12]

Wolff has collaborated with another investigator, Dr. Lawrence E. Hinkle, Jr., in examining the health patterns of over 3,000 people, drawn from five sociocultural groups.[13] It was found that during two decades of young adult life one-fourth of the individuals experienced approximately one-half of the illness episodes. This study confirmed the stress theory in that the individuals who showed the highest susceptibility were those who perceived their total environment to be unsatisfactory and had great difficulty in adapting to it. This study has special significance because it is one of the few epidemiological studies concerned with social stress in relation to illness; most of these studies are relatively small clinical investigations.

This concept of life stress is broader than the earlier psychoanalytic approach. The emotional difficulties may be conscious or unconscious. Sociocultural pressures are regarded as of major importance, as has been demonstrated in a collaborative study by Wolff and Leo W. Simmons, the latter a social scientist.[14] Great emphasis is placed on the individual's own definition of the situation.

Despite this body of mounting evidence of the correlation between psychosocial stress and disease, it was still not possible by studying cases of illness to demonstrate all the links in the chain and why one individual breaks under strain when another does not. Dr. I. Arthur Mirsky and other investigators therefore set forth on another approach, namely, to try to discover which individuals were most likely to develop a disease, before it actually occurred.[15] In a large population group of normal individuals

---

[12] Wolff, *op. cit.*, pp. 148–151.

[13] Lawrence E. Hinkle, Jr., and Harold G. Wolff, "Ecologic Investigations of the Relationship between Illness, Life Experiences and the Social Environment," *Annals of Internal Medicine,* Vol. 49, No. 6 (December 1958), pp. 1373–1378.

[14] Leo W. Simmons and Harold G. Wolff, *Social Science in Medicine* (New York: Russell Sage Foundation, 1954).

[15] Herbert Weiner, Margaret Thaler, Norton F. Reiser, and I. Arthur Mirsky, "Etiology of Duodenal Ulcer," *Psychosomatic Medicine,* Vol. 19, No. 1 (January–February 1957), pp. 1–10.

(over 2,000 men being inducted into the military service) they discovered that a small proportion had a high rate of gastric secretion combined with certain personality characteristics. It was predicted that these persons would be possible candidates for duodenal ulcer and actually the majority of them, when later subjected to social stress, did develop the disease. Mirsky summarizes his theoretical approach as follows:

> From the preceding it would appear that there are three parameters which may contribute to the precipitation of duodenal ulcer: A physiological parameter, which determines the susceptibility of the duodenum to ulceration; a psychological parameter, which determines the relatively specific psychic conflict that induces psychic tension; and a social parameter, which determines the environmental event that will prove noxious to the particular individual. Accordingly, a duodenal ulcer should develop when an individual with a sustained rate of gastric hypersecretion and the aforementioned psychic conflict is exposed to an environmental situation that mobilizes conflict and induces psychic tension.[16]

Similar findings in relation to other diseases—pernicious anemia, diabetes mellitus, hyperthyroidism—suggest that interacting physiological, personality, and social factors are necessary to produce what has been known as psychosomatic disease.

During this period when medicine has been developing its concepts and theory, the recognition of multiple factors in the etiology of disease was always present, even though some groups might temporarily overemphasize one or another factor. It can be observed how the focus in medical thinking is increasingly converging on the patient as a person. The concept of *comprehensive care of the patient*[17] was developed by some medical clinicians and teachers to stress the need of seeing the patient "as a whole"

---

[16] *Ibid.*, p. 2.
[17] *Medicine and the Neuroses: Report of the Hershey Conference on Psychiatric Rehabilitation* (New York: National Committee for Mental Hygiene, 1945). *See* remarks by Dr. David P. Barr on p. 27. It is to be noted that the concept appears in various forms such as *comprehensive medical care* and *comprehensive medicine.*

and of including regularly within the medical picture the interrelated physical, emotional, and social factors. Because medical specialization fragments the patient, comprehensive care clinics have been established to teach and demonstrate the co-ordinated approach to the patient's needs. Dr. George G. Reader, the medical director of one such clinic, states the central concept as follows:

> ... comprehensive medical care is basically the preservation of health and the prevention as well as the cure of disease. In practice this implies attention to emotional and psychiatric as well as physical factors, and continuing supervision of the patient in clinic, hospital or home for a sufficient period of time to bring him through convalescence and rehabilitation to an optimal state of health and productivity, and to maintain him in it. Comprehensive care also implies compassionate care; human consideration for the patient as a person. It solicits his cooperation and imparts to him a willingness to help without invading his rights as an individual.[18]

In its emphasis and intent the concept of comprehensive care resembles that of psychosomatic illness. Both point the way toward the practice of good medicine and will probably no longer be needed when the approach which they emphasize has actually been incorporated into medical practice. Meanwhile, the idea of comprehensive care of the patient is steadily gaining ground and proving helpful, since it is a straightforward idea that is easily grasped. It conveys a sense of unity and does not perpetuate the body-mind dichotomy which has been a problem with some other terms.[19] Furthermore, it emphasizes that the essential service must actually reach the patient (as through a medical team composed of physician, nurse, social worker, and others), with the necessary continuity and with concern for him as a person.[20] Thus

---

[18] George G. Reader, "Comprehensive Medical Care," *Journal of Medical Education*, Vol. 28, No. 7 (July 1953), p. 34.

[19] Stanley Cobb, "A Pain in the Neck," *Harvard Medical Alumni Bulletin*, Vol. 34, No. 2 (February 1960), pp. 9–12.

[20] George G. Reader, "Organization and Development of a Comprehensive Care Program," *American Journal of Public Health*, Vol. 44, No. 6 (June 1954), pp. 760–765.

this concept of comprehensive care brings together the current trends in medical thinking in a formulation congenial to social work. The idea of *comprehensiveness* is applicable to various facets of illness and medical care: the concept of disease, the care of the patient, and the planning and offering of community medical services.

Social Work Attitudes Toward Medical Theory

Medical social workers find it necessary to be aware of the progress of medicine as a whole. Basic research in medical science is pressing toward greater understanding of cell structure and function, and of physiological processes. This research bids fair to cause far-reaching changes in disease concepts. Progress in treatment methods also changes the very nature of medical social problems. The use of new drugs in treatment of syphilis and gonorrhea has so radically changed the incidence and course of these diseases, which formerly presented complex social problems, that they have almost disappeared from the social work caseload. The devastating problems produced by such conditions as bacterial endocarditis and meningitis are also disappearing. Improvements in surgical techniques produce gains for the patient but also new psychosocial problems, as in the area of chest surgery. Cardiac operations have introduced a new phenomenon, the problems associated with suddenly being made whole after a life of limited activity. Medical staffs in hospitals often expect such patients to take on new responsibilities at a tempo beyond their adjustive capacity.

Because the theory of a psychogenic factor in disease is so congenial to their own approach, social workers—particularly those without grounding in biological concepts—sometimes accepted it uncritically. Since they were already working with emotional problems, some caseworkers in nonmedical agencies assumed that they could treat emotionally disturbed individuals with physical symptoms or psychosomatic disease without continual collaboration with physicians. Medical social workers, working close to medicine and seeing a wide range of sick persons in their own practice, observe that in every diagnostic category there is a range of cases, from those with a large organic component at one end to those that are largely psychosocial problems at the other end. The psychosocial component appears particularly large in relation to some diseases but the relative importance of the various elements must be determined by careful examination of each individual situation.

The emerging picture of psychosomatic disease is one of multiple causation. Mirsky's findings regarding interacting physiological, emotional, and social factors in duodenal ulcer suggest a complex pattern, which calls for the collaboration of internal medicine, psychiatry, and social work in the treatment of individual patients. By and large, social workers need to follow new theories regarding disease and to keep an open mind, with awareness that biochemistry and physiology may at any time explain what have seemed predominantly emotional phenomena, and vice versa.

In this connection there should be emphasis on the medical social worker's understanding of disease in terms of its influence on human behavior. Repeatedly it is found, when groups of social workers discuss some problem of deviant behavior, that medical social workers think of the possibility of physiological causation, whereas other social workers tend to think in terms of personality. In a certain proportion of such cases a physical examination will reveal either actual disease or physiological malfunctioning as the basis for the behavior difficulty. The child who is failing in school may be developing a slow and insidious case of rheumatic fever. The housewife who is showing increased irritability toward her husband and children may be suffering from hyperthyroidism. Social agencies sometimes develop costly and elaborate casework plans which miscarry because they rest only on a psychosocial evaluation and do not include an authoritative assessment of the physical status and capacities of the key persons in the situation. Thus social workers, who readily see the influence of mind upon body, need to be more aware of the opposite influence of body upon mind, in order to give much needed and timely help to many individuals who are themselves unaware of what is happening to them. This is but one illustration of the importance of a balanced approach to the whole individual, without excessive emphasis on any one phase of his functioning.

PREVENTIVE APPROACH

Because public health has been more clearly focused on prevention than medicine or social work, which have only recently been moving in this direction, public health knowledge and theory in relation to preventive effort are further advanced. Three aspects of public health may be selected as of particular significance to medical social workers.

Epidemiologic Approach

In clinical medicine the individual patient is the focus of concern but public health is concerned with whole populations. "The epidemiologic focus of observation is a *group* of individuals, and the observations refer to the whole group, both the afflicted and the non-afflicted." [21] While epidemiology originally referred to epidemics only, its usage has broadened to cover all manifestations of disease. A recent definition is as follows:

> ... that field of medical science which is concerned with the relationship of the various factors and conditions which determine the frequencies and distributions of an infectious process, a disease or a physiologic state in a human community. It seeks to advance rational conceptual schemes of causation of the various ills that affect mankind medically speaking. To the extent that this body of knowledge is advanced and valid, it becomes possible for appropriate community agencies to take effective measures directed toward prevention, control or eradication.[22]

The epidemiologic approach is valuable for medical social workers because it carries them beyond the clinical and casework approach to think in terms of whole groups of people. In current hospital practice, social work cases are most frequently obtained through individual referral by the medical staff. In public health programs, the individuals with health problems must be identified from among a larger group of healthy individuals.

---

[21] Leavell and Clark, *op. cit.*, p. 42.
[22] Kenneth F. Maxcy, *Rosenau's Preventive Medicine and Public Health* (New York: Appleton-Century-Crofts, 1956), 5th ed., p. 1289.

Social workers should explore how social work insights can be translated into convincing social data and theory through the epidemiological approach. They are acquiring experience through participating in public health research studies which follow the best epidemiological principles.[23] Progress toward the epidemiological approach in social work can best be made by analyzing the occurrence and distribution of social phenomena among various groups with whom social workers have natural contact. Analysis of a group should not be limited to those members thought to have "problems" but should cover the whole group. While not itself an epidemiological study, Janet Thornton's investigation of the social component in the medical care of one hundred patients in a hospital ward suggests how a social hypothesis about a group of unselected patients, not referred to social service, can be set up and carefully explored.[24]

Epidemiology offers a disciplined way of analyzing total groups so as to discover individuals with common problems and to describe the characteristics and interrelationship of factors producing these problems. Social workers now practicing in public health programs and teaching in public health schools find this approach increasingly important for medical social workers as they move toward preventive activities.

Levels of Prevention

While social work clearly identifies goals for prevention of social dysfunctioning and promotion of improved social functioning, as stated in the *Working Definition of Social Work Practice*, experts in preventive medicine and public health have defined more explicitly the nature of preventive goals. Their concept places the features of health promotion and disease prevention within a frame-

---

[23] Ruth M. Butler, "Mothers' Attitudes toward the Social Development of Their Adolescents," *Social Casework,* Part I, Vol. 37, No. 5 (May 1956), pp. 219–226, and Part II, Vol. 37, No. 6 (June 1956), pp. 280–288; Florence E. Cyr and Shirley H. Wattenberg, "Social Work in a Preventive Program of Maternal and Child Health," *Social Work,* Vol. 2, No. 3 (July 1957), pp. 32–39.

[24] Janet Thornton, *The Social Component in Medical Care* (New York: Columbia University Press, 1937).

work based on the natural history of illness. The following levels of prevention are defined:

Health promotion: These are measures undertaken to further general health and well-being.[25] Illustration: health education.

Specific protection: "This is prevention in its conventional sense and comprises measures applicable to a particular disease or group of diseases in order to intercept the causes of disease *before* they involve man."[26] Illustration: immunization.

Early diagnosis and prompt treatment: "The obvious objectives of early diagnosis and prompt treatment are (a) to prevent spread to others if the disease is a communicable one; (b) to cure or arrest the disease process in order to *prevent* complications or sequelae; and (c) to *prevent* prolonged disability."[27] Illustration: case finding in the early stage of disease.

Disability limitation: "This level includes prevention or delaying of the consequences of clinically advanced disease. Only delayed recognition due to incomplete knowledge of disease processes serves to separate this level of prevention from the previous level. . . . The fact that the departure from a state of health has been so extreme points to the failure of prevention at some earlier phase in the natural history of the disorder."[28] Illustration: treatment of arthritis to prevent crippling.

Rehabilitation: "This is more than stopping a disease process; it is also the prevention of complete disability after anatomic and physiologic changes are more or less stabilized. Its positive objective is to return the affected individual to a useful place in society and make maximum use of his remaining capacities."[29] Illustration: physical training for amputees.

This analysis of preventive effort is based on a more exact knowledge of the natural history of the problem (disease) than is now available in relation to social dysfunctioning. It does, however, suggest to social workers a logical way of analyzing and classifying preventive efforts, which is suggestive for similar analysis of social

---
[25] Leavell and Clark, *op. cit.*, p. 21.
[26] *Ibid.*, p. 23.
[27] *Ibid.*, p. 25.
[28] *Ibid.*, p. 26.
[29] *Ibid.*, p. 27.

effort. Rice has made a beginning in applying the public health concept of prevention to social work practice.[30] In social work, for instance, health promotion is illustrated through activities aimed toward better preparation of young families for the experience of pregnancy and the acceptance of responsibility for the new infant. Such a contribution is possible in any obstetrical clinic where young mothers come for prenatal care. Similar effort toward preparing families for the assimilation of the child into the school is possible in a pediatric clinic. Specific protective measures in some ways similar to immunization are offered when medical social workers help to prepare patients and families for hospitalization and surgery, so that the known trauma of these experiences is thereby lessened. The preventive contribution made by medical social workers to early diagnosis and treatment of disease, lessening of disability, and rehabilitation is well recognized.

Initiative in Offering and Giving Service

Implicit in the epidemiologic and preventive approaches is a third concept not yet as clearly expressed in public health but of significance for social workers. Since public health workers think in terms of promoting the health of the whole population, they obviously cannot wait until individuals apply for service, because by then the problems have already appeared. Thus have been developed methods such as health education and case-finding, in which the public health worker takes the initiative in reaching out to the person—in his home, at his place of work, wherever he can suitably be found. This philosophy and method, which emphasize public health responsibility for initiative in offering help, contrast with the traditional attitudes of medicine and social work, which leave to the individual the initiative for seeking such help. While medical social workers have always reached out to patients in hospital casework, they were not aware of the full implications of the idea until they met it in public health, with its greater sweep and vigor.

---

[30] Elizabeth P. Rice, "Concepts of Prevention as Applied to the Practice of Social Work." *American Journal of Public Health,* Vol. 52, No. 2 (February 1962), pp. 266–274.

As they broaden their own approach to include an increasing amount of work with groups and communities, and increasing emphasis on prevention, medical social workers are finding the ideas derived from public health practice—epidemiologic approach, levels of prevention, and initiative in seeking out individuals early —useful in suggesting a similar approach to their own activities. The testing out of these ideas is still in its early stage, however, and little has as yet appeared in social work literature about this direction of thinking.

REHABILITATION APPROACH

Another important direction of thinking is rehabilitation, which overlaps with and reinforces much that has already been said about the concepts of health and disease, and prevention. One of the features of recent years is the increasing emphasis on rehabilitation. This approach has appeared not only within the health field but also more broadly throughout society. It relates to both the physically and mentally handicapped. It has grown concurrently with, and in relation to, the emphasis on prevention.

Because of the many ways in which the concept of rehabilitation has been used, there has been considerable diffuse and even confused thinking.[31] Rehabilitation can best be understood as having several major aspects: (1) as a broad concept expressing social values and social policy, (2) as a social movement incorporating these values and goals, (3) as a process through which the knowledge and skill of many professions are combined and related to the needs of the handicapped, and (4) as a specific program within which services are organized and made available to handicapped individuals. It is clarifying to keep these aspects distinct from each other. In this discussion rehabilitation is not regarded as a sepa-

---

[31] There is a tendency to extend concepts such as comprehensive medicine, psychosomatic medicine, prevention, and rehabilitation until they all have the same meaning, namely, the best adjustment and functioning of the individual. In this discussion, effort is made to use such terms in their central and most characteristic meaning, in order to avoid the confusion that results from vagueness and overlapping.

rate field of practice. Its medical aspects are included within the health field.

Medical social workers have always considered the rehabilitation of the patient as one of their goals and much of their service has been rehabilitative. They were held back in their efforts, however, as long as other groups in society had such limited views regarding the scope of medical and social services. During the first half of this century, two world wars and a great industrial depression focused attention on the human problems and social costs resulting from physical handicap. The need to deal with large groups of physically handicapped military and civilian personnel stimulated exploration of the problem and rapid development of techniques.

During this period there emerged an enlarged dynamic concept of rehabilitation, which had in it the force to produce remarkable increase in social activity and program development. The radical change in the medical attitude toward chronic disease and permanent handicap is striking. Patients who were formerly regarded as "hopeless," such as individuals with arthritis and hemiplegia, are now received with positive interest in many clinics and hospitals. This response has stimulated the search for new knowledge and for improved methods of treatment. An enormous literature, dealing with all types of handicap and methods of rehabilitation, has developed. Thus the new concept and movement in rehabilitation are contributing to the growth of comprehensive medicine.

As usually formulated, the rehabilitation concept refers to the goal of optimal functioning for the handicapped individual. Frederick A. Whitehouse points out that it should cover not only the return of the handicapped to social functioning, but also the preparation of the young handicapped individual to take on his future roles and responsibilities in life, and the retention of the capacities of the aged. It is thus best conceived as the cultivation, restoration, and conservation of human resources.[32] The rehabilitation concept seems particularly valuable as an over-all frame of refer-

---

[32] Frederick A. Whitehouse, "Rehabilitation as a Concept in the Utilization of Human Resources," in *The Evolving Concept of Rehabilitation* (Washington, D. C.: American Association of Medical Social Workers, 1955), pp. 21–23. (Monograph I in NASW series "Social Work Practice in Medical Care and Rehabilitation Settings.")

ence for bringing together many activities and values previously separate but now integrated, with resultant benefit to society. Mental handicap has been included along with physical handicap. The knowledge and skills of vocational guidance and placement have been combined with those of medicine to produce an expanded and more continuous service. The focus has broadened from concern solely for employability to include the housewife's activities and the seriously disabled person's self-care. Values and goals reinforce each other—the effort to reduce taxes and the emphasis on the human being as the primary resource of our society combine with compassion for suffering and deprivation—to motivate effective action on a large scale. There has been striking awakening in regard to the responsibilities of the professions, the government, and society.

Many professions contribute to the rehabilitative process, which is thus multidiscipline by its very nature. One characteristic not so commonly found in the health field distinguishes rehabilitation, namely, the manner in which the various types of service follow each other as the process moves along. The physician and nurse come first, perhaps followed by special therapists in various types of retraining, who in turn give way to the vocational adviser when the patient is ready for industrial training or placement. All may be on the same rehabilitation team, actively offering service at different times; or the patient may have to move from one agency to another as his needs change. Since the social worker is interested in helping the patient progress through the various steps in his medical care as smoothly as possible, the problems of continuity involved in this succession of services are of special concern to social work.

While there is an increasing number of independent rehabilitation centers (many being built through funds offered through the Hill-Burton Act for hospital construction), the great proportion of what might be regarded as rehabilitation service is being given under existing auspices, such as hospitals, institutions, and special schools. A beginning is being made to see what can be done for the hitherto neglected patients in nursing homes. The successful injection of rehabilitation into an ongoing program involves new value orientations as well as techniques.

The question may be asked, whether rehabilitation is really new, since many of its aspects seem familiar and the concept is already recognized in our society. It would seem that what has developed is a new synthesis, by which motives, ideas, and services are being mobilized and integrated to a degree that would not have been deemed possible a few decades ago.

KNOWLEDGE AND CONCEPTS FROM MEDICAL CARE

The medical social worker also finds it essential to use knowledge and concepts drawn from organized medical care and health services. In the discussion of integration of social work within the health field in Chapter IV, two propositions were advanced: first, that social work should maintain its appropriate and consistent psychosocial focus, and second, that it should be a part of the field in such a way as to share responsibility for the services and contribute to the total program. In the preceding sections the knowledge necessary to understand the central problem, that of health and disease, has been considered, with emphasis on its psychosocial implications. Attention is now given to the knowledge necessary for "being a part" of the operative health services. Since knowledge in this area is less well conceptualized than that related to health, the medical social worker must seek and gather it from many sources.

As a background, all social workers bring from the generic social work curriculum some basic knowledge of the health services at the national, state, and local level, including the hospital as a social agency and community health programs. They have also learned something regarding the major programs and methods for bringing service to various population groups, the methods of payment (particularly tax support and insurance), the relation between socioeconomic factors and medical care, and the availability of and major gaps in service. There is usually also some knowledge regarding the health professions and methods of working with them, varying greatly according to the student's field placement and actual opportunities to work with these professions.

Medical social workers naturally learn a great deal about the methods of physicians and other health professions by practicing with them. They should, however, have in addition formal knowledge regarding these professions, their goals, training, and standards of practice. This knowledge should also cover their ways of thinking and the nature of their professional relationships with patients. Such knowledge is essential for effective collaboration.

Community Programs and Services

From the viewpoint of social work, knowledge regarding programs for community medical care is still an undigested mass of information. In the past, the attention of social work focused on agency administration, co-ordination of agency service in the community, and influencing social legislation through social action. More understanding is needed regarding the nature of social policy, especially the processes by which social needs and policies are defined and embodied in community services.[33] This knowledge and the relevant principles will be derived from such sources as administration, political science, social psychology, and cultural anthropology, all of which have to do with understanding of community forces and the development of community services. In this area of practice, medical social workers are, of course, most concerned with the social aspects of health service and customarily work closely with others—health and social agencies, community groups, health professions—in moving toward development of necessary services.

In many ways the concept of *program,* in the sense of a cluster of interrelated services, has seemed more meaningful to medical social workers than that of agency function as used in social work. Since medical care follows logical steps and disease has a natural history, health services tend to be grouped within programs, the various phases of which are sometimes under a single health agency but are frequently not under the auspices of any one agency, or

---

[33] *See* Irving Weissman, *Social Welfare Policy and Services in Social Work Education* (New York: Council on Social Work Education, 1959).

even within the same community. Diagnostic service, ward care, convalescence, and rehabilitation may all be offered in different places and yet be part of a concerted plan for a patient. Dr. Samuel M. Wishik shows how the adequate treatment of cleft palate involves a complex series of steps beginning at birth and carrying on through vocational guidance and first job placement, all part of a clearly conceived program of services for individuals with this severely handicapping condition.[34] In some ways, therefore, the public health thinking about health programs has been more suggestive for medical social workers than the material emanating from their own profession.

Discussion of medical care raises the question, whether the principles of comprehensive medical care at its best, as medical social workers view it, have ever been put into effect in any specific program in this country. Some authorities consider that the principles and standards established by the United States Children's Bureau for its grant-in-aid programs, particularly the Crippled Children's Services, do represent such an approach and that these programs as actually carried out in many states can be regarded as examples. They have been outstanding in their emphasis on the whole patient, recognition of psychosocial aspects of care, high medical and professional standards, and availability to all persons without discrimination.[35] Unfortunately these programs and principles have never been fully set forth in the professional literature; hence this accomplishment is known only to those who are directly familiar with the program and has not had the influence it could have had in stimulating the improvement of medical care services throughout the country.

Social Science Approach

Social scientists have in recent years been showing increasing interest in the health field. A Division of Medical Sociology has been

---

[34] Samuel M. Wishik, "To Restore the Child with Cleft Palate," *The Child*, Vol. 15, No. 8 (April 1951), pp. 141–143, and 151.

[35] *Medical Social Services for Children* (Washington, D. C.: United States Children's Bureau, 1953), pp. iii–v, and 1–9.

established in the American Sociological Society. Sociologists, social psychologists, and anthropologists have collaborated with administrators, physicians, and nurses in the hospital and with public health workers in the community to explore a wide range of phenomena.

One area in which progress in conceptualization has been made is that of the reciprocal roles of physician and patient in our society. Talcott Parsons, in his analysis of the physician's professional role, identifies high technical competence, emotional neutrality, and orientation toward the interests of others as essential characteristics. Since the patient must place his life and body in the physician's hands, these attributes (and also confidentiality) are requirements. The "sick role" of the patient, on the other hand, requires that he be exempted from normal social responsibilities, that he be taken care of, that he should regard the state of being ill as undesirable and should want to get well, and that he should seek and co-operate with technically competent help. It can be seen that these complementary responsibilities of physician and patient interact to meet the needs of both individual and society in dealing with illness as a social deviation.[36] Similar types of analysis, with appropriate variations, are being developed in relation to the nursing profession.

Active theory-building is also in process around the hospital as a social system, subculture, and therapeutic milieu. The social structure of the hospital, the roles and status of the various professional and nonprofessional groups, their place in the hierarchy, and their social interaction as they carry out their various functions are analyzed in great detail and from different social science approaches.

Social scientists point out that just as society defines the expected behavior of its members, so the hospital defines the expected behavior of the patient. The phenomenon of the "good" or conforming patient and the "bad" or nonconforming patient is easily recognized by all familiar with hospitals. The physician's recommendations, the rules and regulations of the hospital, and the

---

[36] Talcott Parsons, *The Social System* (Glencoe, Ill.: The Free Press), pp. 433–443.

attitudes of professional staff members, all contribute to this concept of patient role, which is assumed to work for the patient's best welfare. Those patients who can follow these expectations usually do benefit. But those who have difficulty in conforming may find the hospital environment a stressful one.[37] Because of the need for disciplined action in dealing with illness, as well as other factors, the social system of the hospital tends to become increasingly rigid. Physicians and others are usually not aware of the impact of their attitudes upon the patient. It may even become a question—as Dr. Hugh Cabot pointed out—whether the hospital is being run primarily for the good of patients or for the doctors.[38] Under these circumstances the hospital, instead of helping many of its patients, may be increasing their problems and, because of the emotional disturbance and frustration involved in hospitalization, may actually be exacerbating rather than alleviating the illness for which treatment is being sought.[39] The teaching in many medical schools, which emphasizes concern for the patient as a person, tends to counteract the development of overrigid policies and procedures in medical care. Psychiatrists and social workers are also working constantly to influence the hospital's social system toward greater flexibility in regard to needs of individual patients and reduction of stress.

There are many specific lines of social science inquiry that have meaning for medical social workers. The current analysis of the power structure of the community throws light on the role of the hospital and the health professions in health and welfare programs.[40] Studies of the influence of social class membership on attitudes suggest that deference shown by a member of a lower class for a professional person (such as physician or social worker) may mask his true feelings about the situation and his treatment. A growing body of theory about small groups is bringing increased

---

[37] Simmons and Wolff, *op. cit.*, Chapter 6.
[38] Hugh Cabot, "Doctors or Trustees—Which?" *Modern Hospital*, Vol. 62, No. 6 (June 1944), p. 48.
[39] Simmons and Wolff, *op. cit.*
[40] Alan F. Klein, "Social Work in Non-Social Work Settings," *Social Work*, Vol. 4, No. 4 (October 1959), pp. 92–97.

understanding of the natural groupings that develop among patients and their families in hospitals and other medical institutions.

This social science theory and these specific studies are significant for medical social workers in a number of ways. They are stimulating because they appraise familiar problems from a new orientation. Since the hospital structure crystallized in the period when medicine and nursing were the only professions concerned with patient care, newer professions such as social work have faced difficulty in finding a place in such a highly organized environment. While the position of the newer professions on the medical team has undoubtedly been accepted in a general sort of way, problems of status, position, and role must be met in establishing a place in any specific medical institution or program. Medical social workers have always been aware how the perception of their role held by others, such as physicians, has affected positively or negatively what they could contribute in the health field. They have been less aware, however, how their own perception of the medical setting, of the professional roles of physicians and others, and of their own professional role either limits or enlarges their capacity for rendering effective service.[41] These social science concepts provide a clearer frame of reference than has previously been available. Through knowledge thus acquired social workers can become more understanding of their occupational environment and more aware of the factors that affect acceptance and integration of their services.

Many of these investigations of the professional role of the physician and nurse focus upon the goals and satisfactions of the worker himself, his concept of his role, and his struggle for advancement. At times the welfare of the patient seems submerged by the concern for professional status. Medical social workers, in using social science concepts to analyze their activities, will wish to be certain that they employ a conceptual framework which always keeps attention directed toward the primary purpose of the professional activity, which is service to individuals and groups.

---

[41] Otto Pollak, "The Culture of Medical Social Work," *Medical Social Work.* Vol. 3, No. 3 (July 1954), pp. 81–89.

8

knowledge from medical social work

Having considered some of the areas of knowledge that the medical social worker selects from medicine, public health, and medical care, the next step is to consider what knowledge comes directly from medical social work itself. Unquestionably, medical social work is building up its own body of knowledge out of its experience in practice and teaching, but this knowledge has not yet been formulated. Therefore, only a beginning can be made here, in order to suggest the quality and flavor of this knowledge.

The reader should be aware of the shift in position that is here taking place. Communication theory emphasizes the importance of *the position of the observer*. In the report of a series of interdisciplinary conferences that were exploring the possibility of a unified theory of human behavior, Jurgen Ruesch repeatedly pointed out the confusion and misunderstanding that resulted from failure to make clear the speaker's position; this means, literally, where are you standing in relation to the phenomenon—looking at it from the outside? if so, from what distance? participating in the ongoing process yourself? if so, in what way? These and similar questions must be kept continually clear, if any particular frame of reference is to be used without misunderstanding.[1]

Each social institution, field, and discipline has its own characteristic position. Special disciplines organize and use their bodies of knowledge within their own frameworks. It can be seen that some of these frameworks are closer to the social work orientation than others. While both medical and psychiatric social work function within medicine, psychiatric social work and psychiatry seem to be largely within the same framework, whereas medical social work and medicine (in spite of overlapping in the social area) seem to be operating in different frameworks. It has not been sufficiently recognized how greatly the problem of integration of service is increased by the degree of such difference; and, at the same time, how much greater is the opportunity to make a significant contribution of something new because of this very difference.

It is important for social work to be aware of, and to maintain, its own position and framework. Premature use of frameworks from other disciplines, without careful testing in social work practice, can pull social work away from its particular orientation. This is why it is so important to identify the peculiar characteristics of social work thinking. Other professions indicate the existence of a difference by their difficulty in following social work thinking, a difficulty which they usually ascribe to our peculiar terminology. Our deficiency in clear concepts and expression may not, however, be the whole explanation. The gap in communication may result partly from an appropriate and inevitable complexity in social work thinking because of the nature of the entities with which social work deals and the position of the professional worker in relation to these phenomena.

A professional committee in medical social work, which for some years has been trying, with research consultation, to identify some of these characteristics of social work thinking, finds that social work knowledge can be captured by generalizations that are rela-

[1] Jurgen Ruesch, "The Observer and the Observed: Human Communication Theory" in Roy R. Grinker, ed., *Toward a Unified Theory of Human Behavior* (New York: Basic Books, 1957), Chapter IV.

tively close to the empirical level. It finds that the deliberate effort to express "practice knowledge" in a disciplined way does decrease the vagueness of the generalizations but not their complexity. Few are represented by a single noun. Until more exploration is done, it cannot be determined how far these characteristics are an accident of social work thinking which can be eliminated by more disciplined formulation, or how far they are due to the essential nature of the social work approach to phenomena.[2]

Progress can best be made at present by working on those portions of social work thinking that seem clearest and best established. In discussing the nature of social theory, Herbert Blumer points out that definition and precise concepts cannot yet be attained but that what is needed at this stage of development is what he calls "sensitizing concepts." Although they cannot be standardized, such concepts can be communicated. This is done, Blumer says, not by formal definition but by exposition which yields a meaningful picture, aided by apt illustrations. These concepts can also be tested, improved, and refined through careful study of empirical instances which they are presumed to cover.[3] This seems to be exactly what we can do best in medical social work at present—namely, describe certain facets of our thinking and activity that seem clearest and recognize others that are still only vaguely conceived.

In examining samples of medical social work thinking, it should be recognized that some of the knowledge now used by social work is tested and thus scientific, but much of it is still in the untested stage, particularly that which is unformulated and imbedded in social work experience. At this stage of the profession's development, therefore, we shall have to be satisfied with a relatively small increment of "hard" tested knowledge and a large proportion of tentative but verifiable findings, tested only through daily social work practice. We should not, however, underestimate the importance of this testing in daily practice over the years, since

---

[2] William E. Gordon and Harriett M. Bartlett, "Generalizations in Medical Social Work: Preliminary Findings," *Social Work,* Vol. 4, No. 3 (July 1959), pp. 72–76.

[3] Herbert Blumer, "What is Wrong with Social Theory?" *American Sociological Review,* Vol. 19, No. 1 (February 1954), pp. 7–8.

many concepts presented in social science have received less practical and consistent testing. The first step is to push toward making the knowledge more explicit and thus more accessible for use and testing.

This chapter makes a beginning in setting forth some of the concepts and knowledge from social work practice in the health field. The shift in viewpoint from the health and medical orientation of the preceding chapter should be clear. There we were considering knowledge and concepts that social work selects and makes its own through use. Here we are seeking social work's own knowledge and concepts, that grow directly out of social work thinking and experience and are eventually verifiable. The emphasis in this discussion is on practice, but the contribution of medical social work teachers to conceptualization should be clearly recognized. It is the viewpoint of this discussion that neither social work nor medical social work are yet ready for building a single comprehensive system of theory. In line with the general purpose of this discussion, what appear to be promising directions of thinking from various approaches are presented, without attempting to bring them together into one organized body of theory.

EARLY THEORY IN MEDICAL SOCIAL WORK

Examination of early attempts to conceptualize the knowledge of medical social work indicates both the values and limitations of these earlier efforts. Medical social work was fortunate in having a clear and useful framework for thinking early in its history. In 1930, in the first of a series of studies of the functions of medical social work, Janet Thornton presented the following analysis:

> Social factors which appear in hospital practice fall into three main categories:
> 1. Social conditions which bear directly on the health of the patient, either inducing susceptibility to ill-health, or helping or hindering the securing and completing of medical care.
> 2. Social distress caused to others by the illness of patients; such as, loss of income, neglect of children, etc.
> 3. Social problems not having direct cause-and-effect

relation to the health condition, but collateral to it. Such problems would exist independently of the sickness.

These factors exist in many possible combinations.[4]

This approach was sound and valuable, since it required medical social workers to identify those social factors that were actually influencing the medical situation and to describe the nature of the interaction. Because of the tendency for social problems to spread, situations in which social difficulties can be regarded as collateral to the medical situation (the third category) are not frequently found. Furthermore, factors in the second category, social distress caused to others by illness, tend to react upon the patient in turn. For example, when a man is unable to support his family because of illness, he becomes anxious and not infrequently wishes to leave the hospital and return to work before his physical condition permits. Thus the first category eventually proved to be the most important one for medical social work. It became known as *the social component in illness and medical care* and has been widely used as a basic concept in medical social thinking, both in practice and teaching. The concept has proved useful in establishing the position of social work in medical care, since the demonstrated interaction of medical and social factors calls for social work as a part of the care of the patient, to assist both in understanding of medical social problems and in dealing with their effects.

As the psychiatric approach began to permeate social casework, there was increasing emphasis in medical social work on *the meaning of illness to the patient* and his family. This idea—which can best be regarded as a general theme rather than a specific concept—was discussed in one of the later studies of medical social work practice and is currently a part of medical social work thinking.[5] Its value is that it has turned the attention of practitioners and teachers toward the individual patient's own definition of the situation, with recognition that it must be understood in every instance and is usually the starting point for social work

---

[4] *The Functions of Hospital Social Service* (Chicago: American Association of Hospital Social Workers, 1930), p. 59.

[5] Harriett M. Bartlett, *Some Aspects of Social Casework in a Medical Setting* (New York: National Association of Social Workers, 1940. 6th printing, 1958), Chapter III.

activity. The idea has been interpreted to cover what are now regarded as the psychosocial aspects, that is, a full diagnostic analysis of the patient's behavior, including his adjustment to the problems of illness and medical care. The emphasis is upon the individual nature of each patient's response, *i.e.,* the difference in the meaning of illness for every person. Thus, while the general idea of the meaning of illness to patients might have operated as a starting point from which medical social workers could explore and make more explicit what they know about medical social problems, it has not been so used by the professional group. The theme itself was too broad to lead to precise thinking at an abstract level and no set of subconcepts or subcategories has been built in to extend and clarify its implications.

All through the history of medical social work, practitioners and teachers have talked and written about the social implications and psychological meaning of the problems associated with the particular medical conditions with which they were working and regarding which they had special knowledge. While a considerable proportion of the literature of medical social work relates to specific medical conditions, such as heart disease, cancer, blindness, or amputation, the conclusions to be drawn from these materials are not easily identifiable or definitive. The difficulty seems to be that social workers writing from their own experience about the psychosocial problems of these various conditions have not yet succeeded in distinguishing those problems that are common to all illness, or perhaps to chronic illness or handicap, from those that are peculiar to the particular condition under discussion. It is possible that more knowledge might be gained by focusing attention on certain recurrent psychosocial problems of illness in their own right, rather than following the medical classifications. Medical social workers undoubtedly possess and use much useful knowledge of this kind that has not yet been organized, classified, and formulated in manageable form. Analysis of this literature and exploration of the whole subject with practicing social workers are indicated, to determine how these generalizations could be better focused.

Another concept widely used in medical social work was that of the *medical setting*. It was an application of the basic concept of *setting* used throughout social work. It was useful in describing the sanction and auspices under which social work was practiced but was too narrowly limited to the administrative aspects and omitted other important features of the field of practice, as has been pointed out.

CONCEPTS FROM GENERAL SOCIAL WORK

At this point, before considering some current approaches to knowledge from medical social work, it will be well to review several concepts that are gaining acceptance in all social work thinking. It has already been pointed out that the concept of *social functioning* is being widely used as indicative of the central concern of social work. If social work is going to use social functioning as a central concept, it must identify the focus and components of the concept from a social work viewpoint. Unless otherwise indicated, the concept can be taken to refer to outer behavior, as observed from society's viewpoint, with primary emphasis on conformity with social codes and expectations. The social work concept of social functioning includes the idea that individuals are functioning with reasonable satisfaction of their own needs and without excessive stress. The self-fulfillment of the individual is a major value of social work. The concept of social functioning must encompass both the psychic and social, the inner and outer aspects, with neither dominant. Because of its value system, social work identifies with the person and this is its primary orientation. Situations are assessed first in terms of their meaning to the individual and then in their broader societal context. Most behavioral sciences (with the exception of social psychology) select one focus, either that of society or that of the individual. Social work has a particularly complex task in constantly maintaining and integrating the two orientations. Since this is where its characteristic contribution lies, this approach must not be lost in the effort to conceptualize the professional focus. At present it is doubtful if the social work focus can be expressed in any one concept or brief statement. No single term like "role" or "interaction" is adequate. We must be satisfied with rather extended exposition of concepts, which will not yet fit together smoothly, in order to be certain that all the essentials are covered. This discussion will use social functioning in the dual sense indicated above, to include both the psychic and social aspects of behavior.

Along with the idea of social functioning and its converse, social dysfunctioning, goes another pair of concepts, those of *equilibrium and disequilibrium,* which are so basic that they are employed by many scientific and professional disciplines. (Sometimes the concept of homeostasis has been extended beyond the organism to apply to other levels of functioning with a similar meaning.) In social work the reference is to the problems which arise from disequilibrium between the individual, the family, or group and their environment, and the efforts of individuals and groups to regain their equilibrium.

The concept of equilibrium, which implies a steady state, can become static. Social work has always stressed the importance and possibility of *growth,* both as a value and as a scientific concept. Psychoanalytic theory has been cast in negative and pathological terms, with defenses as a basic concept. There is need to conceptualize the positive elements in human behavior. One such formulation of human potentialities is that of Gardner Murphy, which was mentioned in the discussion of social work values. He presents the idea of three human natures—the first consisting of the organic make-up, capacities, and cravings, and the second developing through the impact of culture and reaction with the environment. The third human nature he describes as man's insatiable craving to make contact with reality and to understand the world around him, the impulse toward curiosity and discovery observed in all human beings from the small child to the greatest scientists. Murphy's emphasis upon the potentialities for human growth, if this creativeness can be better understood and more fully developed than is possible in our present society, is congenial to and promising for a similar direction of thinking in social work.[6]

Another important concept in active use in scientific thinking is that of *stress.* Its use in medicine has already been discussed. In social work, the reference is particularly to *psychosocial stress.* Because of the many ways in which the concept is being employed

---

[6] Gardner Murphy, *Human Potentialities* (New York: Basic Books, 1958).

today, there is need for each discipline to define carefully its own concept. Social workers should be clear that the concept covers not only pressures, burdens, and conflicts but also deprivations, *i.e.*, anything that is stressful. Thus loneliness, the lack of an essential social relationship, is regarded as a form of psychosocial stress because of its impact on the individual. Man's various ways of dealing with stressful situations, at the biological, personality, and social levels, should be understood. The variations in the impact of stress at different periods of the life cycle are also important. It is generally agreed that illness of any degree of severity is stressful for all individuals and families. More precise analysis and description of these various interrelationships is yet to be accomplished by the various disciplines concerned with problems of health and disease, including medical social work.

The relation between stressful situations and professional intervention is being studied with particular interest today. In the past social workers customarily described their activity in terms of *helping persons with problems*. The concept of *professional intervention in a stressful situation* is being increasingly used by other professions and disciplines as well as by social workers. These are situations where the problem is so difficult or overwhelming that the usual problem-solving methods of the individual or family are not effective.[7] There is temporary disruption of the habitual pattern of behavior, with accompanying emotional tension and disturbance. Such a situation is sometimes described as a *crisis*. The search for solutions often leads to new patterns of behavior which may be strengthening but on the contrary are frequently disabling or handicapping to the individual and family. Professional intervention aims to bring about the direct facing of reality

---

[7] Medicine and social work have been concerned mainly with severe stress beyond the adaptive capacity of the organism, which leads to disruption of normal functioning. For a discussion of such stressful experiences from a social work viewpoint, *see* Henry S. Maas, "Problems in the Use of the Behavioral Sciences in Social Work Education," in *Education for Social Work* (New York: Council on Social Work Education, 1957), pp. 86–88. It should be noted that stress is not always bad or painful. Life is full of stressful experiences which, when successfully integrated by the individual, produce stimulation, satisfaction, and growth.

and constructive methods of problem-solving. It has been observed that a relatively small amount of professional help given at the crucial moment enables an individual to reverse a regressive trend in behavior and to marshal his strengths to deal positively with the problem.[8] A man with hypertension, who had been carrying two jobs concurrently before his physical breakdown and who was taking a correspondence course leading to training for a less strenuous occupation, wrote to his social worker, "My blood pressure dropped ten points every time a lesson arrived." Such gains are often permanent and therefore a way toward furthering improved social functioning. The importance of timely intervention, which means bringing help before the stress or crisis situation has seriously undermined the individual's strength or disturbed his social relationships, is emphasized. The degree to which illness has invaded the individual's life situation will determine the goals of intervention. The earliest possible intervention, perhaps in a mother-child situation in a well-baby clinic, will often achieve complete prevention. In the situation of a chronic invalid in a wheel chair, the goal of the intervention may be limited to maintaining the individual's capacity for self-care.

It is interesting to note that several of these important concepts can be traced back to biological science and medicine. One other concept that should be mentioned comes distinctly from social science. That is the concept of the *family as a social unit*. The basic importance of the family in social work and illness is evident. Caroline H. Elledge describes a situation showing clearly this interdependence of family roles. A previously adequate father of a family reacted to his wife's serious illness and hospitalization by developing physical symptoms and emotional regression that completely incapacitated him. Thus the wife awoke to the disturbing realization of his immature dependency upon her at a time of family crisis when she was least able to face it because of her own illness.[9]

---

[8] Gerald Caplan, *Concepts of Mental Health and Consultation* (Washington, D. C.: United States Children's Bureau, 1959), pp. 144 and 258.

[9] Caroline H. Elledge, "The Meaning of Illness," *Medical Social Work,* Vol. 2, No. 2 (April 1953), pp. 62–64.

Because of concentration on the individual client, the family concept was for a period given little attention in social work practice, and contacts with family members, particularly in the home, were reduced to a minimum. There is now renewed interest in the family. Medical social work has usually seen the individual patient as a part of the family and has worked with relatives as key figures in the illness situation. Much more needs to be done, however, in visualizing the *family as a unit in illness,* in understanding how the health or illness of one member contributes to the illness or maladjustment of other members and to the total functioning of the group as a social unit. This is knowledge which is yet to be formulated.

FOCUS OF MEDICAL SOCIAL WORK

We are now ready to look more closely at medical social work thinking as it is taking shape today. In describing the integration of social work practice within the health field, one of the important characteristics was identified as the constant focus upon the psychosocial aspects of health needs. This medical social focus can be identified not only through observing practitioners working directly on individual situations but also through noting how they describe and analyze their knowledge and experience in the professional literature. A number of such papers are here briefly summarized, as illustrative:

1. Elledge, in a paper on the meaning of illness, says: "The effects of illness on an individual, his family, and his close associates can have as many different meanings as there are possible combinations of such factors as personality development, social conditions, environmental pressures, ways of becoming ill or handicapped, methods of treatment, and possible end results." [10] She describes the meaning of illness from the viewpoint of attitudes of professional persons caring for patients, members of patients' families, and the patient himself. She gives particular attention to "the specific emotional vulnerability" of individuals involved in the illness situation and the deep significance to the individual of bodily

---

[10] *Ibid.,* p. 49.

change brought about by illness and medical treatment, particularly surgery.[11]

2. In a paper on medical social work in an epidemic of poliomyelitis, Alice A. Grant describes the behavior and attitudes of the families of 172 children. This was under wartime conditions when because of shortage of professional personnel the physicians had to concentrate their efforts on the children and could not take time to see the relatives. The author describes how the families came to stand outside the isolation building in the evening, calling to their children, being fearful that medical treatment was not being carried out, comparing their situation with other patients, and becoming disturbed over imagined points of difference. The report analyzes the degree of disturbance, showing that 29 percent of the parents were markedly distressed over the separation from the child and could not accept it, in spite of efforts made by the social workers to help them understand and meet the situation.[12]

3. Ruth D. Abrams, in a paper on social casework with cancer patients based on a multidiscipline research project covering 60 cases, analyzes the ability of patients to accept and face the problems of cancer and describes their responses. The hypothesis of the study was that "the patient is usually concerned with, and often aware of the fact that he has cancer and is reacting to it—whether he says so or not." [13] Some patients in the study were able to express themselves realistically and spontaneously while others denied their symptoms or used aggressive behavior as a defense against anxiety. Among terminal patients a feeling of rejection was found to be common. The conclusion is that an appreciation of the reactions of patients and "an understanding of the dynamics of their defenses are essential in setting goals and improving casework techniques." [14]

4. In an analysis of medical social service in a tuberculosis sanatorium, based on a three-year period of practice, Pauline

---
[11] *Ibid.*, pp. 49–65.

[12] Alice A. Grant, "Medical Social Work in an Epidemic of Poliomyelitis," *Journal of Pediatrics*, Vol. 24, No. 6 (June 1944), pp. 691–723.

[13] Ruth D. Abrams, "Social Casework with Cancer Patients," *Social Casework*, Vol. 32, No. 10 (December 1951), p. 426.

[14] *Ibid.*, pp. 425–432.

Miller offers "a picture of the interrelationship of social and emotional factors with the medical condition of the individual patient." [15] The patient's relation to his family and social responsibilities are stressed throughout the discussion. This paper offers an interesting contrast with a similar discussion by a psychiatrist that focuses on the patient's attitudes toward himself and his illness.[16] The two papers, taken together, show rather clearly the distinction between the focus of social work and that of psychiatry in approaching problems of chronic illness.

5. Community resources can contribute to a patient's recovery when he has poliomyelitis, says Elizabeth Maginnis. "A link must be forged, however, between these agencies and the child who has polio. Someone on the hospital staff who knows the child's situation and also knows the potentialities of the community's resources to help him and his parents is a logical liaison. This forger of the link is more than an intermediary; she not only knows the facets of the child's needs, what services the agencies have to offer him, and how to bring them into play, but she also knows how to get the patient ready for the services. She appreciates what steps are necessary in his progress before outside assistance can benefit him. In other words this staff member has the skill to help a patient—even a very young one—to understand the next move after his own fashion and to feel ready to take it. This readiness of the child is one of the elements that make for success in the whole plan for restoration." [17] The medical social worker's role in co-ordinating community resources for a sick child and in helping him to use them constructively toward recovery is presented here.

6. Using the experience of medical social workers over many years in working with blind children, Eunice W. Wilson describes the handicapped child. Questioning the tendency to regard handicapped children as so "different" that they must be placed in

---

[15] Pauline Miller, *Medical Social Service in a Tuberculosis Sanatorium*, Public Health Service Publication No. 133 (Washington, D. C., U. S. Public Health Service, 1951), p. 5.

[16] Jerome Hartz, "Human Relationships in Tuberculosis," *Public Health Reports*, Vol. 65, No. 40 (October 6, 1950), pp. 1292–1305.

[17] Elizabeth Maginnis, "When a Child Has Polio," *The Child*, Vol. 15, No. 9 (May 1951), pp. 166–169.

special environments for care, she stresses that the child must be understood as a complete individual, like any other child; that all children find their greatest sense of security within the family; and that segregation on the basis of handicap alone should be avoided. The warmth and interest of professional people in whom they have confidence enable many parents to develop a constructive program for their handicapped child in a manner that they could not have undertaken without help.[18]

These six papers from the medical social work literature show a central concern for the individual patient and his family, similar to the medical practitioner's approach to an individual case. Each paper is based on the experience of the medical social worker in working with numbers of patients and families, all of whom were facing a similar problem. Insofar as their material permits, the authors offer tentative generalizations regarding the problems presented by illness and medical care, and the responses of patients and professional persons. The identification of these social workers with the patients and families about whom they are writing and their efforts to understand the stressfulness of the experiences stand out clearly. The discussions are carried on within a framework of thinking which consistently emphasizes the relation between medical and social factors in these various situations and the psychosocial implications of illness.

CLASSIFICATION OF MEDICAL-SOCIAL PROBLEMS

Some preliminary steps (mentioned earlier in this chapter) have already been taken by the professional group to examine medical social work literature and practice in order to discover in what form medical social workers are generalizing their knowledge, taking these generalizations at a level as close to actual experience as possible.[19] No generally accepted system for problem classification in social work or in medical social work is at present available, but much attention is currently being directed to this basic gap in

---

[18] Eunice W. Wilson, "The Handicapped Child," *Pediatrics,* Vol. 5, No. 3 (March 1950), pp. 569–573.

[19] Gordon and Bartlett, *op. cit.*

professional thinking, particularly by research social workers.[20]

A comprehensive diagnostic and treatment classification gives a profession better control over its activities and is eventually a necessity for effective professional judgment and action. Physicians can set up a clear categorical list of the causes of disease and methods of treatment, which goes a long way toward describing their professional practice. But because of the fluid nature of social work, the "units" with which we deal cannot be so clearly identified and classified. As has been shown, the medical social worker customarily thinks of disease and its social implications together, either in general or in terms of their meaning to the individual patient. The steps in medical care are viewed in terms of the patient's readiness to move through them. A single factor is usually not viewed as separate but related to others, in terms of its psychosocial implications, which is the social work frame of reference.[21]

The first attempts to capture the characteristic patterns of medical social work thinking are likely to be only partially successful. It is important, however, to begin with such tools as we have at our command and to press forward toward increasingly effective formulation as the control of our material and our experience improve.

Medical social workers have tended to follow the medical pattern of thinking in classifying medical social problems. The social and emotional problems of patients in various medical diagnostic groups, such as cancer, poliomyelitis, asthma, and other diseases, or of patients with various types of medical conditions, such as

---

[20] Alfred J. Kahn, "Some Problems Facing Social Work Scholarship," *Social Work,* Vol. 2, No. 2 (April 1957), pp. 54–62; Lola G. Selby, "Typologies for Caseworkers: Some Considerations and Problems," *Social Service Review,* Vol. 32, No. 4 (December 1958), pp. 341–349.

[21] Probably the most comprehensive coverage of medical social work concepts is to be found in an outline of curriculum content to be taught in schools of social work, prepared by a group of medical social teachers in 1951. *See Education for Medical Work: The Curriculum Content* (Washington, D. C.: American Association of Medical Social Workers, 1951). Additional concepts are recognized and are being taught in schools but are not available anywhere in the professional literature.

chronic disease, physical handicap, or blindness, are analyzed and discussed. This approach is useful and appropriate in working with physicians but does not show the full characteristics of social work thinking and lacks precision for general classification, since the problems discussed are often not distinctive of the particular medical condition but are found among other patients also.

It is not possible at present to develop a comprehensive scheme of classification for all medical-social problems. The most practical way to begin is to attempt classification of certain clusters of problems, in a manner relevant to the way problems are met and dealt with in social work practice. Since the focus of medical social work is upon the relationship between medical and psychosocial phenomena, a classification scheme based on the nature of this relationship offers promise. The relative *dominance* of these major entities in any situation is of significance to the social worker in classifying and assessing such a situation. One simple but useful beginning might therefore be to devise a scheme to show the relative dominance of medical and psychosocial components in situations, starting with dominant medical problems at one end and moving through the intermediate range to situations involving dominant psychosocial problems at the other end.[22] An initial scheme for such an analysis might be drawn up as shown on page 146. This classification is primarily intended for use with individuals and families but has applicability for larger groups. The illustrations under each category are suggestive only and do not attempt to be inclusive of all such phenomena. The important point is the possible usefulness of such an approach.

The problems grouped in the left-hand column are frank and serious manifestations of illness and handicap, with the concomitant phenomena of medical treatment procedures and disability. These problems are stressful for all patients and their families. When social work is needed, its service is mainly supportive and clarifying. In well-adjusted patients and families, the need for help is frequently acute but usually self-limiting because of their ability to function and to carry on by themselves after the first

---

[22] Eunice W. Wilson and Harriett M. Bartlett, "Referrals from Hospitals to Social Agencies: Some Principles and Problems," *Social Casework*, Vol. 36, No. 10 (December 1955), p. 459.

TYPES OF MEDICAL-SOCIAL PROBLEMS IN TERMS OF RELATIVE DOMINANCE OF MEDICAL AND PSYCHOSOCIAL ELEMENTS

Medical Problems Dominant	Medical and Psychosocial Problems Equally Important	Psychosocial Problems Dominant
Overwhelming stress from serious illness and handicap	Minor or temporary interrelated medical and psychosocial problems	Personality disturbances or defects
Sudden impact	Static or recurrent moderately limiting illness or handicap associated with psychosocial difficulties	Social maladjustments
Threatening medical procedures		Family disequilibrium
Severe handicap, limitation, and disfigurement	Major medical and psychosocial problems chronically linked together in patient's life situation	Socioeconomic problems (income, living and working conditions)
Progressive and terminal illness		*associated with*
associated with		Physical symptoms and
Psychosocial problems resulting mainly from the medical situation		Minor medical problems

difficult adjustment is over. In the instance of families with less strengths and particularly in the many instances where illness creates new psychosocial problems, more extensive help is needed. In chronic illness, the patients are likely to remain under the care of the health agency for long periods. The social work activity tends to fluctuate with the changes in the medical problem.

The problems in the middle column result from the combination of illness with previously existing psychosocial difficulties. There is always complex interaction of factors in these cases. The psychosocial problems may be partly responsible for the illness or disability. They frequently contribute to its further progress. Sometimes the dominant problems occur at the socioeconomic level, while in other instances they are to be found in deeply rooted emotional conflicts. Too often these cases are referred too late to the social worker. The slow and insidious interaction between the illness and the psychosocial elements produces maladjustment and invalidism in individuals and breakdown in families. When the medical problems are severe, any of the problems listed in the left-hand column may also occur in these cases. Patients and families originally classified under dominant medical problems may later move into the middle column, as the psychosocial problems created by the illness slowly grow and spread. The cases where chronic illness becomes permanently linked with the ongoing life situation of the patient and family are characteristic and major problems for the medical social worker.

The patients whose problems are grouped in the right-hand column come to the health agency with physical symptoms and complaints of various sorts. The patient feels ill or is so regarded by others, as in the instance of a child with a behavior disorder who is brought to a pediatric clinic by his parents. There is, however, no significant illness or physical defect. The problem is actually one of psychosocial maladjustment and malfunctioning. Physicians formerly told such patients that there was "nothing wrong with them" and showed no further interest in their difficulties. Medicine now recognizes responsibility to try to help these individuals, who are coming in increasing numbers to medical clinics and general practitioners' offices. Many of them exhibit mild psychiatric symptoms—anxiety, depression, and hypochondriasis.

They are the people who are reacting to life stress and deprivation through various combinations of physical and emotional symptoms, not serious but often persistent and disturbing to the patient. How they can best be helped is still to be determined. When the individual and family recognize their psychosocial difficulties, they can sometimes be helped by referral to a social agency. Some individuals, however, see their problems as medical, have confidence in the medical institution and their own doctor, and resist being transferred or "sent away." A few have sufficiently severe psychiatric difficulties to be transferred to psychiatric clinics. For others, physicians in general clinics are working with medical social workers, sometimes with psychiatric consultation, to explore what medicine can and should offer to them. The problem of time and effort can become serious because of their great need. When psychosocial problems pervade a whole family, such situations fall within the sphere of family welfare agencies, although health agencies may have continuing responsibility in relation to health maintenance even if there is no organic illness.

The caseload of any social service department, and probably of any individual worker, will exhibit the full range of these medical social problems. The problem classification is suggestive also in relation to groups of patients and families. Groups of patients falling in any one category can sometimes be helped by discussing their common problems together. Sometimes the most effective approach is by modifying policies and procedures, or developing new services in the agency or community, so as to lessen the impact of the problem even if it cannot be entirely eliminated. Medical social workers also have occasion to give consultation to other professional workers who are concerned with many of these problems in their own practice.

Other types of classification are needed. Eleanor Cockerill and Helen Gossett demonstrate the value of the life cycle as a framework for medical social workers. They point out that social work practitioners have particular opportunities to help individuals deal with certain life events and crisis experiences, because of the setting in which they practice and the characteristic points of contact with people this setting affords. Medical social workers have repeated opportunities to serve individuals at certain points in the life continuum, when they are dealing with such life events as pregnancy and birth and such experiences as illness, injury, surgery, and bereavement.[23] The analysis prepared by Cockerill and Gossett shows these points of contact and the professional responsibilities of the medical social worker, with emphasis upon the promotion of mental health. All phases of the life cycle are covered from the prenatal period to old age. The types of intervention and the varying focus upon individual, family, and community are presented. A fresh orientation such as this stimulates the medical social worker to perceive new points of intervention and ways of helping. It can be regarded as an application to medical social work of the general orientation to knowledge of human growth and behavior through understanding the potential for social functioning at each phase of the life cycle, as suggested by Butler.[24]

Once we begin considering classification of the phenomena with which medical social work is concerned, many other useful approaches come to mind. One is a scheme for judging "adaptation to life stress," ranging from successful adaptation to regressive immobilization, which was developed in connection with a psychosomatic study of coronary artery disease.[25] A classification of patterns of family reaction will also be needed, ranging from those situations where illness causes only temporary disturbance of equilibrium to those where illness comes to dominate the family pattern of living, just as it does in the instance of some individuals. Some logical classification of health services and programs from the social work viewpoint, in terms of their effectiveness in meeting the psychosocial problems of illness and medical care, may eventually be possible. A classification of cultural attitudes toward

---

[23] Eleanor Cockerill and Helen Gossett, *The Medical Social Worker as Mental Health Worker* (New York: National Association of Social Workers, 1959), p. 1.

[24] Ruth M. Butler, *An Orientation to Knowledge of Human Growth and Behavior in Social Work Education* (New York: Council on Social Work Education, 1959).

[25] Henry H. W. Miles, Samuel Waldfogel, Edna L. Barrabee, and Stanley Cobb, "Psychosomatic Study of 46 Young Men with Coronary Artery Disease," *Psychosomatic Medicine,* Vol. 16, No. 6 (November–December 1954), pp. 462–466.

illness and handicap would also be useful. These approaches are examples of the kinds of schematic thinking which will later be possible and valuable as tools to increase the analytical capacity of social workers in the health field. As attempts to find devices for analyzing medical social situations, they are only a beginning in getting at the nature of social work knowledge and thinking.

Some categorical schemes attempted in social work and social science seem to destroy the essential nature of the thing they analyze. It is possible that some of these devices create more problems than they solve. The test will be whether they bring clarification rather than confusion. If such first attempts as these prove unsuccessful, however, the search should still go on because it is clear that social work in general and medical social work in particular need to find their own appropriate and meaningful ways of analyzing their practice.

CONCEPTS DERIVED FROM PRACTICE

Having considered the background and focus of medical social work thinking and some schemes of problem classification, we are now ready to assess the potentials for developing significant concepts and generalizations out of current practice. An effort will be made to formulate certain concepts that are proving useful to medical social workers and appear characteristic of their thinking.

Stressful Situations in Medical Care

Medical care presents many problems to patients and their families. It is possible to identify certain potentially stressful situations in medical care that are difficult for most people, as follows: being admitted to the ward or clinic, waiting to hear the diagnosis, frequent change of doctors or nurses, lack of privacy, receiving services for which one cannot pay, wearing an appliance, taking injections, facing surgery, taking anesthetics, going to bed for a long period, facing a doubtful or poor prognosis, adjusting to a chronic treatment regime (medication, rest, diet), keeping regularly under medical supervision over long periods. Most individuals need some sort of help from some member of the medical team in preparing for and going through these experiences. Only selected patients, for whom one or more of these situations is particularly stressful, need medical social work assistance.

As medical social workers observe patients and their families moving through the process of medical care, it would appear that one of the most stressful aspects is that of *uncertainty*. Removed from his normal social contacts, stripped of his clothes and possessions and put to bed in a hospital, visited by a succession of strange people, moved about the medical institution for tests and consultations, the patient has continually before him the questions: What is going to happen to me? What will the doctor find? Will he be able to help me? What will the treatment be? Will I be disabled? How will my family be affected? Diagnostic procedures require time, and in many cases the diagnosis is uncertain over long periods. When doctors disagree, anxiety mounts. If the hospital staff is so hurried or impersonal that little attention is given to the patient as an individual, his increasing social isolation and fear of loss of control may lead him to question his own identity. "When this illness is over and I leave the hospital," he thinks, "will I be the same person I was and can I resume my previous role in life?" The clinic patient has similar difficulties, usually less acute but often more protracted because of the frequent need to make many visits before the medical picture is clear.

Because of the threatening nature of illness, *fear and anxiety* are the emotional reactions which the medical social worker meets most often in working with patients and families. They are normal responses to this stressful reality experience.[26] Medical social workers find, however, that individuals react to the different phases of reality according to their past life experience and way of defining the situation. Thus some have particular fears of helplessness, others of "being cut," and others of losing control through loss of consciousness; all of these responses are aspects of the stressful

---

[26] Fear is an immediate and direct response. Anxiety is an ongoing, painful uneasiness in anticipation of some future threat or impending ill. Anxiety is in this sense related to reality and should be distinguished from the pathological anxiety reaction of the neurotic individual.

medical care situations listed above. These reactions range from the rational at one end toward those that are more in the nature of fantasy. In working with apprehensive individuals, medical social workers endeavor to identify what particular phases of the situation are most threatening for them. These reactions are further discussed in an earlier study of medical social work.[27]

Fear and anxiety are practically universal among hospital patients. The medical social worker knows that one way to offset the stressfulness of the hospital experience is to insure that the patient have *opportunity for the fullest possible participation in his medical care*. The patient who is prepared for each step in medical care, who is kept informed by physicians and nurses as to the reasons why certain things are being done, can move along with the medical team more confidently and take responsibility for his own share in the process. From a viewpoint diametrically opposed to that of social work, some physicians believe that patients have no "right" to ask or know about their condition. "They should trust the doctor and leave everything to him," is the implication. Such an attitude is felt by all but extremely passive patients as belittling to human dignity. The child with diabetes who learns to give himself insulin and the adult patient with chronic disease who understands the nature of the medication he is taking are better prepared to face the reality of their illness. Experience shows that patients should be helped to take part in their own care as fully as their physical, intellectual, and emotional capacities permit. Under such circumstances, patients with adequate personality strengths can still come through the experience of illness to greater personal growth and maturity, even though they suffer relatively severe bodily damage and physical limitation.

Sequential Phases in Psychosocial Adjustment to Physical Illness and Handicap

There are a number of concepts and areas of partially formulated knowledge in medical social work which have added value when viewed in relation to each other. The attempt is made here to set forth some of these general ideas which have to do with the indi-

---

[27] Bartlett, *op. cit.*, pp. 117–123.

vidual's adjustment to successive phases of illness and recovery.[28] These phases are presented in the order in which they occur with many patients, with recognition that the sequence and combination of problems may vary in any individual situation. Understanding of these phases or steps in recovery from physical illness is important for medical social work, in order that patients may be given the necessary help. Such understanding also aids diagnostic ability to discern that point in the ongoing illness when the patient can, and should, be expected to move toward his usual and more mature pattern of behavior. If there is delay in this process, casework help at that time is sometimes crucial.

Regression is a term used with widely varying meanings in general medicine, psychiatry, psychoanalysis, and social science. As used here, it refers to a temporary phenomenon associated with relatively severe bodily disease, *i.e.,* the tendency of patients to revert toward less mature types of behavior. It results from the interaction of physiological, emotional, and social factors. The physical condition causes weakness, helplessness, and a narrowing of the psychosocial horizon. The patient's attention is turned in upon himself. He is to an extreme degree dependent upon others to meet his daily needs. There is often marked emotional lability and irritability. Under such conditions of serious illness the patient needs and demands the care and treatment accorded a child.[29]

In working with seriously ill patients, medical social workers are constantly aware of this phenomenon of regression. Distinction is made between these temporary manifestations of behavior due to illness and the patient's normal personality pattern, which will not be revealed until a later stage of recovery.[30] Persons who do not

---

[28] *See also* Henry D. Lederer, "How the Sick View Their World," in E. Gartly Jaco, ed., *Patients, Physicians and Illness* (Glencoe, Ill.: The Free Press, 1958), pp. 247–256. This description of the patient's passage through the various phases of illness, done from a psychiatric approach, did not come to the author's attention until after the above medical social analysis had been completed.

[29] Bartlett, *op. cit.,* pp. 130–134.

[30] The social worker will seek to obtain through the family and other sources an understanding of the patient's personality and behavior pattern previous to the illness but needs to recognize how illness is temporarily obscuring and modifying the normal picture.

understand this type of regression tend to classify these individuals as immature personalities. Medical social workers know that during a regressive phase patients need extra support and acceptance, that they cannot be expected to face reality, make difficult decisions, or carry their various home and social responsibilities.

> Using this knowledge to guide her first contact with a depleted and anxious young woman with duodenal ulcer in a hospital ward, a medical social worker reached out to the patient throughout the interview, assuring her that worries and fatigue are real and do cause real pains, that she needed to be spoiled a bit, that she had been carrying a heavy load. Having been rejected by some of her family for what was regarded as imaginary illness, the patient's response to the social worker's understanding was immediate and positive. Like other individuals who feel understood, she said, "You are the only one who ever said that."

One of the medical social worker's contributions is to help the family and others in the community concerned with the patient's welfare to modify their expectations and lessen pressures or burdens placed upon the patient during this period. Doctors and nurses understand and accept the phenomenon of regression in their care of sick patients. They know it is temporary, partly due to physical weakness, and in most instances will disappear as the patient gains strength. What the medical social worker adds to the concept is its meaning in terms of the individual's diminished capacity for social relationships and ability to carry his usual social responsibilities.

A characteristic emotional reaction in physical illness is *depression*. This is likely to appear early in the hospital period at the point where the patient is emerging from the initial psychic shock of illness or accident and first becoming aware of their implications. The reaction may appear as frank depression or may be masked in other forms. It can also appear at any phase of ongoing or chronic illness when the situation becomes overwhelming for the patient. Medical social workers are learning to recognize the symptoms of such reactive depression and to work with these patients within appropriate limits. The distinction between this type of depression and psychotic depression is important but not easy to make. Because the depressive reaction is common in illness, medical social workers need better understanding of this phenomenon.

Another type of emotional response commonly found in physical illness is *emotional dependency*. This is a natural concomitant of the already described factors in the illness situation, such as physical helplessness, psychic lability, and diminished capacity for social functioning. Medical social workers are aware that while emotional dependency is characteristic of the initial stage of any casework relationship when help is being sought, it is likely to be deeper and more far-reaching in illness. Thus the handling of the casework relationship becomes a delicate matter of meeting the patient's needs and yet not enlarging or prolonging the emotional dependency through the operation of the professional relationship itself.

As the patient moves out of the regressive phase of illness the medical social worker watches to note the emerging individualized pattern of adjustment to the illness. If the disease leaves him with some bodily damage or physical handicap, can he accept his changed condition and circumstances? Can he come to grips with them as his returning strength permits? Some patients require considerable time and help to take this step and some never succeed, thus remaining invalids all their lives. The diagnostic signs as to whether a patient is denying his illness are not always easy to identify. A patient may be overoptimistic in the face of severe handicap; he may criticize the doctors and the hospital; he may block at some step in medical treatment; he may project his difficulty onto his family or employer; he may become withdrawn and passive; or he may react in still other ways. Dr. Grete L. Bibring has presented several such instances showing varying patterns in reaction to tuberculosis in three patients in a hospital ward. One patient required special sympathy because of a dependent need for attention, and two regarded illness as weakness but reacted quite differently, one avoiding discussion of the subject, the other showing aggressive resistance. Bibring indicates how such individuals can be helped if their behavior is understood, but unfortunately in hospitals such understanding on the part of the staff is not always available.[31]

There are some individuals whose personal identity has been so invested in their body that they suffer severe personality damage when the body which they value so much is injured or mutilated. Until they can incorporate the change within their self-image, these individuals are blocked in returning to normal activity.[32] In working with problems of handicap the medical social worker looks first for the patient's motivation. A young married man with both legs paralyzed by poliomyelitis was convinced that he was like a child again. He had always been taller, stronger, and faster than others his age and that was how he kept up with and passed them. Now he felt that he had to grow stronger physically and could see no other way to grow as a person in order to take up his responsibilities as a breadwinner.[33] If, as in this instance, the individual cannot face the reality of his physical loss or limitation, it is doubtful if he can be helped toward rehabilitation without psychiatric help, no matter how promising the resources and opportunities available to him. The social worker therefore realizes what great effort is needed early in a case to enable an individual to accept the reality of his handicap so that he can move to the next step of doing something about it.

After the acute crisis in illness comes a period which has not been conceptualized in medical social terms but is known in medical terms as *the convalescent period*. It begins in the hospital and continues outside, at home or in another institution. In serious illness convalescence lasts for weeks or months. Early ambulation is shortening the hospital stay but not necessarily the duration of the convalescent period. Physicians, particularly surgeons, still tend to underestimate the length of time needed by many patients

---

[31] Grete L. Bibring, "Psychiatry and Social Work," *Journal of Social Casework*, Vol. 38, No. 6 (June 1947), pp. 209–211.

[32] The psychoanalytic concept of *body image* has been used to explain this phenomenon. The concept is not being employed in this discussion because it has many interpretations. If a clearer formulation is eventually attained, it will undoubtedly be helpful to medical social workers.

[33] Anonymous, "Medical Social Work in Microcosm: A Polio Case Record," *Medical Social Work*, Vol. 2, No. 3 (July 1953), p. 119.

for the physiological, emotional, and social adjustments that must take place in this intermediate phase of recovery. Some disabled patients are still working on acceptance of their handicap at the beginning of this period but if they have not completed this step by the end of convalescence, the social worker knows that the prognosis for social recovery is becoming less favorable. It is not unusual to see a temporary period of depression during convalescence, as the individual first realizes his limitations and perhaps tries to force his strength. The curve of increasing activity should in the long run be upward.

As the individual moves toward increased activity there is likely to be a conflict between the wish to get well and the hesitation of leaving the protected condition of illness. For most persons the losses involved in being ill provide a strong motivation to get well and return to active life. For some individuals, however, the advantages of being cared for and protected from life's problems—sometimes described as "secondary gain"—become so important that they cling to illness. Special help and stimulation are indicated to prevent such patients from losing their momentum toward recovery. By the end of convalescence the patient should be moving toward return to active social functioning, even if the first steps are slow and faltering. The social worker who is sensitive to the degree of readiness of each individual helps each one to progress at his own tempo.

The next advance is the definite acceptance of one or more steps toward realistic social functioning, in the light of the individual's handicap. When there is relatively severe physical handicap, many individuals obtain special training as preparation for such return to activity. The housewife receives training so that she can return home in a wheel chair to take care of her family. The man often returns to some less strenuous occupation in his old place of employment or may have to seek an entirely new occupational role. Sheltered employment is sometimes necessary, as a transitional phase or permanent arrangement. Medical social workers find that some of the disabled patients who have progressed through the earlier phases of recovery block at this later stage because they cannot adjust to the *changes in their social roles necessitated by their physical limitations.* The insecure father of a family whose personality has been bolstered by his success as a worker and a wage-earner cannot accept a change that lowers his status in the eyes of his wife and children. The adolescent youth who must give up high school athletics cannot face this loss of prestige in his peer group. A Japanese woman, who had made good progress in the early stages of physical therapy for hemiplegia, kept returning for exercises after she was considered ready for a job. Her feeling that she was a disgrace to her family, because of the attitudes toward physical handicap in her cultural group, was found to be an important factor impeding her further expected progress. These individuals are more likely than those who have difficulty with the earlier stages of recovery to be able to make a good start in a rehabilitation program. But as time goes on, problems begin to appear and it eventually becomes evident that the individual is not likely to complete the rehabilitation plan until he has come to terms with the changes in his social roles and relationships which will be required by his physical limitations.

A Psychosocial Concept of Disability

The preceding discussion of the patient's movement through the various steps toward recovery leads to a consideration of the nature of disability. Disability is a central problem and a core concept in medical social work. A clear analysis and formulation regarding this phenomenon are thus essential. One prevalent but oversimplified interpretation identifies disability with the observable and measurable physical handicap.[34] Compensation systems which classify all individuals according to percentages of physical loss are of this type. The general public, and also many physicians, tend to accept this definition because it is the most objective and straightforward to grasp. Observation of a group of individuals falling within a single classification of this type, such as 50 percent disability, will show, however, that their life-functioning varies all the

---

[34] Unfortunately the terms "handicap" and "disability" are used interchangeably in the literature of medicine and rehabilitation. Regardless of the terms used, great care must therefore be taken to distinguish between the two separate concepts, namely, actual physical loss or limitation (here described as handicap) and limitations in capacity for social functioning (here described as disability).

way from total invalidism to fully adequate performance in all social roles. In fact, it is well known that some individuals are spurred to even greater success than they would otherwise have attained through the effort put forth to overcome physical handicap.

Thus it is clear that the realistic physical handicap, while it is the first essential component, is only one part of the larger picture of disability as a total phenomenon. A more effective way of analyzing disability is to be found in assessing what the individual can do, *i.e.,* the nature of his social functioning. This should include not only his actual performance but also the degree of satisfaction and relative lack of emotional disturbance associated with his various activities. For adequate understanding, certain knowledge and skills are important. There must be a searching evaluation of the patient's physical condition as a basis for judging his capacity for activity and for bearing life stress. Medical social workers must be prepared to ask physicians the right questions to elicit this knowledge. The once popular recommendation of "light work" is now recognized as useless. In addition to the usual attention to the patient's motivation and life experience, there is special concern for his interests, intellectual capacity, and vocational aptitudes, for the measurement of which many specific tests are now used. As in any instance of illness, it is important to know the patient's position in the family group and the degree of understanding support he receives from the various members, and also his participation in other social groups. Finally, an assessment of the sociocultural environment is of immediate practical importance. The resources in the community represent the patient's opportunity for retraining and rehabilitation. The prevalent cultural attitudes toward disease and handicap, as held by employers, employees, and the general public, all too obviously favor or limit his functioning.

The full range of factors involved in assessment of disability is shown in a penetrating analysis presented in a workshop at the University of Pittsburgh School of Social Work.[35] It becomes clear that all of these interacting components are important in arriving at

---

[35] "The Concept of Disability: Summary of a Panel Discussion," in Eleanor E. Cockerill, ed., *Social Work Practice in the Field of Tuberculosis* (Pittsburgh: School of Social Work, University of Pittsburgh, 1954), pp. 139–151.

a comprehensive description of disability in any one instance. Since physical and personality factors are most frequently recognized, the medical social worker would particularly emphasize the social components, such as the amount of support accorded the patient by the medical team and by his family, as well as the availability of assistance through the community. The patient lacking these social supports is to that degree more severely disabled, when compared with another equally handicapped individual in a more favorable environment. Because of the number of interacting variables and their susceptibility to change, either through treatment or other influence, the state of disability is regarded as fluid rather than static.

What have been called the "sequential phases" in the patient's movement toward recovery are obviously related to the concept of disability. They represent stages through which most patients must pass and problems which most patients must solve in relation to their illness. They are similar to the "eight stages of man" as described by Erik H. Erikson, the life phases through which each individual moves in attaining maturity.[36] At any point in this forward movement through illness and recovery the patient's progress can be delayed or completely blocked. This occurs not only because of the particular meaning of the experience to him as an individual but also because of the chance occurrence of other developments in the situation which increase the stress—piling up of problems in the social environment, breaks in the continuity of his medical treatment so that he lacks needed support at a psychological moment, and similar factors. If the stress becomes excessive, breakdown in adaptive capacity occurs. Then in some instances *illness and disability become permanently linked with the life situation* and this becomes the subsequent pattern. Illness and disability are from then on the dominant theme in the individual's life. Since psychosocial factors are so important in disability, medical social work can play a significant preventive role in these situations. Too often social workers who are working with chronic invalids realize what opportunities for giving help were missed at an earlier point before the invalid pattern became fixed.

---

[36] Erik H. Erikson, *Childhood and Society* (New York: W. W. Norton and Co., 1950), Chapter VII.

Psychosocial aspects of rehabilitation. Disability and recovery as here discussed are closely related to the concept of rehabilitation of the physically handicapped. Rehabilitation requires much technical knowledge and highly specialized services. It is an area of extremely rapid change and experimentation, because medicine itself is working out measures for reducing the effects of mental and physical handicap, while new specialists are also being brought into the rehabilitation team. Medical social workers have been drawn into many new types of multidiscipline teams, often including specialists who have not previously worked with others in the medical setting, such as clinical psychologists and vocational advisers. Some of these teams may include as many as nine or ten different specialties. Most of them, in refocusing medical objectives toward an emphasis on rehabilitation, offer promising opportunities for social work participation. Examples are teams concerned with the evaluation of cardiac patients for employment, the rehabilitation of patients with amputations, the return of chronically disabled and aged institutionalized individuals to community living. As always happens when social work is practicing in a changing milieu, social workers find it necessary to re-examine their own contribution in order to clarify its relation to the particular goals, values, knowledge, and methods of the program.

Medical social workers have thus become aware that they have been functioning with insufficient knowledge in certain important segments of their work, as in the psychosocial aspects of vocational training and work adjustment. They are being stimulated to explore these areas and determine what new concepts and principles are essential for their own practice. They are also recognizing the peculiar relevance of their own knowledge and experience, which falls squarely within the area of rehabilitation. The manner in which the handicapped person's social relationships—in the medical setting, in his home, in the community—facilitate or impede his movement toward optimal social functioning is a major concern of medical social work. Examination of present thinking and practice in rehabilitation suggests that greater emphasis is being placed on the psychic and organic aspects of the problem and that breakdown of rehabilitation plans not infrequently occurs because sufficient attention was not given to the individual's social environment as it affects his movement toward recovery. Here, as in other phases of medicine, the social concept needs to become more operative. Thus we have another reason for the urgency of formulating and focusing social work knowledge and experience. Mary A. Stites demonstrates this social work viewpoint convincingly in an analysis of a group of rehabilitation cases.[37]

Rehabilitation is thus an important area for medical social work practice. Because of its rapid growth, technical aspects, and many specialties, it requires seasoned practitioners who have sufficient security to bear the pressures and uncertainties while working to identify more clearly the social work role and contribution in widely differing situations in this practice.[38]

Illness and Social Roles

The impact of illness upon the social situation and the whole train of interactions that ensues are a matter of major concern for the medical social worker. Because of its very obviousness, it has not been given the attention it deserves. Social workers in all fields are now coming to realize that the "social" aspects of their psychosocial focus must be conceptualized and put in orderly form in the same manner as the psychic aspects. Social science concepts are being actively explored, particularly the concept of *social role,* as it relates to the social functioning of individuals. In a very general way social roles are patterned behaviors resulting from the individual's position in society (as from age or sex) and membership in certain groups (as in the family or the work group). The concept is useful in explaining personality growth through socialization. It parallels Freudian theory in demonstrating how the individual must learn and master essential social roles at each successive phase of the life cycle.[39] It is further useful in helping

---

[37] Mary A. Stites, "Psychosocial Diagnosis in Vocational Rehabilitation Services," *Social Casework,* Vol. 39, No. 1 (January 1958), pp. 21–27.

[38] Ruth D. Abrams and Bess S. Dana, "Social Work in the Process of Rehabilitation," *Social Work,* Vol. 2, No. 4 (October 1957), pp. 10–15.

[39] Talcott Parsons and Robert F. Bales, *Family, Socialization and Interaction Process* (Glencoe, Ill.: The Free Press, 1955).

the social worker to understand better in social terms the problems of major social work concern, since it clarifies how the individual's potential for social functioning is fulfilled or frustrated through his various social roles. An individual of a certain personality type functions more easily in some roles than others. There may be stress because of conflict in roles or because of differing interpretation (of the individual and those around him) of the same role. Such consideration of social roles brings a greater emphasis on the social interaction phase of behavior and thus a better balance in social work theory.[40]

In recent social work writing two uses of the role concept have been suggested in relation to medical social work, one focusing on the role of the patient in medical care and the other on the role changes resulting from illness and physical handicap.[41] Every patient faces certain tasks that he must meet and carry through because of the nature of his illness and medical care, such as giving up his regular activities, being dependent on others, and suffering pain. He also is influenced by and must adjust to the expected behavior for patients as defined in the particular environment where he is receiving care. These elements—the realities of illness and the expectations of those caring for him—largely define his role as patient. The range of characteristic roles in illness and the manner in which individuals respond to them are fruitful matters for further investigation by medical social workers.

In its second usage, that of social role modification as a result of illness and physical handicap, the concept seems particularly con-

---

[40] At a conference of social scientists and social work researchers considering the use of social science concepts in social work research, the current limitations of role theory and the need for clearer definition of the role concept, which has a wide range of meanings, were pointed out. The particular contribution of role theory up to this time was indicated as the emphasis on the situational determinants of behavior. See Edgar F. Borgatta, "Role and Reference Group Theory," in Leonard S. Kogan, ed., *Social Science Theory and Social Work Research* (New York: National Association of Social Workers, 1960), pp. 16–27.

[41] Werner W. Boehm, *The Social Casework Method in Social Work Education* (New York: Council on Social Work Education, 1959), pp. 113–114.

genial to medical social work thinking.[42] Illness and handicap always cause changes in social relationships. During illness there is temporary withdrawal from active life and more or less complete social isolation. If the individual is left with physical limitations, his social activities undergo modificaton. Radical readjustments take place among the members of a family because of the heavy financial burden of chronic illness and the inability of the chief wage-earner to maintain the former standard of living. Some families concentrate excessive concern upon a handicapped member, while others reject him or place him in the role of scapegoat. These phenomena have always been recognized as of major significance in medical social work. There should be exploration to determine in what ways the social role concept brings added understanding of the problems involved.

The integration of the social role concept with the concepts regarding personality that are already incorporated in social work thinking is a task that lies ahead. The balanced emphasis upon the psychic and social aspects of situations has been described as characteristic of social work and ways must be found to maintain this balance in the expanding conceptual framework. One constellation of ideas that ties the two together is that relating to stress and adjustive capacity. The stress resulting from role conflicts of various types may overtax the individual's adjustive capacity and the resulting emotional disturbance may contribute to the development of illness. Dr. Nathan W. Ackerman describes such conflict as follows:

> In the process of adaptation, the social role of the individual may serve either a positive or a negative psychological function. In mature, well-integrated personalities, a social role can reflect the strength of the individual expressed positively in participant group action. Here there is no conflict between the individual and the social components of self. They are mutually reinforcing. In weaker persons, handicapped by specific emotional disabilities and generalized immaturity, the individual and social aspects of self may come

---
[42] Henry S. Maas, "Social Casework," in Walter A. Friedlander, ed., *Concepts and Methods of Social Work* (Englewood Cliffs, N. J.: Prentice-Hall, 1958), pp. 62–64.

sharply into conflict. The effort of integrating a particular social role may exact an excessive price in terms of anxiety and conflict within the individual self; or conflict within the individual may damage or prevent the effective execution of a given social role. Such discord between individual and social aspects of self are common in a variety of psychopathological types.[43]

It might be added that severe piling up of social stress may exceed the adjustive capacity of even relatively well-balanced personalities.

Sociocultural Aspects of Illness and Medical Care

From the medical social worker's viewpoint, other valuable applications of sociocultural theory are found in the analysis and demonstration of the manner in which membership in various social groups, such as the family, religious, and ethnic groups, affects the individual's perception of his illness, handicap, or medical care and his relationship with various members of the health professions.[44]

Medical social work knowledge regarding sociocultural aspects of illness and medical care is scattered and uneven, but it is beginning to assume more orderly form. The aspect that first caught the attention of social workers had to do with the customs and values prevalent within ethnic groups that influenced attitudes toward illness and medical care. Dietary restrictions, taboos and superstitions, social regulation of women and children, all fall within this category. The writer recalls vividly being drawn into a case as a young worker by agitated ward physicians, who had failed to persuade a Jewish rabbi, recovering from perforating gastric ulcer and still dangerously ill, to take any nourishment. The patient lived alone, had no visitors, and spoke no English. Through an interpreter it was learned that he was refusing hospital food because it was not prepared according to his religious tenets.

---

[43] Nathan W. Ackerman, *The Psychodynamics of Family Life* (New York: Basic Books, 1958), p. 61.

[44] Stanley H. King, "Social Perception, Culture, and Illness," in *Perception of Culture: Implications for Social Caseworkers in Medical Settings* (New York: National Association of Social Workers, 1960), pp. 9–24.

Thus for several days the young caseworker carried to the ward from the patient's residence, in a congested neighborhood near the hospital, pitchers of soup specially prepared by his landlady—continuing this emergency service until a friend of the patient could be found to take it over. Incidents of this kind impress us forcibly with the impact of cultural norms on scientific medical care.

Medical social workers also noted characteristic patterns of reacting to pain, illness, and handicap among different cultural groups.[45] The stolidity of the North European patient in facing physical suffering contrasted sharply with the excitability of the South European. It was observed that the passivity of some Orientals in giving in to fate prevented them from putting forth effort toward rehabilitation, while the need of members of other cultural groups to preserve face prevented them from discussing their problems freely. Medical social workers were aware of these phenomena as being due to cultural differences, not personality, and used this knowledge in their practice in a common-sense way.

Religious goals and standards have been of particular importance, since religion is so deeply concerned with problems of suffering and death. Medical social workers have worked closely with representatives of the various religions in bringing comfort to dying patients and their families. When individuals regard their illness as a punishment for sin, the problem falls within the sphere of religion. The social worker's understanding and use of religion as a social, moral, and spiritual force in relation to problems of illness is an important subject that requires more attention than it has received.

The medical social worker observes how some sociocultural norms and values give support to the sick person, but others create problems for him. The acceptance of illness in our society and the many resources for care represent the positive side. Medical social workers inevitably tend to have their attention turned toward the problems and limitations resulting from social attitudes and values. Two kinds of fears that are widely found in American society today present barriers that many sick persons must surmount. In this

---

[45] Mark Zborowski, "Cultural Components in Responses to Pain," in Jaco, ed., *op. cit.*, pp. 256–268.

pioneer culture, with its emphasis on individual effort, there is a public attitude which assumes that giving help will create dependency. Workmen's compensation laws, which might seem to confirm this fear, are administered with inadequate understanding of the relation between illness, money, protracted litigation, dependency, and neurotic invalidism. Social workers know that help appropriately given at times of stress does not create dependency but frees the individual to use his own strengths; however, this has not yet been convincingly demonstrated to the public. In spite of the Judaeo-Christian tradition of protecting the weak and handicapped, there also tends to be an attitude of fear, repulsion, and rejection toward the chronically ill and handicapped, which is rather widely prevalent in our society.

Under these circumstances, the handicapped person is regarded as "different," unworthy, sometimes reprehensible and dangerous. His associates tend to place him in an inferior position or isolate him through their own withdrawal. If there is some objective sign of handicap, such as deformity, coughing, or fits of unconsciousness, he is further stigmatized. These attitudes largely go back to unconscious fears and impulses; thus they are difficult to influence by direct education. The sick person's real needs and capacities become obscured under this cloud of evasion and fear. The sick and handicapped are thus frequently prevented from attaining the best social functioning of which they are capable because of these sociocultural barriers.

As part of the recent social science interest in the health field, attention is being directed outside the hospital to these cultural components of illness and medical care as basic concepts. One of the most comprehensive studies, undertaken by a sociologist and a physician, Simmons and Wolff (mentioned in the preceding chapter), is concerned with the relations between social science and medicine, with emphasis on the links between sociocultural stress and disease.[46] A study by Lyle Saunders of the manner in which cultural differences affect the utilization of medical care by the Spanish-speaking people of the Southwest illustrates a large litera-

---
[46] Leo W. Simmons and Harold G. Wolff, *Social Science in Medicine* (New York: Russell Sage Foundation, 1954).

ture which is accumulating on this general subject.[47] Some of the most significant investigations have appeared in the public health field and have to do with acceptance of public health services in all types of cultures and communities, from the most primitive to the most modern.[48] These investigations demonstrate that "folk medicine" and scientific medicine represent two distinct patterns of behavior, which can be integrated only through full knowledge and careful planning.

MEDICAL-SOCIAL APPROACH TO COMMUNITY HEALTH PROGRAMS

From their experience in working with people, medical social workers have considerable knowledge as to how health programs affect the persons they serve and also as to unmet needs. It is agreed that this knowledge is not being used as effectively as it might be. This discussion can only suggest a few points in relation to the nature of this as yet unformulated social work knowledge. There are two concepts commonly used in relation to health services to which social work might make a significant contribution, namely, *accessibility and continuity of service.*

Medical social workers should join with others in testifying to the general need for medical care, with concern for provision of the essential services, their adequacy in terms of quantity and quality, and their geographical distribution. Medical social workers are too small a group, however, to influence greatly the general availability of health services. Their greatest contribution can come through attention to aspects within their specific area of practice—the psychosocial aspects of medical care—regarding which others often have less concern and opportunity for direct observation. The medical social worker is particularly concerned with

---

[47] Lyle Saunders, *Cultural Differences and Medical Care* (New York: Russell Sage Foundation, 1954).

[48] Benjamin D. Paul, *Health, Culture and Community: Case Studies of Public Reactions to Health Programs* (New York: Russell Sage Foundation, 1955).

the psychosocial factors in health problems which block or delay use of the services and thus interfere with their *accessibility* to the persons who need them. The means test for the medically needy family is an outstanding example. Another example is complex legal and administrative procedures related to medical care, particularly those which are difficult to understand and cause people to fear they are losing control over their lives or those of their children. Hospital admission policies also present many barriers to persons needing medical care. The emotional implications of such situations and the manner in which they influence use of health services are not well understood or generally accepted. If medical social work knowledge is to be effective, it must be clearly formulated and buttressed with convincing supporting data. An illustration would be the manner in which the medical social workers in the Division of Health Services of the United States Children's Bureau have from time to time worked with the states in gathering social data as a base for policy determination or for the organization and structuring of health services.[49]

There is considerable discussion of the importance of *continuity of care* as a basic administrative principle, but the problem imposed on individuals and families through lack of such continuity have not been presented in convincing fashion. The medical social worker, who moves with the patient as he progresses through the various steps in medical care—from his home to the clinic or physician's office, into the hospital, out to the convalescent home, nursing home, chronic hospital, or rehabilitation center—witnesses probably more vividly than any other professional worker the difficulties presented to patients by our loosely organized and over-categorized system of health services. Patients who should be under care too often give up through ignorance, confusion, and discouragement.

One important approach to this problem is through measures to fill the gaps, remove the restrictions, and improve the co-ordination of community health services. Social workers are already working with their health associates toward such objectives but only a

---

[49] *Medical Social Services for Children* (Washington, D. C.: United States Childrer's Bureau, 1953).

beginning has been made. Medical social workers are keenly aware of additional aspects that are often not even recognized by other workers. The tremendous importance to the patient of feeling that the members of the health team are genuinely interested in him and the potency of this attitude in motivating patients to carry through the successive steps in their medical care are well known to medical social workers, but they are not generally recognized as an important factor in influencing continuity of care. This aspect would be difficult to demonstrate but with careful thought and imagination such demonstration should be feasible.

These are two illustrations of the nature of social work knowledge and the ways in which it must be organized before it can become effective as a tool for improving service in the program area.

SOCIAL WORKER'S OWN ATTITUDES AND RESPONSES

In social work the self-awareness of the worker is customarily thought of as part of the development of the professional self, which is taught in relation to the teaching of skill. Self-awareness is discussed here as knowledge because it begins with recognition that the social worker's own attitudes are vital in influencing performance, and with understanding how these responses operate. Each individual has to learn this through his own feeling and doing, not intellectually. But for the profession as a whole it is part of the body of professional knowledge.

Furthermore, in each field of social work practice there are particular situations, characteristic of that field, which present crucial problems to the social worker in terms of his own attitudes and responses. Successful performance in the field depends upon ability to deal with one's own attitudes in relation to these recurrent situations.

These characteristic experiences in the health field are well recognized, although relatively little has been written about them. They are customarily discussed by medical social work teachers in schools of social work, in the classroom and in the field, and by medical social supervisors in practice. One group of such phenomena has to do with illness and physical handicap, and their concomitant elements, which are disturbing and often shocking to most people. Helplessness and dependency, and the threat and coming of death are the most common and serious problems associated with illness. Deformity, disfigurement, and mutilation are problems which come as by-products of illness and accident. The emotional impact of all these phenomena is only too clear. Since much of the individual's response is unconscious and repressed, most social workers need supervisory help in learning to deal with such situations.

A second group of emotion-evoking situations has to do with the conditions under which work is carried on in a health setting. Can the social worker accept the discipline of sharing the patient with medicine and the other professions? This means readiness to assume the appropriate social work role in the medical team, with acceptance of medical authority and recognition of the middle-level status of social work. It also means acceptance of the tempo and inevitable interruptions of medical care without too much frustration. These are factors that operate less starkly than those related to mutilation and death, but they are still disturbing to most social workers and must be faced.

No social worker ever forgets the first time he faces a patient he knows is going to die, when the patient himself is ignorant of his prognosis. The impact of this knowledge on the member of the helping profession is at first numbing and shocking, to the degree of producing temporary immobilization and withdrawal. But the worker who is going to remain in the field knows that he cannot help by withdrawing and so, step by step and case by case, learns to develop a way of behaving in which the normal response of compassion is combined with that degree of professional discipline that permits the giving of help. While much more study and understanding of the medical social worker's responses and ways of handling them is needed, present evidence suggests that the emphasis on self-awareness has enabled workers to handle their feelings directly and continue in a helping relation with patients and families to a degree that is creditable and encouraging in view of the known threat and stressfulness of the situations involved.

CONCLUDING COMMENT

The subject matter discussed here as knowledge emanating from the experience of medical social work has to do with psychosocial aspects of illness and falls within the medical social worker's characteristic focus. Other disciplines are concerned with these problems, but the effort has been made to show the approach and insights characteristic of medical social work. When these concepts and this knowledge are thus brought together, the values of this consistent focus both in service to the patient and in contribution to the total health team can be rather clearly perceived. The need for deepened knowledge and skill is equally evident.

The present discussion is only a beginning. These concepts and generalizations require refinement and testing. Furthermore, there are many additional areas regarding which medical social workers have special experience and knowledge that require formulation. Some of those that might be explored are:

1. The hospital as a therapeutic milieu; the strengths and limitations of the hospital as a social environment in helping patients toward physical recovery and return to social functioning.

2. Problems of illness and handicap which cannot be helped through medical and psychiatric therapy but require "social therapy," that is, modification of social relationships as the indicated method of helping.

3. The family in relation to illness; disequilibrium in the family as affecting and as affected by illness; the multiproblem family in which illness is a dominant problem.

4. The interaction between psychosocial and economic aspects of illness and medical care; financial stress related to illness; anxiety over costs of medical care; problems of the medically needy.

5. Some special skills used in medical social work, such as reaching out to the individual or family that has not applied for help; giving support to persons under overwhelming stress; timing of help in relation to various phases of illness and recovery; triangular interviews between patient, physician, and social worker; multidisciplinary conferences between two or more members of different professions; collaboration with hospital and public health nurses.

6. The social work approach to use of resources within the health agency and the community—professional skills, health and welfare resources, lay groups—in carrying through comprehensive medical care for patients; the knowledge and skill needed to prepare patients and families for participation, to select appropriate resources and to co-ordinate an ongoing plan that may last for months or years.

7. Community attitudes (sociocultural approach) as they strengthen or limit medical and social services to the sick and handicapped.

8. Methods of identifying the relevant psychosocial factors in various types of health and medical care programs and of including measures within the programs that meet the needs as identified.

As attention is turned in these directions, undoubtedly additional areas of medical social work knowledge will be recognized and those most fruitful for immediate exploration will be identified.

9

social work methods

Knowledge and values are applied in social work practice through use of various methods, in order to influence, modify, or change problems and situations considered to be within the scope of the professional worker's competence. The social worker's action in each instance is based upon a professional assessment of the situation. The aim of such assessment is to identify the problem and arrive at a judgment as to whether it falls within the scope of social work and, if so, what should be done about it. In now moving into discussion of social work methods, attention will first be given to the social worker's assessment of medical social problems, with particular concern for the individual patient and his situation, but with awareness of implications for assessing broader types of problems.

ASSESSMENT OF MEDICAL-SOCIAL SITUATIONS

To define the medical social problem is a difficult intellectual and social process because of the number of issues and persons involved. It might seem to one unfamiliar with the field that all any social worker without experience in the medical setting needs is to gain some additional knowledge about disease and medical care from books and doctors, and to add this to the body of social work knowledge. However, the process is not that of adding one and one to make two, but of identifying subtle interactions in a constellation of organic, psychic, social, and cultural factors. The increasing knowledge about psychosomatic illness and cultural stresses has added further dimensions to what was already complicated enough when the major elements were regarded as only medical and social factors.

Much of the theory regarding social work with individuals has emerged from the family and children's fields, where in defining the "casework problem" with the client the worker customarily depends mainly upon the body of theory regarding personality and family relationships that is basic for all social workers. It has not been sufficiently noted that in some other fields of social work practice workers consistently use an additional body of knowledge and theory (as in relation to illness or corrections) which must be integrated with the basic knowledge regarding behavior from the beginning and throughout the case. This appears to affect the pattern of social work thinking in these fields, since a persistent effort is required to keep the various streams of thinking related for the client's best interest and to use the important knowledge about the specific problem (which the worker has and the client may not have) to help the latter solve it in his own way.

In considering the nature of the problem or situation as it is perceived by the social worker in the health field, it becomes clear that what we have is not an individual coming with a problem and carrying on interviews at a desk with a social worker, according to a pattern described in some fields of social work. In medical social work practice, patient and social worker move together through a complex field of forces and persons. The conceptualization which seems best to describe the medical social worker's practice is that of the person (or group) in a social situation in which health, illness, and medical care represent the central concern. This idea of person-in-situation is a characteristic and essential social work concept that appears and reappears throughout its history.[1]

---

[1] The social situation covers the social relationships (social interaction, social transactions) of a person or group at a given time. The concept of situation is not as inclusive as, and is more transient than, that of environment or field. It is broader than the concept of case-

Sometimes there is greater emphasis on one or another facet of the constellation but the concept always persists.[2]

The characteristics of what might be called the "medical social situation" and the manner in which the social worker keeps integrating the medical, social, and emotional aspects within this framework, can be visualized through the following two illustrations:

> The first situation concerns a 33-year-old man, who is completely immobilized in a ward bed with severe rheumatoid arthritis and isolated from all family contacts. An early marriage with an immature neurotic young woman had been broken up. In spite of apparent good intelligence, the work history showed irregular employment at unskilled jobs. The man had a great need to appear strong and adequate, thus had difficulty in accepting his disability and dependence on others. He used hostility and humor to cover his deeper feelings. Because of his negative reaction to authority, the medical staff, at first interested in the patient, later rejected him. The social worker moved very slowly into a relationship. Knowing that such a socially isolated, depressed, and hostile handicapped individual could unconsciously find a way out of his difficulties through becoming permanently disabled, the social worker hoped to prevent such a linkage of handicap and life problems. Because of the patient's lack of support from family, doctors, or other social relationships,

---

work diagnosis, since the social worker in the non-social work setting, in deciding upon appropriate social work action, must take into account the impact of the setting itself and the relation of social work activity to that of the other professions active or potentially active in the problem. That is, the relevant aspects of the setting and the other professions' activities are included within the social situation, since they can bring either help or stress to client and family.

[2] In 1937 Ada E. Sheffield, following Gestalt theory in psychology, suggested that the unit with which the social caseworker deals should be the *situation*. Her analysis of social work thinking about the social situation is clarifying and has not received the attention it deserves. See Ada Eliot Sheffield, *Social Insight in Case Situations* (New York: D. Appleton-Century Company, 1937). In recent years attention turned toward the personality aspects, sometimes to the degree of almost abandoning the outer or situational aspects of the constellation. Currently there is a swing toward a better balance between the two aspects.

she reached out to him through the casework relationship and found that he could use help through this medium. As he talked with her about his past experience and hopes for the future, he began to ask for help with his current problem. He was able to move into a rehabilitation plan, improved enough medically so that he could complete special training, and a year later was working successfully as an accountant.

In a second situation a well-adjusted, intelligent 18-year-old girl of Italian background was in a hospital for exenteration of the orbit of one eye because of carcinoma of the lacrymal gland. A young physician, himself under stress, had conveyed the situation to the patient as far as he felt able. In talking with the patient afterward the social worker found that the girl knew her eye would be removed but thought she would be able to wear an artificial eye and did not realize the extent of the disfigurement. She was very anxious about taking ether and apparently had no awareness that she had cancer. (The mother was informed of the diagnosis.) The worker considered what reality the girl would have to face in order to go through the several episodes of surgery that lay ahead. Since it seemed important for the patient to realize the extent of the surgery, the worker helped the doctor and patient toward clearer communication on this subject. The girl talked freely to the worker, telling how she had dreamed about her eye. "I won't be the same person," she said. The worker gave her close support during the necessary surgery, on one occasion standing by to hold her hand during painful changing of surgical dressings. She listened to the girl's fears about anesthesia but decided that further insight was not necessary, since acceptance of surgery was not blocked. The worker talked with the patient's mother and thought that as time went on the girl perhaps realized her diagnosis but did not need to talk about it directly. The worker maintained the casework relationship long enough to make certain that the patient was not being unduly disabled by this traumatic experience. Actually she made an excellent recovery. Within a year she had returned to her old job and, in spite of the patch over her eye, was going with a boy friend.

One sees in these situations how the social workers are using their knowledge of human behavior and medical care to consider what steps the patient must or can take, with what readiness, at what tempo, and with what need of support and stimulus. The thinking and action are attuned to these various aspects.

Elements in Assessment

Examination of selected cases showing "good practice," such as these, suggests that certain elements are consistently taken into account for arrival at an adequate assessment of the medical social situation. Pursuing this line of thought, the writer developed the hypothesis that medical social workers follow a regular and orderly method of thinking, and that it thus would be possible to identify certain elements that are constant in their assessment of medical social situations met in practice. After reviewing more than fifty fully recorded cases, the writer constructed a chart setting forth these elements. Several groups of practitioners or advanced students in medical social work were asked, in informal discussion, to indicate what elements they thought they took into account and it was found that each group regularly mentioned all the areas in the chart except one (to be discussed later). Furthermore, when shown the chart, they reacted to it positively and stated that it was clarifying to them and an aid toward better understanding of their own way of approaching their work.[3] The chart appears on page 179.

The hypothesis (requiring verification and revision through study) is that the medical social worker consistently takes these or similar elements into account in a case. In simple situations some elements can be reviewed almost in a flash and discarded as irrelevant. In complex cases all are carefully explored and weighed. The most important are identified and their interrela-

---

[3] A group of five caseworkers at the Massachusetts General Hospital also worked on a special project in 1959–1960, involving the analysis of three cases each and a series of eight conferences for discussion of the method and material. When asked to identify in one of their own cases the elements which in their judgment were important for their assessment of the medical social situation, without being given any suggested categories, the workers spontaneously produced material which in coverage and arrangement corresponded closely with items in the chart, with very few gaps. When asked to repeat the analysis, using the suggested scheme, with the same and other cases, they reported that it fitted "naturally" into their thinking. More carefully controlled examination of a larger sample would be necessary to identify the characteristics of practitioners' thinking in an authoritative manner.

CONSTANT ELEMENTS IN ASSESSMENT OF A MEDICAL-SOCIAL SITUATION

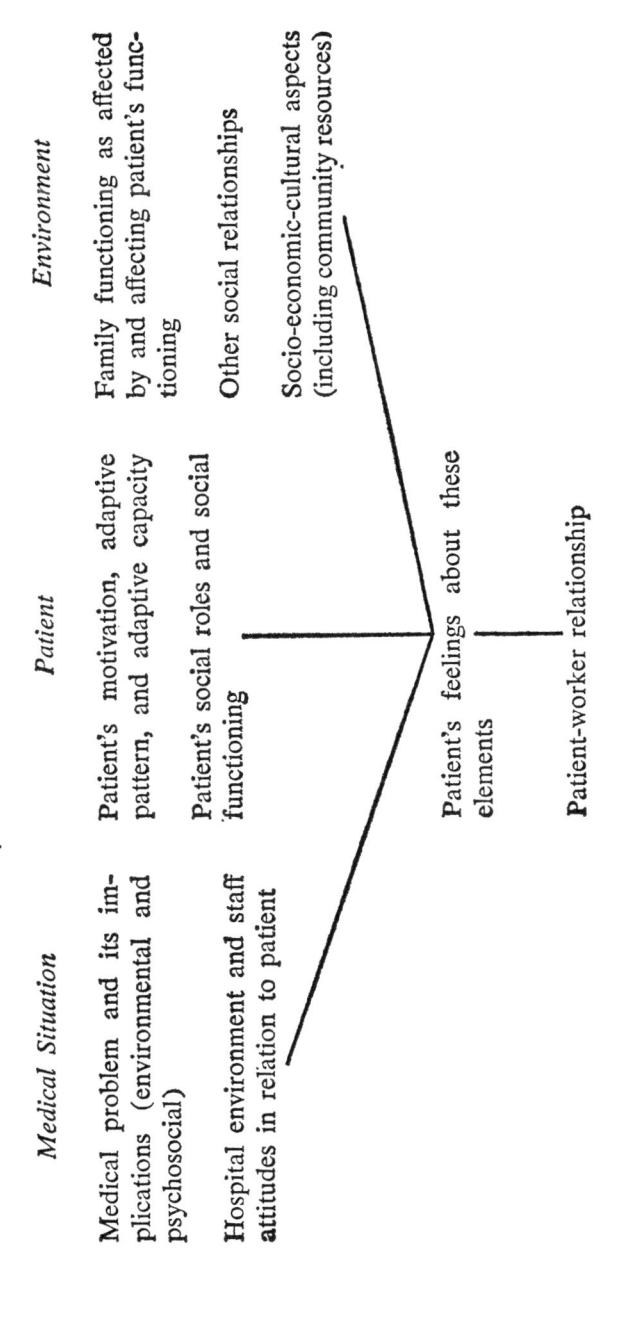

Medical Situation	Patient	Environment
Medical problem and its implications (environmental and psychosocial)	Patient's motivation, adaptive pattern, and adaptive capacity	Family functioning as affected by and affecting patient's functioning
Hospital environment and staff attitudes in relation to patient	Patient's social roles and social functioning	Other social relationships
		Socio-economic-cultural aspects (including community resources)

Patient's feelings about these elements

Patient-worker relationship

tionship defined. In conformity with the psychosocial focus of social work, the social worker is concerned in knowing both the facts of the situation and their meaning to the individual. Personality diagnosis is necessary but is only part of the total assessment. The breadth and depth of the social study vary with the problem. Within the assessment of the total relevant situation, the social worker wants particularly to learn the patient's own definition of the problem. The patient's and the social worker's definitions may not agree, but the social worker knows that the beginning must be made at the point where the patient wishes and can use help.

This kind of assessment is carried through at least once in any piece of activity which is significant enough to be regarded as a "piece" of professional social work practice. In more complex situations it is repeated at intervals, as required by the changing medical and social situation. Since this is medical social work, the assessment, when adequately done, produces some meaningful analysis of the interrelationship of the most significant medical and psychosocial elements. This analysis will enable the social worker to arrive at a decision regarding the appropriate goals and role of social work.

According to the evidence from practice, any of the elements given in the chart, or any combination of them, may dominate in a particular situation. As has been suggested in Chapter VIII, in some situations the medical problem is overwhelming, whereas in others the psychosocial problems predominate. In many instances the problem centers in the patient's emotional needs and in others in the pressures of outer realities. In all situations the patient's relation to his family (or lack of family) is important. For some time medical social workers have recognized that the family, as well as the individual, is a "unit of illness."

Most of the elements covered in the chart are discussed in the general casework literature in comparable terms, with the exception that the medical elements are, of course, less emphasized. It is clear, for instance, that all caseworkers assess not only the psychosocial aspects but also the client's way of relating to the social worker as an index of his probable ability to use casework help. One item, however, requires special attention because it is not usually mentioned. In discussion with social workers and in observation of other outlines listing the items in assessment of a medical social case it was noted that there is little or no mention of the item here called "hospital environment and staff attitudes in relation to patient," although medical social workers consistently take this factor into account in assessing the situation and defining their own role.[4] As was shown in discussion of the social worker's role in multidiscipline practice, if the medical team and others in the hospital show acceptance and understanding of the patient, then the social worker can move right along with them. If, however, as sometimes happens, physicians are tending to withdraw their interest from an incurable patient who can no longer be helped by medical treatment or if a certain patient has come to be regarded as "difficult" by various team members, the social worker will take this into account in defining the action to be taken. Special effort to bring the medical team closer to the patient might be attempted. If success in this direction does not seem likely, the social worker may decide to reach out to the patient and offer a larger measure of casework help than his problem would ordinarily require. In other words, the degree of support and understanding offered the patient by the hospital definitely influences the shaping of the social work role. This seems logical and appropriate but is rarely recognized by workers unless called to their attention.

Readers will think of other elements that might be included in the assessment. The nature of the social worker's working relationships with the medical team caring for the particular patient are usually taken into account. Group workers point out that the patient's role in various patient groups should be regularly considered. In order not to make the chart too complex, some of these additional elements, which are frequently considered in assessing the situation, have not been included at this preliminary stage of thinking.

The chart has purposely been set up in the form of a constella-

---

[4] *Program Guide: Social Work Service* (Washington, D. C.: Veterans Administration, Office of the Chief Medical Director, 1957), p. 39; Eleanor Cockerill, "A New Philosophy of Social Work in Chronic Illness," *Public Health News* (New Jersey State Department of Health), Vol. 38, No. 2 (February 1957), pp. 57–59.

tion of factors in a field to suggest an important characteristic of social work thinking. Observation of practice indicates that medical social workers early in their assessment move rather rapidly to obtain an overview of the "whole" person and situation. This overview should not be regarded as an attempt to understand the total person or situation, which would be excessively time-consuming and not relevant to the task, and hence overambitious and inappropriate. The aim is to identify and relate, insofar as possible, the essentials of personality and situation. The social work emphasis upon the uniqueness of the individual means that the worker cannot be satisfied with understanding only segments of behavior or environment. Although the process is still not too well understood or described, social workers do seem to carry it through characteristically and with skill. In a multidiscipline group, for instance, it can be observed that social workers seek to understand this "wholeness" of individuals, groups, and situations more immediately than do other team members, and discuss the problem more naturally in these terms. Having obtained this overview, the social worker then proceeds to pursue those selected aspects of the situation which are judged most pertinent to the social work assessment and action. This search for the "whole" underlines the observation that in social work we are dealing, not with social functioning or social roles as abstract phenomena but with persons who are involved in various types of social situations. It further shows the need for a type of theoretical framework which allows room for and highlights this characteristic social work approach.

In order to describe fully the characteristics of medical social work thinking in assessing practice situations, several successive phases would need to be considered, as follows:

1. Constant elements in assessment of medical social situations (which guide the social worker's thinking).

2. The process by which these constant elements are evaluated and interrelated in order to arrive at a judgment as to what the social worker's action should be.

3. The refocusing of the social work assessment and judgment for presentation in multidiscipline medical conferences.

4. The characteristics of joint professional thinking about med-

ical social situations in medical conferences (physicians, nurses, medical social workers, and others).

In the foregoing discussion effort has been made simply to identify the constant elements and to set them up in some logical way so that they could be viewed as a constellation. The process by which the essential data are obtained and the manner in which they are evaluated and interrelated in order to arrive at the assessment and to reach a judgment regarding action to be taken is complicated and requires much more exploration than can be undertaken in this monograph. It resembles the diagnostic process as discussed in the casework literature but covers a somewhat wider area.

The process of evaluating and relating the elements in the medical social situation is more fluid than the similar evaluative process in medicine. Unlike the medical student, the social worker is not taught to do the examination in a certain order or to apply knowledge and theory according to certain clearly defined theoretical systems. It may be that individual social workers follow differing patterns in seeking and analyzing the essential knowledge and that more than one approach will actually be found valid. Social workers find it difficult to describe their own thinking processes in practice. It is possible that younger workers depend to a considerable degree upon their work situation to stimulate and move them along through the process of assessment. They respond to the demands of the conference with the supervisor or medical team, the preparation of a social summary for the medical record, the referral to another agency, or a crisis in the patient's situation by undertaking the kind of comprehensive analysis of the data which is required in such instances. Mature workers probably develop more disciplines and controls within themselves. No concerted study of diagnostic thinking and assessment has been made in medical social work to provide answers to these questions.

Observation confirms, however, that the medical social worker follows an orderly pattern of thinking in assessing a case situation. It seems likely that a social worker who is carrying a case alone in a social agency can control this process better than the medical social worker, who shares the patient with other professional workers and must move with the patient through the often rapid changes in the illness situation. Analysis of cases, observation of social workers, and conferences with them suggest, furthermore, that trained and experienced medical social workers consciously follow a characteristic pattern in keeping the medical and psychosocial aspects consistently related and in teaching young workers to do so. Werner A. Lutz has done an interesting analysis to show how the social worker would move through a logical diagnostic process in social casework, if this process could be controlled.[5] The writer believes that the foregoing description of medical social work thinking is closer to current practice, in that a formal structure such as Lutz outlines is not currently practical but a general pattern of orderly sequence and analysis is possible and actually being employed. This pattern is not fully revealed in the traditional case record. Better understanding should come from observing practice and conferring with social workers as to how they operate in their practice.

This discussion of medical-social assessment has focused on the situation of the individual patient. A similar orderly process of thinking is developing in relation to medical-social problems of groups and of families, as well as to problems of community health. With fuller understanding, it will also be possible to identify the constant elements in these newer types of assessment.

SOCIAL CASEWORK IN THE HEALTH FIELD

The *Working Definition of Social Work Practice* identifies the major social work methods as social casework, social group work, and community organization. Practice and theory are more advanced in social casework but the other methods are advancing rapidly. Until recently social casework was also the dominant method in the health field and all medical social workers received

---

[5] Werner A. Lutz, *Concepts and Principles Underlying Social Casework Practice* (New York: National Association of Social Workers, 1956). (Monograph III in series "Social Work Practice in Medical Care and Rehabilitation Settings.")

basic education in social casework. Now group work is moving into the hospital and convincingly demonstrating its value there. Community organization method is also becoming relevant for social work in the health field, although its application awaits more effective demonstration. Thus, although somewhat unevenly applied, all these methods are to be found in the health field.

Starting with social casework, it is conceived as that method of study, diagnosis, and treatment of individual and family problems, based on understanding of human behavior, which is taught in schools of social work and presented in the professional literature. The concept as used here covers not only the direct work with the client but also purposeful working relationships with the family and other persons in the agency and community, when these relationships are a part of rendering service to the client. At present, some of these activities are given relatively little emphasis in student instruction and hardly receive recognition as being important components of casework.

Social casework is the most fully developed and best-known social work method. It is a clinical method similar to that employed in medicine. Casework has made a major contribution to social work through developing its own theory and through selection, testing, and adaptation of psychiatric knowledge and theory in relation to social work practice. Medical social workers responded cautiously at first to psychiatrically oriented casework, because of their association with conservative and scientifically minded physicians who raised questions regarding the new theory. As a result, medical social work did not follow the extreme casework trends of "passive therapy" and treatment of the individual client in isolation from his family and social situation. As the dynamic casework approach was increasingly taught to all students in social work schools and as supervisors oriented in the new theory were brought into social service departments, a consistent concept of casework permeated social work practice, including medical social work.

Social casework reached its period of predominance in medical social work during the forties. The official statement of standards for hospital social service departments in 1949 said, "Casework service to the individual is the primary and fundamental activity of the department. All other activities of the department depend upon sound, continuous social casework practice." [6]

The psychosocial diagnosis in medical-social casework, as has been pointed out, is concerned with a person in a social situation which has some significant health implications. A wide array of elements relating to the person himself, his social functioning, his immediate and wider social environment, and the medical problem must be assessed. The purpose of this assessment is to determine the treatment goals and the focus of treatment. There is no etiquette or custom in the medical setting that limits the medical social worker in deciding whether to work with the patient, the family, or others in the situation. The worker is free to work with any or all, according to the indications in each situation. One of the important decisions, therefore, is who appear to be the key persons toward whom treatment should be directed. In the case of a deafened child, for instance, the school teacher's failure to understand his needs and problems may be the crucial element affecting his ability to develop security in his peer group.

While formal data are not available, informal review and analysis of many cases indicate that medical social workers make contact with one or more family members in the majority of their cases and probably direct part of the casework effort toward them in a similar proportion. A woman often needs help in taking over additional responsibilities when her husband's role changes through illness. A relative's attitude frequently blocks a handicapped patient in moving toward rehabilitation. Distinction should be made between the customary casework concern with the interrelationships between individual family members and a direct focus on the family as a functioning social unit. In earlier discussion of the assessment of a medical social situation, it was suggested that the social worker always must assess the equilibrium of the family in terms of its ability to meet stress relating to the illness of a member and also to carry its essential functions. The assessment

---

[6] *A Statement of Standards To Be Met by Social Service Departments* (Chicago: American Association of Medical Social Workers, 1949), p. 3.

guides the social worker's decision whether social treatment can be directed toward one or more individual members (within the family context) or must be directed toward the family as a whole.

In the past, attempts have been made to set up certain classifications of casework treatment which will help the social worker gain a better understanding and control of his activity. The tendency has been to make a distinction between effort directed toward modification of the environment and that directed toward working directly with the client himself. The current recognition that the social worker is concerned, not with emotional problems alone, but with social functioning and social interaction lessens the sharpness of this distinction. The client is seen as the center of a field of social forces which influence his behavior and which he, in turn, can and does influence. These forces must be visualized as being potentially within the scope of casework treatment and frequently to be dealt with if treatment goals are to be achieved. When treatment is directed toward key persons, they become an active part of the problem situation rather than just one aspect of the client's environment.

Better understanding of the casework relationship with the client is also important in giving a clearer base for analysis of treatment. Helen Harris Perlman describes the casework relationship as follows:

> Warmth, receptivity, sympathetic responsiveness; acceptance of the person as he is and expectation that, with help, he will strive toward change in himself or his situation; purposiveness, objectivity, and goal; the ability and willingness to be of help; authority of expertness and of charge—all these characterize the caseworker's professional relationship. Within this dynamic matrix of acceptance and expectation, security and stimulation, the conscious work of problem-solving takes place.[7]

It is important to recognize that certain elements of support and stimulus are inherent in the worker-client relationship. Lacking this recognition, the concept of environmental modification be-

---

[7] Helen Harris Perlman, *Social Casework: A Problem-Solving Process* (Chicago: University of Chicago Press, 1957), p. 83.

comes arid and is consequently devalued. If it is clearly perceived that all the social worker's activity in the helping process with the client and his family is carried on through such a medium, then the distinctions in treatment become less artificial.

The psychosocial assessment of the situation may define problems outside the agency's scope and lead to referral to other sources of social work help in the community. Since the decision to use these other health and social resources is arrived at through the casework relationship, it involves the fullest possible participation by the patient, or his family if he is too ill to participate or if the problem centers in the family. Persons who do not understand casework tend to think that referral to another agency or resource is simply a matter of giving a little information and encouragement, after which the client will take the necessary step. Social workers themselves have underestimated the nature of their service in this area. The preparatory help given the client toward clarifying his problem and using other resources is definitely a professional service, whether accomplished in one interview or over a period of months and years.

Some Implications of the Health Setting for Social Casework

Since medical social casework deals with the reality problem of illness, which concurrently evokes emotion and affects social roles, psychological support and environmental modification are commonly used together. Treatment which emphasizes psychological support is now recognized as giving support to the individual's strengths and constructive defenses, in order that he may maintain a reasonably adequate social adjustment or achieve a better one.[8] Recent formulations of casework treatment stress two broad emphases, one which "supports" and "maintains" adaptive patterns and a second which "modifies" these patterns. Both aim to improve social functioning. Some degree of increased self-awareness, insight, or personality change is assumed to result from the second

---

[8] Lola G. Selby, "Supportive Treatment: The Development of a Concept and a Helping Method," *Social Service Review*, Vol. 30, No. 4 (December 1956), pp. 400–414.

treatment approach. Clarity and agreement are still lacking, however, as to what really happens in each form of treatment. How far the second approach, "modification," involves uncovering of previously hidden material and does, or does not, require psychiatric consultation, is at present not clear. It is evident that such concepts as "support," "insight," "clarification," and "interpretation" require definitive analysis, if they are to used in treatment typologies in social work.[9]

The two features of the health field which probably affect casework practice more than any others are: (1) the sharing of the relationship with the patient with other professional persons, and (2) the interweaving of the casework process with the ongoing illness and medical care.

In some cases one or more members of other professions will be carrying the responsibility for care of a particular patient over relatively long periods. Under such circumstances, the relationship of each to the patient and their relationship to each other become of major importance in the treatment. There may be a triangular relation between physician, patient, and social worker. A nurse is often included in such a treatment team. Such situations move most smoothly when each member of the team is clear as to his own professional role and there is frequent communication among the members. The social worker aims to strengthen the patient's relationship with the physician and with other professional workers, as indicated. With the exception of the psychiatrist, the social worker is at present trained to be more aware of relationship as a therapeutic tool than the others. Physicians and nurses, however, are becoming increasingly conscious of this aspect of patient care. It is now not unusual to have a physician recommend to a social worker that a patient needs emotional support and to

---

[9] Florence Hollis, "Personality Diagnosis in Casework," in Howard J. Parad, ed., *Ego Psychology and Dynamic Casework* (New York: Family Service Association of America, 1958), pp. 83–96; *Method and Process in Social Casework*—Report of a Staff Committee, Community Service Society of New York (New York: Family Service Association of America, 1958); Eleanor Cockerill, *et al., A Conceptual Framework for Social Casework* (Pittsburgh: School of Social Work, University of Pittsburgh, 1952).

indicate the kind of support he himself is ready to give in his role as physician. The social worker is flexible in adjusting the social work role in relation to what is being offered by the others, such as physician and nurse, whether a psychiatrist is involved in the treatment plan, and similar factors.

When the professional staff is changing rapidly or the patient is moving about from one part of the hospital or medical care program to another, the medical social worker may be the only staff member who has a continuing relation with him. This relationship then becomes of major significance to the patient, who will look primarily to the social worker for help in understanding his highly fragmented medical care and in dealing with the special difficulties his medical problem presents to him. This whole matter of interprofessional relationships in patient care is an enormously complex matter, of which greater understanding is needed. These aspects are not ordinarily shown in case recording and thus not available for study.

The necessity for carrying on casework as part of medical care places special demands upon the social worker for timing and flexibility. Patients are frequently inaccessible for social work interviewing because of their physical condition or because of the various medical procedures. Sudden changes in the illness or in medical recommendations can completely disrupt social work planning. Action by others in the health agency—professional or nonprofessional workers—can interrupt or distort the social work relationship with the patient in ways that cannot be foreseen. Such situations can be frustrating, even to an experienced worker. However, since the progress of disease in individual cases cannot be predicted, the medical social worker has to learn to meet such rapid changes. In fact, it can be said that a certain attitude of readiness for surprise and ability to modify casework planning quickly is an essential in this field of practice.

On the other hand, there are the positive aspects of timing, by which casework is really integrated with the patient's care. Looking back on their cases, medical social workers can often recognize that being available to a patient at a certain critical moment in his ongoing medical care made all the difference in his ability to deal with it. There is, also, a rhythm by which casework and medical care move along together. In recurrent illness the curve of need rises and falls with each exacerbation of the disease, and in progressive illness the intensity of medical and social care tend to rise together. When patients with chronic illness are attending the clinic regularly, they are likely to come to see the social worker before or after the visit to the doctor. In some phases of medical social work, such as problems of child behavior in a pediatrics clinic, regular weekly interviews with the social worker, not so closely correlated with the medical visits, may be indicated.

Linkage of Life Situations and Chronic Illness

This discussion cannot attempt full analysis of medical social casework today. Some characteristic problem situations, however, are presented, with indication as to the social worker's use of knowledge, values, and skill in the problem-solving process.

One important cluster of situations characteristic of medical social work is that in which life situations are in the process of becoming, or have become, permanently linked with illness. Increased medical and social diagnostic skill is permitting recognition of more of these situations at an early stage. The following is an illustration:

> A shy, immature youth of eighteen was under examination in a gastro-intestinal clinic for persistent digestive symptoms. No organic cause was found and it was considered that the symptoms were due to emotional strain related to the family situation. The boy was the only child of separated parents. Since the father, who had deserted, was not providing family support, the boy had left school and gone to work in an office. The mother was holding him closely tied to her through her own neurotic need. He was in conflict over his wish to be free of his mother's domination and his guilt over wishing to break away. Before the medical social worker could work out a treatment plan, the boy's mother was admitted to the ward with a cerebral hemorrhage, which progressed rapidly to a fatal termination. In response to his mother's illness, the boy's anxiety became so extreme that the social worker accompanied him to the ward and sat outside the door of the room when he visited his mother. Under

the severe stress his emotional and physical status deteriorated still further. He was described as looking as though he had been "put through a wringer." The internist, recognizing a clinical picture which often precedes serious gastric disorder such as ulcerative colitis, referred the patient to psychiatry. For a year the internist, psychiatrist, and social worker worked closely together in this boy's treatment, each giving support and help in his own area of competence. At the end of the treatment period the patient was eased of his anxiety and guilt, had made gains in living independently, and was in good physical health. With the social worker's aid he had completed a rehabilitation course in mechanical drawing, was living in the YMCA and supporting himself through a job with a business firm.

Social casework in such a situation requires full knowledge not only regarding personality and social functioning but also regarding digestive disorders as a form of psychosomatic illness. The physicians and the social worker were equally aware that they were working to prevent a serious and disabling type of chronic illness, ulcerative colitis, to which this youth was particularly vulnerable in his stressful psychosocial situation. The role and contribution of each member of the clinical team was clearly defined and carried out in sensitive relation to the others. The social worker was the team member most accessible to the patient, who could call her on the telephone or see her in her office when needed. She not only gave him the support he required because of his mother's death but also helped him to relate appropriately to the internist and psychiatrist during the treatment period and gradually to return to an adequate pattern of social functioning. This was a piece of genuine preventive work because the members of the clinical team knew what problem they were trying to prevent. By treatment of a vulnerable individual undergoing a critical life experience they were able to save him from becoming a chronic invalid.

As chronic illness advances, linkage of illness and the life situation becomes stronger and results of treatment cannot so frequently be successful. The following situation illustrates a more advanced case of chronic illness in which the psychosocial situation was a major component.

A thin, nervous woman in the middle thirties, the mother of two children of school age, was in a hospital ward recovering from a severe bout of duodenal ulcer. She had a ten-year history of illness, with shifting medical diagnoses and several surgical operations, yet had persistent symptoms. Her background revealed early deprivation and insecurity due to the death of both parents. She was currently under stress because of her double role as housewife and factory worker, complicated by friction with her husband's family (who refused to admit her real illness) and her husband's inability to give the affection and support she needed. When seen by the social worker, she was regressed, dependent, and weeping. She said, "I can't answer back. I just cry." The social worker reached out to her and accepted her dependency. The medical team, all greatly interested in the patient, gave united support, which was continued in the clinic over more than a year. The internist, feeling that the psychosocial situation was of great importance in this case, looked to the social worker to play a major role in treatment. The patient saw the social worker each time she came to the clinic. At first the patient had bloody diarrhea, was tense, and easily upset. She obtained relief through the social worker's acceptance of her feelings. Gradually, as the patient's strength permitted, the social worker encouraged her to face the situation more directly. (It had become evident that the patient was the stronger of the two marital partners and that little help could be expected from the husband.) At the end of six months she had made striking gains. Although the social problems in the family were only partially solved, the patient told the social worker, "I'm fighting my own battles now." Several years later she returned to the hospital to say that she had continued well and had no recurrence of her ulcer.

This is the type of case that particularly requires that understanding of regression, depression, and dependency described in Chapter VIII, "Knowledge from Medical Social Work." The social worker at first allows the patient to be regressed and dependent but steadily helps her to recognize and make use of her strengths, as the acute illness subsides. Careful handling of the worker-patient relationship is necessary to prevent undue prolongation of the emotional dependency.

In approaching such a problem of chronic illness the medical social worker has a background of knowledge and theory regarding this particular condition and psychosomatic illness in general, but is careful not to make any assumptions regarding the patient's personality and behavior pattern. Each case is fully studied and assessed in terms of the individual findings, without theoretical bias. As a means of clarifying the life pattern, some physicians and social workers have found useful the life history chart, in which the significant events in the development of illness are charted chronologically in relation to the events of the patient's life.[10] When illness and life stress occur together in a recurrent pattern, the nature of the patient's problem can be better understood. There must be evidence that these events are more than correlated in time, however, and that they have been actually disturbing to the individual. Often it can be observed that conflict in social roles, as in these two cases, contributes to the stress preceding the physical breakdown.

Many patients with chronic illness present a surface appearance of serenity and passivity which appears incongruous to doctors and social workers who know the severity of their illness and life problems. In these patients the emotional phase of the reaction is buried beneath the façade of physical illness. In some way the illness meets their need, as through bringing love and attention from others, punishment for guilt, or permission to give up the struggle of being independent. These chronic patients are frequently the "good" patients, who carefully conform to medical recommendations but still do not get well. This is, however, an instance of the body's use of inept defense against stress. The chronic illness can go on and more seriously disable or kill the patient. Difficult decisions must be made as to whether the problem is near enough to the surface so that the patient can be helped to face it directly and thus arrive at a better life adjustment which may diminish both his stress and illness. Medical social workers use their knowledge of the physiology of emotion to guide them in their interviews with all seriously ill patients. Through their own observation and consultation with the medical and nursing staff, they assess with greatest care the sick person's ability to discuss potentially disturbing matters.

---

[10] Stanley Cobb, *Borderlands of Psychiatry* (Cambridge, Mass.: Harvard University Press, 1943), Chapter I, "Body and Mind."

Early Intervention in Crisis Situations

Another group of characteristic problems relates to those situations which prove temporarily overwhelming to individuals and families. Their response to such crises appears in the form of disorganization of behavior, as in withdrawal, blocking, or excessive anxiety.

One of the most frequent of such problems to come to the medical social worker is that of the patient who is blocked in carrying through some particular step in medical care because of the psychosocial difficulties it presents to him. This may happen at any point in ongoing medical care. Sometimes the step is one that is difficult for most people; sometimes it has peculiar meaning to this particular individual. Sometimes the problem centers in the environment, sometimes in the person, but it always appears in some type of social interaction. Such a situation is illustrated in the following case:

> An intelligent, high-strung, young single woman, whose father was dead and who had been supporting her mother as "head of the family," was examined in a public health clinic because her mother had been admitted to a tuberculosis sanatorium. The patient's diagnosis was advanced pulmonary tuberculosis with positive sputum. She refused sanatorium care and showed great hostility toward the health department, asking that no one be sent to visit her. The public health team at the clinic requested the social worker to take the initiative in the situation and to see if she could gain the patient's co-operation, in the hope that more authoritative methods would not become necessary. The social worker went to the home and was able to establish a relationship with the young woman, who discussed her feelings about her father, mother, and married younger sister, and also her changed role in the family as a result of this illness. She said that she wanted to be free, like her father, but always did the things that were expected of her. The social worker gave assistance in relation to certain environmental problems, such as a threatened eviction and the patient's wish not to be placed in the same ward with her mother at the sanatorium. There was some contact with the married sister, who was co-operative and understanding. The patient responded to case-

work help by changing her attitude and six weeks after her violent refusal of medical care, voluntarily went to the sanatorium.

This situation illustrates a brief piece of casework offered to an individual at time of crisis. A person who had previously functioned adequately was temporarily breaking under the piling up of medical and social stress-provoking factors. The impact of illness brought out previously repressed feelings centering on role conflicts. In spite of certain personality difficulties, it appeared that she had sufficient ego strength to carry on herself after this limited but timely help.

This social worker had to be in command of full knowledge of the program of her agency and of the disease, tuberculosis. She had to be able to function competently as representative of the public health team which had requested her to solve this problem. In going out to seek this resisting patient, the social worker was following a pattern characteristic of medical social work and given even stronger emphasis in public health. Unfortunately medical social workers have not contributed to the social work literature any analysis of this aspect of their casework practice. Through long experience they have learned that the individual does not have to apply for casework help himself. His need may be recognized by someone else, such as the physician, who brings the social worker into the situation. By enabling the patient to talk about his situation, the social worker permits him to decide whether he wishes to use casework help; the majority of patients do. In its sensitivity, patience, and respect for the individual's own readiness to move, the process maintains the patient's right of self-determination in the fullest sense.

Many referrals which come to the social worker's attention because of problems related to one step in medical care are the result of relatively transient psychosocial stress which can be alleviated through a brief type of contact and service. Problems of adjusting to the wearing of apparatus, whether in an adolescent or aged person, are not infrequently of this type. Often, however, the difficulty over one step in medical care is only a symptom of deeper underlying problems. A mother who reacted with extreme anxiety on first hearing her young son's diagnosis of epilepsy could deal with her guilt and stress through a single long interview with a social worker, in which she confessed how she dropped him as a baby. The mother of a diabetic girl who was using the insulin injections to punish her child and a young woman with a leg amputation who had gone without an artificial limb for years presented problems that required a long period of treatment by the social worker and others.

In these stressful situations the medical social worker knows the value of being readily available to the patient at the time the problem first appears and of being part of the ongoing situation. The social worker recognizes the stress and reaches out to the patient, who responds by talking about the problem, feeling release and support, leaning temporarily on the social worker, gaining enough perspective to make a choice among alternatives of action, and finally taking up again his own independent activity. In a weekly tuberculosis clinic patients who had just been informed that they had active tuberculosis and must go to a sanatorium were regularly asked to see the social worker. The shock of such a revelation—particularly if it is the first diagnosis—was obvious and the opportunity to help was great. Interviews with patients facing surgery offer a similar opportunity. The social worker helps the patient to deal with the immediate stress and then prepares him for what lies ahead, so that he is fortified to take the steps with less trauma. The social worker also informs the medical team of the patient's responses, so that stress is further lessened through the ability of the environment to adapt to his particular needs. This kind of professional service represents a characteristic opportunity of the health field, where the social worker is actually on hand and becomes a participant in the ongoing situation.

Medical Care Services

As was pointed out in Chapter III, each field of practice requires certain characteristic services peculiarly related to its program. The responsibilities assigned to the school social worker in relation to the child truanting from school and to the corrections worker in relation to the individual who has broken parole are of this nature. In the health field this responsibility relates to the enabling and extension of medical care. These referrals, which usually come from physicians, resemble those described above, in which the patient needs assistance in taking some step in medical care, but differ from them in that the need is less in the patient and more in the medical institution's responsibility for facilitating the care of its patients. Most frequently some planning is required which is beyond the usual scope of the physician or nurse. Planning of aftercare for ward patients (frequently called "discharge planning") is a common example. Helping patients to obtain and adjust to complicated and expensive appliances that are made outside the hospital would be another example. Medical social workers often feel frustrated over these cases and question whether they are appropriate for professional workers.

Actually, more study of these medical care referrals is needed for adequate assessment of the problems and skills involved, and also of the social worker's necessary output of time and energy. Meanwhile, a number of things can be said about this phase of practice. Observation of these cases shows that many of the situations involve stress, even crisis, for the patients, as can be seen in the following example:

> A middle-aged woman, who had been the dominant member in a family group consisting of her husband and adolescent son, was referred from a medical ward because of disabling illness that made it impossible for her to carry her former role as housewife. Aftercare in a chronic hospital was recommended. In exploring the family situation, the social worker found that the husband and son could bear to let her go more easily than she herself could give up the role in life which had met her emotional needs. It required all the social worker's skill to help this woman to face the change in her life situation involved in going to the chronic hospital and being willing to remain there, under circumstances so traumatic to her personal goals and her own picture of her place in the family.

Observation also indicates that the planning of aftercare is only the first step in many ongoing problems of chronic illness involving serious psychosocial problems of individual personality and family interaction. Thus it appears that some, but not all, of these situations call for the skilled service of a professional social worker.

It is probable that there are two major types of situations included within these medical care referrals: (1) those of sufficient complexity to require professional assessment and treatment, and (2) those in which the need is only for medical care arrangements which could be satisfactorily carried out by a case aide or subprofessional worker in the social service department. What, then, is the best organization of service in terms of economy of workers' time and effectiveness of service? One school of thought advocates that social workers should assess every referral and assign to case aides those not requiring casework service; but this is time consuming for the professional worker. Another school of thought advises that aides be assigned such referrals from the beginning but be trained to recognize when problems are beyond their competence. Whether aides can actually function reliably in this way has not been conclusively demonstrated. Similar questions regarding borderline problems occur in all fields of social work practice. Until the profession defines and distinguishes in an authoritative manner tasks appropriate for workers with different levels of competence, professional and subprofessional, this will remain a troublesome and unsolved issue in practice.

Positive and Preventive Approach

The discussion thus far has emphasized a kind of understanding on the social worker's part that will facilitate timely intervention, at crucial points all through the course of illness before serious problems develop. The question arises whether intervention might be pushed back to an even earlier stage, before any disequilibrium occurs and while stress is only beginning or potential.

All social work is keenly interested in the preventive approach and medical social workers are particularly interested because of their association with public health. Since social casework is a problem-solving process, the emphasis up to now has been mainly upon preventing already developed problems from becoming worse.

The positive emphasis in public health teaches us that it is important to deal with situations at an even earlier point, before they become problems. This, however, becomes something difficult to visualize within the traditional milieu of medical social work. How does the worker manage to be at the proper place, in contact with the proper individual, at the proper time, in order to offer casework service in this positive manner?[11] What is the appearance of this service, so that it can be identified as an entity?

For a while the answer to this question eluded search through many sources in the literature and practice. Finally, however, illumination came through the experience of a family health project, a combined service-study program for health supervision of mothers and infants. A multidiscipline medical team with a psychiatric consultant, working under the auspices of the Harvard School of Public Health, offered comprehensive care to a group of healthy young women in their first pregnancies and to their babies. The medical social case records of three women who made a good adjustment were selected as demonstration of the preventive approach. Each case as presented shows slightly higher incidence of stresses and potential problems.

> 1. A mature, responsible young couple, both from large families, were well suited and prepared for family life and looking forward to their first baby. In early pregnancy the mother was happy and relaxed. The couple moved to a new apartment in preparation for the child's coming. At time of delivery an unexpected stress appeared in that the father, who had a history of gall bladder disease, was suddenly admitted to a hospital for cholecystectomy. As a result, both parents were hospitalized at the same time. Not only was the husband unable to offer support to his wife at a time when she was psychologically in need of it, but his demands on her were necessarily greater than normal and his condition created great emotional and physical strain. The treatment plan was to give the mother extra emotional support through the casework relationship and provide someone to whom she could turn for help with planning if this should become necessary,

---

[11] Eleanor Cockerill and Helen Gossett, *The Medical Social Worker as Mental Health Worker* (New York: National Association of Social Workers, 1959).

hopefully freeing the mother to be able to meet the infant's needs as well as the father's care. With the support of the social worker and her own family, the mother went through this difficult experience remarkably well. The father soon returned to work. The social worker wrote in the record, "This is one of the most consistently good situations I have observed at the Family Health Clinic."

2. This couple was of Greek extraction; the husband was several years older than the wife. She was an immature, conscientious girl, attached to a neurotic, compulsive mother and rather poorly prepared for the sexual aspects of marriage. The couple were genuinely fond of each other. The social worker aimed to provide a warm accepting relationship which would counteract the wife's anxiety-provoking relation with her own mother. The girl was encouraged in her own capacities for motherhood and in a more relaxed attitude toward child care. The infant had a rapid heart rate, which the mother associated with the heart disease of her own father. The child did not eat well and when he refused food prepared by the mother, the father (who accompanied her to the clinic) said that he "got so angry he would like to stuff the food into the baby." In these instances the social worker was present at the time the problem first appeared and was able to participate with the rest of the medical team in enabling the parents to deal with it before it became fixed. She encouraged a more relaxed attitude toward infant feeding and aided the mother in distinguishing the normal heart condition of the child from the actual cardiac disease of her father. By the time the baby was a year old, the parents had become relatively independent of the maternal grandmother in care of their child and although the mother's reactions were still immature, the couple were enjoying the child and all was going well.

3. This couple, an attractive young woman and her serious, competent husband, had both had difficult early years and had no near relatives. Conception had taken place before their planned marriage and the wife was full of anxiety about this, until she perceived that the social worker and her own friends accepted it. Casework treatment was directed toward helping this prospective mother relieve her guilt about the conception, so that this guilt would not be transferred to her relationship with the expected baby. This was an emotionally deprived young woman with inadequate mothering, suggesting her need of extra attention and support during pregnancy and early motherhood. Early in pregnancy the social worker helped the husband to see that his wife needed more support

from him in the form of a more liberal budget to meet her nutritional needs, and love and special attention to meet her dependency needs in pregnancy. Homemaker service was arranged to help when the mother came home from the hospital with the baby. After the baby girl was born, the mother was encouraged to observe the infant carefully in order to see her as a person apart from herself. Later, when circumstances forced the mother to give up breast feeding, she revealed her guilt about this to the social worker, fearing she might not have done the best thing for the baby. Immediate acceptance of this step by the clinic team and discussion of the adequacy of bottle feeding served to ease her conflict. She continued to use casework interviews to think through and test her own ideas about motherhood but was able to devote her strong maternal instincts to her baby in a healthy way without allowing her personal problems to interfere. Healthy development of children in this family seemed indicated and when the mother returned to the clinic for her second pregnancy she used the services of caseworkers and other team members constructively to prepare herself for the experience of rearing two children.

These cases demonstrate specific preventive effort in social work. Too often social workers have been content to assert in a vague way that everything they do is "preventive." But there must be some relation of the professional activity to a known problem which is threatening. Most social case records today do not reveal this relationship, which is convincingly shown in the public health casework records cited above. These social workers had regular contacts with the mothers in the clinic and in the home throughout the pregnancy and the infant's first year. Services offered in the Family Health Clinic were directed toward preventing physical and emotional disorders in the infants born to the women attending the clinic, working through the parents, especially the mother. The goal was defined positively as the promotion of physical and mental health. Special emphasis was placed on preventing disorders in the mother-child relationship by helping the expectant new mother to handle in a healthy way the stresses inherent in the first pregnancy and early motherhood, that is, preparing for her role as a mother.

The social workers were present at the time new stresses or difficulties began to emerge and were able to give casework help directed toward preventing development of real problems. This process can be seen in the instance of the father's attitude toward feeding in the second case and the mother's guilt over weaning in the third case. In both instances serious negative attitudes might have become ingrained and handicapped the child's personality development.

These social workers had skill in casework and were able to intervene in the situation at the psychological moment. What else was essential? They had to have at their full command a body of well-defined and rapidly growing knowledge oriented toward such preventive service. In the Family Health Clinic, as in any medical setting, the characteristic contribution of the social worker in preventing, or intervening in, health disorders (including disorders in the mother-child relationship) was her knowledge of personality development and interpersonal relationships, of family life, and of the broad social environment. Her experience in dealing with pathology in other settings was useful in identifying potentially hazardous situations and in detecting early signs of disorder. She worked directly with the parents to avert possible, or treat existing, disorders and made available specialized knowledge from the field of social work to others on the staff for their use in working with parents and child. Casework treatment was enriched by, and also dependent on, specialized knowledge of other staff members regarding the physical and psychosocial aspects of pregnancy and child rearing. In addition, new knowledge and insights were obtained by the multidiscipline team during the course of the study, thus increasing the body of knowledge regarding both normal and pathological experiences that may occur during pregnancy and the early months of child rearing. The social worker's encouragement of the third young mother to observe her baby carefully in order to see her as an individual was related to the team's observation that some mothers have particular difficulty in separating from their children. Thus these cases clearly reveal a point made earlier in this discussion, that no matter how skilled social workers may be in casework, they could not have rendered this preventive service unless they possessed the highly specialized knowledge required to recognize and deal with a particular kind of problem at its very inception.[12]

Other Areas of Special Concern

A number of additional characteristic phases of social casework can be briefly mentioned. Each is a subject of sufficient importance for a separate discussion in its own right.

The child and his family: Children's problems are treated within the family context. The greatest amount of casework is probably done with the mother. An increasing amount of work is being done directly with the child, particularly when he is separated from his family or suffering from chronic illness and handicap. The aim is to help the child bear the stresses of the situation and participate in his own treatment as far as possible.

The isolated individual: Persons separated from their families and living alone are a special concern for the social worker, particularly the adolescent, the unmarried mother, and the aged. The social worker often supplies the added support which the family might have given, to carry them through the stress of illness.

Resisting patients: The patient who strongly resists medical treatment is being recognized as a person who has strengths and whose motivation, if understood, can sometimes be directed toward participation.

The patient with terminal illness and his family: As would be expected, medical social workers have a great deal to do with terminal illness. The aim is to help the patient and family meet the problem according to their individual readiness and capacity. Assistance in arranging care for the patient either at home or elsewhere is one important phase of service. Another important component is the emotional support given to the patient and family. When the patient is too ill to participate in a casework relationship, the major service is given to the responsible relative.

The family as a unit in illness: While medical social workers do

---

[12] *See* Florence E. Cyr and Shirley H. Wattenberg, "Social Work in a Preventive Program of Maternal and Child Health," *Social Work*, Vol. 2, No. 3 (July 1957), pp. 32–39.

considerable work with family members, there is need for clear demonstration of the manner in which psychosocial problems of illness and disability permeate a family as a whole; how families meet such stresses; the changes that take place in family structure and functioning; and the focus of social casework on a family unit rather than on selected key members.

Rehabilitation: The experience of medical social workers in rehabilitation also demands analysis and formulation. While it is difficult to separate the rehabilitation emphasis from the rest of medical social work, the participation of medical social workers in formal rehabilitation teams and similar undertakings is accumulating to the point where it should offer something of specific value toward understanding the psychosocial problems of physical handicap and the psychosocial component in rehabilitation. One particularly interesting question is arising in regard to the social worker's role. It has been customary to assume that social work activity would terminate when medical care comes to an end. But the psychosocial problems of disability sometimes persist after the physical aspects of the care have been completed. The man with a leg amputation may have his prosthesis but not be using it. The housewife with heart disease, who is resting in a convalescent home, may resist returning to her own home to take up her household tasks. Should the medical care be regarded as completed in these instances? What is further needed is frequently within the scope and competence of medical social work. If these psychosocial problems are really recognized as components of disability and rehabilitation, the question is whether medical social work should continue its service, even after the traditional medical care has ceased, in order to help these patients through the further steps of rehabilitation until they attain more effective social functioning. How far should the physician and the whole medical team consider this as their responsibility and the social worker as their representative in carrying through full rehabilitation as a part of comprehensive medical care? While the medical agency cannot, and should not, continue working with patients for an indefinite period, it does appear that many are at present being dropped before medical responsibility for rehabilitation has ceased.

The special aspects of casework discussed here represent only a sample of the areas of concern to social workers in the health field. The areas included under casework are obviously the ones in which the problem and treatment call for a one-to-one relationship between the social worker and the individual with a problem. We are now ready to consider situations where service can be offered through other types of professional relationships and activities.

SOCIAL WORK WITH GROUPS

Social group work as a well-developed social work method found its place in the health field only recently. Previously the efforts of group workers were concentrated on defining their method in traditional settings, such as settlements and youth-serving agencies.

From the earliest days medical social workers have worked with patients and their families in groups. For many years in one community a group of mothers of children with rheumatic heart disease met regularly with the cardiac social worker to have tea together and discuss their problems. These social workers used informal methods and did not command knowledge of the group process, but it seems probable that such sessions were of considerable help to the participants. Some social caseworkers also worked with psychiatrists and other physicians in varied types of group projects.

In recent years professional social group workers began exploring the possibility of practicing in hospitals. The applicability of the group work method has been recognized and its use is steadily increasing. Some of the kinds of groups worked with have been children on hospital wards, men with chronic disease and handicap in veterans' hospitals, and physically handicapped men and women preparing for rehabilitation. Group members discuss their feelings about illness and handicap, the hospital and its staff, their own use of medical care and rehabilitation, the behavior of other people toward them, and similar subjects. Sometimes games, plays, and music are used. Sometimes the sessions are wholly devoted to group therapy through discussion. Group workers have also worked effectively with physically handicapped children in summer camps.

The group work method helps patients and families in a different way than casework. Members of a group help each other to face life problems, while giving mutual support. Some individuals can participate in, and benefit from, group discussion when they cannot use casework help. The method is particularly relevant at some life periods, such as adolescence, when young people are moving out of the family circle and look to their peers as role models. In an analysis of social group work method, Gisela Konopka presents a processed narrative of a series of seventeen sessions held by a group worker with a group of epileptics in their late teens and early twenties.[13] She shows vividly how they were strengthened through the group process to function with greater security in work and other roles, as well as in everyday social contacts. In her evaluation of the results, she says:

> In following this group we have seen how the group process worked in helping individual members. Group interaction, group discussion, and reality testing were helping agents. We saw the role of the group worker as the one of giving support, of giving information, of helping with some insight, of referral to other community resources. We recognize as the basic goal in this group a re-establishment of self-confidence in individual members, a giving of security through a sense of belonging, a testing of skills, and a beginning of insight into oneself by understanding better one's relationships with parents, family and job.[14]

In 1960 social group workers and medical social workers began meeting together to discuss their common interests and problems under the auspices of the National Association of Social Workers. The first discussions confirmed the principles enunciated earlier in this chapter, that all social workers in health programs pursue the same general purposes but with different use of method. Group workers focus on the psychosocial aspects of illness and medical care, and integrate their activity with the over-all health program, just as caseworkers do. Since group workers are employed predominantly in institutional settings—such as hospitals and camps

---

[13] Gisela Konopka, "The Method of Social Group Work," in Walter A. Friedlander, ed., *Concepts and Methods of Social Work* (Englewood Cliffs, N. J.: Prentice-Hall, 1958), pp. 154–183.

[14] *Ibid.*, p. 183.

—their activity is more closely related to medical care and rehabilitation than to public health at this time.

Group work offers direct service to patients by making use of the natural groups that form in hospital wards or in other places where patients come together, as in recreation rooms. Chronic hospitals and long-stay institutions offer particular opportunities for such activity because of the greater stability and continuity of patient groups. Group work theory stresses understanding of the hospital as a social system, in which staff have certain expectations regarding patient behavior, and patients in their turn arrive at their own definition of the hospital and the attitudes of its personnel. These patient attitudes can be compared with the inmate culture in the correctional institution.[15] As would be expected, the combined use of casework and group work methods has been found to be helpful to many individual patients, as well as stimulating to the social workers themselves. An example of combined group work and casework follows.

> A single man in his early thirties was admitted to a chronic hospital with severe multiple sclerosis. He had used a wheel chair for several years and was unable to stand or walk. He had been living alone with his widowed mother on the top floor of an old house. The hospital had a rehabilitation program that aimed to restore patients to optimal functioning for their condition. The patient found himself a member of an aggressive group of young handicapped patients whose expectation was that they would leave the hospital as rapidly as possible and who turned against the patient because he had decided that he could not return home and wished to remain in the institution. It was decided by the caseworker and group worker that efforts should be made to help the patient deal with this conflict situation.
>
> A week later, when the entire group was assembled at the young adult lounge program, the group worker initiated a discussion of the problem, with the patient receiving support from some fellow patients as well as from the worker. The discussion revolved around why some patients may want to remain in the hospital owing to their need for constant med-

---

[15] Lloyd E. Ohlin and William C. Lawrence, "Social Interaction Among Clients as a Treatment Problem," *Social Work*, Vol. 4, No. 2 (April 1959), pp. 3–13.

ical care. Some patients took the stand that they had been in other hospitals and it would be better to remain here if there was no other adequate place appropriate for them in the community, since they felt that this hospital was one of the better services offered. The result of this meeting was that the patient saw that the entire young adult group was not antagonistic toward him and that he could receive support from them as well as from the staff for his decision. The vocal subgroup still argued for its position, but it was seen by the patient that their feeling did not necessarily hold sway over the entire group.

Two weeks later the matter came up for discussion in the same group and was handled in the same way. Meanwhile the caseworker helped the patient to move along in a plan related to his individual needs. After four months he was discharged to a special hotel in the community, with facilities and living arrangements suitable for handicapped men, where he could have greater independence and wider social contacts than had been possible in his restricted home life.[16]

It appears that casework and group work help were equally important in enabling this severely handicapped young man to attain a more satisfactory level of social functioning.

Group work can be helpful for newly arrived patients who are trying to adjust to the hospital, particularly older patients who are less likely to take initiative in aiding each other. In one hospital such small group meetings were being held for new patients. A group work record describes a woman who appeared quite upset about entering the hospital, with flushed face, looking as if she wanted to get back into bed away from the group. In reply to a question from the group worker she indicated that the woman next to her had been friendly and helped her to feel more comfortable about being in the hospital. This remark sparked a flurry of discussion from the others, with comments such as, "We have to help each other in this mess we're in." "Let's plan some interesting events." "How about getting together for supper?" Thus the

---

[16] This case was used in a group meeting sponsored by the Medical Social Work Section, National Association of Social Workers, on "Implications of Changing Emphasis in Education for Field Instruction in the Medical Setting," at the National Conference on Social Welfare, May 1958, Chicago, Ill.

group was beginning a process in which the members would use the group worker's assistance to help each other meet the difficult hospital experience.

The group worker has the same responsibility as the caseworker to relate his activity to the medical problem. A group worker in a children's hospital helped a group of bed patients on a ward to release their anxiety about illness and their hostility toward doctors through role playing.[17] In a long-term hospital for adults it was demonstrated how such media as games, plays, and music can be used for effective treatment on a nonverbal level. A small harmonica group for muscular dystrophy patients had the threefold purpose of providing musical enjoyment, a socialization experience, and prescribed activity to utilize lung capacity as steps toward rehabilitation. Since group work is not necessarily concerned with pathology, some group activity is appropriately directed toward supporting the strengths of well-adjusted individuals.

Group work has a valuable and pertinent contribution to make in relation to the internal structure and social policy of the hospital. It may take the form of working with ward committees of patients, whose reactions to, and suggestions regarding, hospital policy and procedure can represent a contribution to the hospital as well as an enlargement of patient participation which is of definite therapeutic import. Because of their special understanding of hospital group life, group workers are able to make direct contributions to the hospital administration and medical staff regarding the impact of the hospital program on patients and families, also its relation to aftercare in the community.[18]

The interaction of group workers and caseworkers in medical settings is proving mutually beneficial. Group workers are directing the attention of caseworkers to hitherto little-understood group phenomena among patients, families, and hospital staff and helping

---

[17] Constance Impallaria Albee, "Group Work with Hospitalized Children," *Children,* Vol. 2, No. 6 (November-December 1955), pp. 217–221; and Constance Impallaria, "Some Contributions of Therapeutic Group Working in a Medical Setting," in *Selected Papers in Group Work and Community Organization* (Columbus, Ohio: National Conference of Social Work, 1952), pp. 54–62.

[18] Hyman J. Weiner, "Group Work and the Interdisciplinary Approach," *Social Work,* Vol. 3, No. 3 (July 1958), pp. 76–82.

them to understand how they can relate to the various group processes that are continually going on as a part of institutional life. Caseworkers are helping group workers to understand the psychosocial aspects of illness and disability, and sharing their experience in participating with physicians in medical care. As was pointed out, medical social workers have in the past worked with patient and family groups themselves—alone or in association with physicians and psychiatrists—and are likely to do so increasingly in future. These activities of medical social workers will be more soundly based on relevant theory now that group workers are becoming available as consultants and associates in practice. In general, it appears that the use of group work in the medical setting can be regarded as a growing trend, limited primarily by the supply of qualified professional group workers.

PROGRAM PLANNING AS A MEDICAL SOCIAL WORK ACTIVITY

The *Working Definition of Social Work Practice* recognizes community organization as a social work method. Since theory development in community organization is still at an early stage of growth, it is understandable that medical social work has not yet demonstrated any very effective use of this method. The first step in analysis of this area of practice is to identify the actual activities going on in medical social work which seem to fall here and to consider their logical relationship to the growing theory of community organization. The related method of administration will also be found relevant because of its close connection with community organization.

What is described in medical social work as *program planning* has been going on ever since the early days but was not visualized as a major function until medical social workers moved in considerable numbers into public health programs in the late thirties. Many social workers in the health field are now devoting a substantial part of their effort in this area. However, the activity has not yet taken form in skills and methods that can be clearly distinguished and has not been fully described in the literature. One professional committee attempted for several years to obtain samples for analysis. The fact that they did not succeed suggests that the activity was not yet recognizable as a consistent "piece" of practice.

Some of the currently identified characteristics of program planning in medical social work are as follows:

1. Participation of medical social workers in development of policy and program within their own agency is the aspect usually emphasized first. This phase of activity has been more clearly recognized in public health agencies than in hospitals.

2. Participation in community planning—development, improvement, and co-ordination of services—is the other major aspect. This can be carried on from the base of the social worker's own agency or under the auspices of community councils, professional bodies, research projects, and similar groups.

3. The focus is upon the psychosocial aspects of health, as is true of all social work in the health field. It requires working equally with health and social welfare personnel, sometimes together and sometimes separately.

4. The activity occurs at federal, state, and local levels, and is beginning to become important at international levels.

No over-all definition of program planning has been produced by the medical social group. Descriptive classifications covering the two major segments of the field—hospital practice and public health practice—were prepared and published separately.[19] It has been traditional in medical social work to divide program planning activities into two distinct categories, according to whether they are carried on within or without the agency. Examination of these formulations raises questions as to whether this approach is the most helpful and may even create artificial divisions. When practice in health agencies is viewed as a whole today, it can be seen that planning initiated in the hospital frequently extends into the community and that planning undertaken in public health programs

---

[19] *A Statement of Standards To Be Met by Social Service Departments in Hospitals, Clinics and Sanatoria* (Washington, D. C.: American Association of Medical Social Workers, 1949); and "Educational Qualifications of Medical Social Workers in Public Health Programs," in *A Statement of Personnel Practices in Medical Social Work* (Washington, D. C.: American Association of Medical Social Workers, 1951), pp. 13–22.

frequently encompasses the hospital as part of the community. Thus in this type of planning, hospitals and communities interpenetrate, without definite boundaries. Furthermore, as was pointed out in the descriptive list of activities in Chapter IV, all types of program planning are concerned with policy, standards, and services and make use of the professional methods of administration and community organization. The chief difference seems to be, not in content or method, but in the auspices, that is, whether the social worker is acting under the sponsorship of the health agency or of some other auspice in the community.[20] In general, the likenesses seem more significant than the differences. For this reason both types of program planning are combined in this discussion.

Because auspices influence professional roles, medical social workers should be more familiar with the concept of *representativeness,* which is basic in community organization.[21] They should be clear which aspects of program planning are a part of their position and job in the agency, as in working on internal policies or representing the health agency in community planning. They should also be clear what responsibilities are involved when working on community planning as a representative of one's professional group or as an interested citizen, and how these activities relate to job responsibilities.[22] These are matters for further exploration and clarification in social work practice.

---

[20] If it is found that social workers actually perceive their work differently when it is initiated "within" or "without" their agency, then the distinction should probably be retained. Unless this is demonstrated, however, there seem to be advantages in looking at program planning as one type of professional activity in medical social work.

[21] Genevieve W. Carter, "Social Work Community Organization Methods and Processes," in Friedlander, *op. cit.,* pp. 249–250.

[22] Program planning as here discussed resembles social action and shades into it without clear boundaries. Both activities are concerned with bringing about change of social policy and services. This discussion, however, focuses on those phases of the social worker's activity which are most closely related to his particular professional competence, with an emphasis on the opportunities for influencing social policy within the program of the agency, which in the health field often covers large numbers of people. These opportunities do not seem to have been sufficiently recognized in relation to social action, which stresses social workers' activities outside their jobs.

Medical social workers customarily speak in terms of "participation" in program planning. While this is an accurate description, since the medical social worker always collaborates with others in this activity, the term is open to possible misunderstanding because it seems to imply that medical social work takes part only in activities initiated by others. Actually medical social workers initiate much of this activity themselves and should be doing so increasingly. For the purposes of the present discussion, it seems best neither to adopt the earlier definitions and categories nor to define new ones at this point, but to describe activities and suggest some preliminary ways of thinking about them.

Effort to strengthen the social component in health services—both in their own agency and in the community—has always been major for medical social workers. In the hospital this has been done primarily through casework and educational approaches. It is now realized that this is not enough and that a broader attack is called for. Program planning operates at a different level than casework, and medical social workers must learn to operate comfortably at this new level.

In viewing a health program or health policy, the social worker seeks to understand its impact on the persons concerned. Does the policy for hospital visiting hours cause suffering by unduly separating parents and children? Does the method of administering the means test for public medical care demean the dignity and integrity of applicants to such a degree that many are prevented from seeking such care? Is there such lack of continuity between specialized services that patients become lost and discouraged before they complete their care? Is sufficient explanation given to patients and families so that they really grasp their part in carrying through medical treatment?

In relation to programs and community services, it appears that doctors, nurses, and others on the health team are aware of social factors but do not regularly include them in their assessment of the situation in practical ways as do medical social workers. Ethel Cohen [23] has shown this convincingly in an editorial pointing out

---

[23] Ethel Cohen, "Some Social Considerations about Research and Prolonged Hospital Stay," *Journal of Chronic Diseases,* Vol. 7, No. 3 (March 1958), pp. 264–268.

that knowledge regarding the importance of social aspects has far outrun its applications. Comprehensive studies of medical care are planned and service programs are developed without consideration and inclusion of the social factors, although we have now for decades possessed methods for assessing and dealing with them. In multidiscipline teams working with groups of patients or families it has been observed that members of other professions tend to regard such groups as more or less homogeneous, whereas medical social workers are the first to call attention to the range of possible reactions and differences in response which should be anticipated in planning.

Why, then, it should be asked, have medical social workers not been more effective in influencing health programs and community services? Why does a medical social worker who has first-hand knowledge about what illness means to people—the stresses, the pressures, the failure of others to understand, the gaps in service—and who cares intensely about these things fail to make this knowledge and feeling effective in some type of action beyond the individual case? What blocks the social worker from wider activity? [24]

In an address discussing trends in social work participation in the California health department over several decades, Esther C. Spencer and Constance Grass pointed out that social work consultants are being asked to participate in the planning of a growing number of new health programs, such as chronic disease, mental health, industrial health, and alcoholism.[25] Such participation requires ability to identify the significant social elements in these programs; but social workers are not prepared or accustomed to analyze population problems in this way. We are realizing that our concern with professional methods—whether we should offer casework or consultation—has not prepared us to take the essential steps that must come earlier, *i.e.,* gain understanding of problems as they affect large groups in the community. This matter becomes

---

[24] *Report of the Special Conference on Community Health,* prepared by Kurt Reichert (New York: National Association of Social Workers, 1958).

[25] Esther C. Spencer and Constance Grass, *Perspectives in Public Health.* Paper presented at the Annual Meeting of Medical Social Consultants in Public Health and Public Medical Care Programs, Chicago, May 1958.

even more urgent because of the fact that many public health problems today involve a complex of psychological and social factors, in which the social factors may be more accessible to analysis and treatment for the population as a whole than the psychological problems.[26]

Several problems require solution before medical social workers can function effectively in relation to social policy and social programs. First, there must be motivation toward recognition of responsibility for making a contribution. A good beginning has been made, since many practitioners are aware of the importance of this activity as a part of medical social work and the leadership group has been trying for some years to come to grips with it. It appears, however, that the educational preparation and experience of medical social workers—particularly those in hospital practice—has not yet developed in them that ability to look beyond the urgent needs of the individual to the common aspects of need in groups of individuals. This ability is essential to a comprehensive social work approach. There has also been an attitude that only the head of the social service unit or department has responsibility for policy and program planning, with the implication that practicing workers should limit themselves to direct service.

A conceptual framework is needed which enables medical social workers—in fact, all social workers—to visualize the various components of their job within one compass. In recent years the great emphasis on the individual has limited the horizon of thinking. Work with groups and communities has been too much regarded by medical social workers as "belonging" to certain social work specialists with their own methods. Practical methods and facilities for getting the firsthand knowledge about individuals and families into the form of data, to be used as a base for program planning, are also needed. The research methods taught in schools of social work somehow do not seem to have enabled graduates to take these steps with ease and efficiency.

The particular social work knowledge, theory, and method on which this activity rests are those of community organization. Administrative principles as used in social work are also relevant.

---

[26] *Ibid.*

These are still in an early stage of formulation. As they have been taught in schools and applied in practice, they have not seemed particularly applicable to medical social work, since they have dealt more with independent social agencies and community councils than with the broad programs in which social work characteristically functions in association with other professions. Considerable effort will be needed in order to identify the concepts and formulations which will prove most relevant and useful in medical social work. As a conceptual base for this discussion, Violet M. Sieder's definition of the community organization method is suggested. It is as follows:

> Community organization is a method of social work practice which helps a community determine and achieve continuously more desirable program goals which meet constantly changing social welfare needs by facilitating the interaction of its constituent parts (organizations, institutions, individual leaders, and geographic subdivisions) in such a way as to make maximum use of its internal and external resources while at the same time strengthening its potential ability to undertake the solution of new and more difficult problems. Its focus is upon helping individuals and groups increase their capacity and motivation to work together to bring about progressive change and better integration in the social services of the community. This is achieved by helping the community to identify needs, rank these needs, formulate a plan to meet them, implement the plan of action, and assess this action in terms of its adequacy and consequences. This method is based in social work philosophy, principles and ethics, and depends upon knowledge of the social structure and dynamics of a community social welfare program content, the science of human relations, and the art of professional practice.[27]

Although this definition describes effort as focused upon communities and medical social workers are primarily concerned with specific programs, it will be found that there is much in this statement relevant to medical social work practice. Theory regarding

---
[27] Violet M. Sieder, "The Tasks of the Community Organization Worker," in Harry L. Lurie, *The Community Organization Method in Social Work Education* (New York: Council on Social Work Education, 1959), pp. 249–256.

the relation between social work and social welfare policy, now appearing increasingly in the social work literature, will also prove helpful.[28]

In current practice considerable activity in program planning cannot be identified as a full use of professional method. It appears rather as isolated steps and partial activities which may have some cumulative effect over a period of months and years but are often only loosely related and organized. Some of this fragmented activity may be inevitable and appropriate, but effort is needed to increase the proportion of organized and disciplined problem solving.

Channels and Process

There are two approaches that are useful in attaining a better understanding of program planning in medical social work. One is the description of the administrative channels within which it occurs and the other is the description of the process, with emphasis on its scope and continuity. Taking the first approach, there are a number of administrative channels now being used regularly for program planning in the health field. In some hospitals the social service director or an experienced staff worker is a member of a regular policy-making group, such as a management committee, composed of department heads and presided over by the hospital administrator. In the public health agency the social worker participates in regular staff meetings at which policies and programs are discussed. In the community council medical social workers may be members of planning committees that focus upon one or another aspect of health and welfare.

Under any of these auspices the medical social worker may also be invited to take part in some specific project, such as to formulate standards of practice or to carry through a study. Sometimes the social worker is the first to identify some need and takes the initiative in stimulating action through appropriate channels. These ac-

---

[28] Eveline M. Burns, "Social Policy and the Social Work Curriculum," in Werner W. Boehm, *Objectives of the Social Work Curriculum of the Future* (New York: Council on Social Work Education, 1959), pp. 255–274.

tivities range from local effort focusing on a particular problem, such as a project to establish a new social service department in a community hospital, all the way to planning on a nationwide basis, such as participation in a committee of the American Public Health Association to produce a policy statement on the quality of medical care in a national health program. Since medical social workers are concerned with both health and welfare, they are often in a position to take steps to improve the understanding between health and welfare personnel and to further the co-ordination between their services.

It is particularly important to identify more clearly the social worker's characteristic process in these program-planning activities. When the social worker is participating in one of the administrative or professional groups that meets regularly, the activity is likely to consist of brief contributions regarding the psychosocial aspects of the problem, contributed as each expert present participates from his own special knowledge and viewpoint. The social worker also takes part in decision making by the group, whenever this is indicated, watching to make certain that the psychosocial factors and the relevant social values are taken into account. Except in instances where there is prolonged examination of one problem, the charting of the social worker's activity in such a group would appear as rather loosely related "pieces" of activity, but the total contribution would reveal consistency in purpose, content, and emphasis.

If we are to identify and analyze process, we shall have to start with specific instances in which the beginning and the end of the problem-solving process can be identified. Three illustrations from medical social work follow.

The first shows medical social workers identifying a small unmet need within their agency and taking steps through administrative channels within the agency so that a change is made to meet the need. The knowledge and skills used here are primarily administrative.

> This situation is concerned with payment for medication recommended for certain patients discharged from tuberculosis sanatoria. The usual procedure in this state is that when patients are discharged on drug therapy, arrangements are

made for them to purchase their own drugs if they are financially able to do so or they are referred to the health department in the city or town where they reside for the drug to be provided from this source as a part of continued treatment. In some cases when patients are to receive public assistance on discharge, the drugs are provided through that source. Through information provided by state health department social workers and inquiries from other community agencies, it became apparent to the head social work consultant that some patients discharged from hospitals were unable to pay for their own drugs and were also considered to be ineligible for help through their own local health department, because their residence in the community was not of sufficient duration. Although this situation did not involve a large number of patients, it did represent a hardship for the patients and also made it necessary for the social worker to seek aid through voluntary services to assist patients with the cost of medication used in treatment of a disease which traditionally has been a public health responsibility. As a result of the social work consultant's bringing to the attention of the hospital administration and the director of tuberculosis control the cases of patients who were not eligible for assistance through the usual channels, a budget was established for the purchase of drugs to be dispensed free of charge to patients being discharged from state sanatoria. These funds are used for patients who do not have drugs available to them through the usual community resources.

The second illustration shows how a social worker in a public health agency, when asked by a community agency to participate in a specific plan, uses his knowledge of human behavior and community resources to suggest some of the wider implications of the problem, so that planning will not be premature or too narrowly focused.

A social work consultant in an urban health department is asked to assist a private association for mentally retarded children in planning an institute or a series of institutes for public health nurses. The association, which spearheads local community efforts in behalf of the mentally retarded, believes that many parents of retarded children in the community need advice regarding the management of such children and believes further that public health nurses are in a very good position to give such advice. The association wants to be in a position, when receiving inquiries, to make referrals to public health nurses. The institutes are envisioned as a means of orienting the nurses. The planning committee developed by the association includes various disciplines from the health department and from a specialized rehabilitation center for retarded children in the community, as well as staff members of the association. The social work consultant is included because it is thought that he may be able to give "pointers" to the nurses regarding handling of social problems. In several conferences the social work consultant takes initiative in refocusing his contribution along these lines:

1. He interprets to the committee that parents of mentally retarded children have a range of needs and suggests that such needs must be dealt with in a variety of ways. For example, there is a vast difference between a mother's lack of knowledge regarding methods of child care and a complex family relationship problem related to the retarded child.

2. The consultant suggests more searching consideration regarding range and types of needs through evaluation and study of the data and insights available at the rehabilitation center.

3. He suggests that for certain types of needs community social agencies may be better utilized than heretofore and proposes ways by which these agencies can be included in the over-all planning.

4. He suggests that the suggestions under both (1) and (3) above be pursued prior to more specific planning for institutes for the public health nurses.

The third instance describes social work participation in a multidiscipline group that is engaged in developing policy and standards for a national program.

After the passage of the first Social Security Act, the United States Children's Bureau established a professional advisory committee to give assistance in defining goals, standards, and criteria relating to the Crippled Children's Services. Representatives of the major professional groups concerned with care of crippled children were members. The president of the American Association of Medical Social Workers was invited to join this committee and remained a member for several years. She participated with the other professional

> representatives in outlining goals and standards of service designed to meet the needs of the "whole child." It was the social worker's function to stress those psychosocial aspects which fall particularly within the knowledge and experience of medical social work. These recommendations were later incorporated in the state plans, on the basis of which the various states developed their individual programs. This professional advisory committee was an outstanding example of a group working on high-level social policy at a strategic point in the early definition of an important nationwide medical care program.

This is a clear instance of long-range program planning of broad scope. All three illustrations can be recognized as examples of problem solving, with definite purpose, focus, and continuity.

The following example shows a medical social worker taking the initiative to further community planning and reveals the steps in the process.

> An experienced social work consultant in a state health department was assigned to a geographical area consisting of moderate-sized communities in which there was a considerable number of trained and partially trained social workers giving health and welfare services. These workers did not, however, meet together and the social work consultant could find no effective channel through which to further her own agency's goals and services. The opportunity to improve co-ordination suddenly appeared when several social workers and the public health nurse were having lunch together after having met to discuss a difficult case in a local public welfare office. The social worker raised the question whether they might meet periodically to discuss some of their common interests and problems. She received an enthusiastic response and out of this beginning there developed an organized group of persons consisting of health and welfare personnel from several neighboring towns, who met regularly to learn about each other's services and consider together the problems in their communities.
>
> Workers in other towns within the area heard about this first successful effort at co-ordination and were stimulated to follow its example. By being present at the right time, the social worker was able to participate in the stimulation and development of four more such local groups, all of which

showed real vitality. Knowing her helpful contribution to the formation of the first group, later groups asked her to aid them in their organization. Not herself trained in community organization, she consciously used the basic principles she had learned in social work about working with people. She was careful to move slowly in terms of the readiness of the group. It was important to avoid any appearance of domination by the professional element in social work or by the large state agencies. She was convinced that the groups would survive and be useful only as long as the local people controlled them and felt that they were really their own.

As the writer sat down with this social work consultant to analyze her activity in the formation of these five local groups, it was possible to distinguish certain steps that together assumed a repetitive pattern, as follows:

1. Awareness of the limitations of the local situation and motivation to contribute to the improved functioning of the agencies are the first requirements.

2. Activity begins when "either one of the other workers speaks to you or you speak to them." There is a tentative exploratory phase.

3. A planning committee is set up, the social work consultant being a member but not chairman. Great care is taken in inviting individuals with leadership potential to this committee.

4. The planning committee assesses the situation, defines a program, and sets up an organization. Simple bylaws are prepared.

5. Membership and program committees are established, and a regular schedule of meetings is planned.

6. At the first general meeting the bylaws are discussed and accepted and the group is now a going concern. At this point in the life of the group the social work consultant changes her role. She is ready to participate in committees like any other member and is watching how she can make helpful contributions to the program in a quiet way, but is careful not to assume a conspicuous role.

The social work consultant's opinion was that the groups would carry on without her from this point, as the members obtain both pleasure and benefit from knowing each other and working together.

It is of interest to note that only after several years of slow, patient groundwork in these many communities does the social work consultant have channels for furthering her public health program, channels created through her own vision and persistent effort.

This example shows clearly what Sieder describes as "helping individuals and groups to increase their capacity and motivation to work together to bring about progressive change and better integration in the social services of the community." [29] It implies working co-operatively with others and furthering their efforts, not in relation to their own needs but toward some common social work objective. The goal is not personality change but change in programs and services. As in all social work, there is orderly progression which involves getting facts about the situation, assessing possible alternatives, selecting one line of action, and implementing it through appropriate methods.

We do not yet know whether "participation in program planning," as used now in medical social work, will prove a helpful concept to cover the activities described in this section. Possibly, when we know them better, some other term may be preferable.

There is a tendency for social workers involved in community activities to say rather glibly that they are "doing community organization." It is not clear whether medical social workers can practice in the area of policy and program with only knowledge of the principles of administration and community organization, such as they are now receiving in schools of social work. This seems a minimum. Should they also be drawing on trained community organization workers to help them as partners in some of their major enterprises? If so, in what ways? By collaborating in actual instances of problem solving? By analyzing practice and identifying principles? Should medical social workers also see that some of their own practitioners obtain training in administration and community organization, in order to strengthen this phase of their practice from within? Definite measures of this kind are needed and possibly more than one such approach will be required, if the group is to make its broader contribution to programs and communities in a professional and disciplined manner.

---

[29] Sieder, *op. cit.*, p. 249.

10

methods characteristic of the health field

Having discussed social work's own methods as used in the context of medical care, we are now ready to discuss social work's use of methods and processes customarily employed by a number of other professions. Those most characteristic of the health field—teamwork, consultation, teaching, and research—will be considered. These activities require from social workers almost constant collaboration with members of the health professions and thus represent multidiscipline practice in its most fully developed aspects.

THE TEAMWORK PROCESS

Multidiscipline practice, as previously noted, appears in many forms, some quite loose and some highly organized.[1] We can probably learn most by studying multidiscipline practice in its most formal manifestations, because of their greater visibility and

---

[1] *See* pp. 72–74.

because they have already been discussed to a greater extent in the literature. We will, therefore, begin with the teamwork process. In this discussion, the term "teamwork" is given a precise meaning, denoting one particular aspect of multidiscipline practice, namely, the organized, continuous, and co-ordinated activity of a small group of individuals from two or more of the health professions, working together under the auspices of a single agency to further common objectives, such as patient care or program development. The team must be a real group which gets together at regular intervals for person-to-person sharing of knowledge and joint thinking. It is best regarded as a group of professional workers. Some writers include anyone in the health agency who has any contact with the patient and others insist that the patient himself must be regarded as a member. Obviously the whole purpose of the clinical team is to understand the patient's needs, to serve him, and to enlist his fullest participation. To accomplish this, the patient does not have to be a member. The basic requirements are the co-ordinated activity of specialists toward furthering of common objectives. This interpretation of teamwork seems clearest and most useful for medical social workers. Changes in concepts and practice may lead to a modified concept at some future time.

The general goal of all teamwork in the health field is the welfare of the individuals, groups, and communities being served, and the furthering of specific research. This goal is placed above the particular interests and concerns of any one of the participating professions. Teamwork is an outstanding example of a Gestalt in which the whole is greater than the sum of the parts. Sharing of knowledge and skill, together with intellectual stimulation, leads to greater results than could be obtained by any of the members functioning separately. Moreover, values accrue to those who are being served and also to the members of the participating professions—ultimately to society.

The teamwork process is used not only in the care of patients but in a wide range of nonclinical functions. Effective teams are found among clinical, administrative, teaching, and research groups in hospitals, rehabilitation centers, tuberculosis sanatoria, public health agencies, in fact, throughout the health field. The pattern of teamwork varies according to the setting, objectives, composition, and organization of the team. Many factors affect the ways of working together. Some of them are whether the chairman is a clinical professor, public health officer, or young hospital resident; whether the group is discussing one case, all the patients on a medical service, or a community program; whether the purpose is general care, physical rehabilitation, or preventive services. In the earliest pattern of clinical teamwork, the physician saw himself as obtaining data and recommendations from the other members, on the basis of which he made the final decision regarding the patient's care. This is still the pattern in the strictly medical aspects of care, since these must be medical decisions. Increasingly, however, decisions regarding other aspects, such as the way the team will work with the patient or the plan for aftercare, are being made through full discussion by the whole group. Sometimes the group includes a psychiatrist who does not work with patients directly but acts primarily as consultant to the team in helping the members to understand the emotional aspects of the problem and their own attitudes toward the patient and each other. Groups that work together over a sustained period without too frequent changes of personnel, as in a research project, are likely to develop the smoothest teamwork, because they have learned to adjust to each other and to make the most of the contribution of each member.

A process of such complexity, involving professional workers from so many different backgrounds and with differing personalities, presents many problems. The practical ones arise from the fact that it is time consuming, and also difficult to get so many busy people regularly together in one place. The subtle problems in interaction are even more important. Insecurity, domination, competition, fear of assuming responsibility, and other emotional phenomena interfere with the best functioning of such a group. Intellectual differences and disagreements also present obstacles. It is not for this discussion to evaluate such complex problems but only to attempt to clarify essentials and present some issues.

The description of interprofessional teamwork in the literature tends to focus on clinical teams. We need more consideration of teams working on problems of social policy, program planning, teaching, and research, in order to see if there are important differences. Observation and analysis of teamwork usually are limited to the formal conferences. A full analysis should deal with the total process, that is, the events relevant to collaboration that occur between conferences as well as during them. The final test is in the outcome of the joint thinking as actually applied in practice.

Problems of communication bulk large in interprofessional teamwork. Difference in expertness means that the members are usually operating from within different frames of reference and using different terminology, and these factors create barriers. Members have to become familiar with each others' concepts and values.

In the discussion of leadership there has been confusion, since the distinction has not been made between (1) the co-ordinating role of the chairman, (2) the authority of the senior profession, and (3) the initiative appropriately assumed by one or another member at various times because of the nature of the problem. In clinical teamwork, the physician carries the ultimate responsibility for diagnosis and treatment (both professionally and legally); hence, he must carry the over-all authoritative role by virtue of his position. In the medical setting, he is usually the presiding officer. It is possible that such a clinical group may at any time assign to some other of its members—such as medical student, nurse, or social worker—the responsibility for taking initiative on a case; this can in one sense be thought of as temporary leadership.

Much helpful analysis has been undertaken from the psychiatric angle. Since this deals with the difficult emotional adjustments demanded in teamwork, it has had the effect of emphasizing problems of personality interaction before the positive requirements of this type of collaboration have been clearly defined and accepted.

A still relatively unanswered question relates to the ability of the patient to work with multidiscipline teams. Their combined knowledge undoubtedly increases diagnostic accuracy, but how does it feel to the patient to be working with such a group instead of one physician, as in the past? Such evidence as is now available suggests that a patient does, and can, work successfully with all the members of a relatively large team if he is clear as to the function of each member and convinced that all are working together in his interest. Actually, since under conditions of modern medical practice the patient always has to work with many people in a hospital or health agency, he probably finds his contacts eased and improved as the degree of teamwork increases. Some teams make a point of selecting carefully those of their members who can work best with a certain patient and delegating to them responsibility for carrying out the agreed-upon treatment measures.

It is a principle of teamwork that each member should make his own distinct contribution, but this is more easily said than done. There is much overlapping between professions, which has been called the "gray area." [2] This overlapping is particularly evident in relation to the psychosocial aspects, since all the health professions are moving to include more of this content in their education and practice. Thus the "gray area" is a special problem for the social worker on the health team: When several professions work together, distinctions can more readily be made between the concerns that are in the central focus of each than in trying to demarcate their boundaries. Social workers will feel more secure if they have in mind that it is their long-range contribution that will stand out as characteristic, not what occurs in any single conference. There are times when the whole team appropriately works together on what is primarily a medical social problem, but in the long run the social worker will stand out as the member who represents this psychosocial focus.

The total process of multidiscipline teamwork can be viewed rather simply as an activity in which (1) each member comes with his own contribution, (2) there is joint assessment and planning, and (3) each carries out his own role. It can be seen as a continuous in-and-out movement, a coming together at proper moments to heighten the collaboration and integration, and then going out to carry through the implied activity. Such a description as well as some of the limitations in the current analysis of the teamwork process raises the question, whether we have found the right model to give the greatest amount of insight into this activity.

---

[2] Elizabeth P. Rice, *Team Work in Medical Social Work* (New York: National Association of Social Workers, 1957), p. 7. (Mimeographed.)

Would joint thinking or joint effort suggest more accurately its essential character? Perhaps we should have more than one model to guide our thinking. Possibly medical social workers have been clinging too much to a single model of teamwork, influenced by the medical tradition, that of the physician as leader working with representatives of the associated professions. Observation of a few of the most brilliantly successful teams suggests that more emphasis should be given to the way the group as a whole works together. Out of such groups there seems to emerge a kind of interchange, growth, and creative thinking which transcend anything that individual members could attain by themselves.

As yet there has been no strong motivation or movement in the health field to analyze and define the essentials of teamwork and to consider teaching it to professional students, even though it is being widely used in health practice. Since the teamwork pattern runs counter to the pattern of individual practice traditional in medicine, a period of adjustment is necessary before physicians can be expected to understand and accept this modification in their professional role.

An Example of Multidiscipline Teamwork

At this point an example of teamwork is presented in some detail in order to suggest the kind of analysis that will be helpful in furthering the much-needed understanding of this professional process. This is a team concerned with a family health study, described in Chapter IX. It was giving care to young mothers having their first babies. The clinic had a multidiscipline staff consisting of obstetricians, pediatricians, nutritionists, a public health nurse, social workers, and a consultant psychiatrist, all of whom were available to serve the patient and family. The atmosphere was planned to promote preventive health services to the pregnant woman. A unified treatment plan was emphasized. The social worker usually saw the patient at each clinic visit and made a home visit at a certain planned point in the case. The various members of the team whose action is described had been working together for from one to three years. The example follows:

The case is that of young parents who were living with the husband's mother because he was having difficulty in finding work. The patient, a young woman of British ancestry, had experienced considerable insecurity and stress in early life because of her mother's long illness and death from tuberculosis when the patient was a child. From that time until her marriage she had lived with various relatives. While at first showing little feeling about her baby, she soon began to manifest anxiety which persisted throughout the pregnancy. She exhibited excessive concern regarding her mother-in-law's attitudes, particularly after the baby came. The parents continually talked and planned about moving to their own home but did not accomplish this during the period of clinic contact.

Being a stable staff engaged in research, this team met together more regularly than is possible in the usual treatment clinic.[3] They came together briefly before each clinic session to discuss any special needs of patients scheduled for visits and held postclinic conferences after every session. The social worker's record notes fifteen such conferences where this patient's progress and problems were discussed. In addition there were two very full conferences with the psychiatric consultant. It was felt that this patient needed more help than many of the mothers because of her persistent anxiety. Her behavior was characterized by avoidance of aggression either in herself or in those around her, an emotional pattern developed as a result of her early history and mother's death at a time when she was particularly vulnerable. The following team conference was held when the baby was five weeks old, just after the social worker had made a home visit:

A brief resume was given by the social worker of the progress of the case to date and the present social situation. In brief, the data presented were as follows: Mrs. A had delivered a four-pound, twelve-ounce baby girl and the baby had been discharged home. Mrs. A had pumped her breasts during this period and was feeding the baby by breast quite successfully. There had been intrafamilial tensions resulting from differences in child upbringing in the generation of the mother-in-law and Mrs. A, with specific difference center-

---

[3] The complete course of the patient's care included ten prenatal visits, the delivery of a premature baby at the hospital, and twelve visits to the pediatrician and three for postpartum supervision of the mother within the first year of the baby's life. In the total period of care the social worker had over twenty interviews with the mother, including one visit at the hospital with the public health nurse and one home visit.

ing around picking up the baby and "spoiling" her. Mrs. A's mother-in-law had been antagonized by the visit from the public health nurse in addition to service offered by the visiting nurse, and especially by personal questions asked her about her own circumstances as was required by law in establishing suitability of home and care for a premature baby. Because of the mother-in-law's feeling about visitors Mrs. A had been reluctant to have the social worker call but the senior psychiatrist at a general postclinic conference had suggested that intervention seemed definitely indicated. He suggested placing the burden of responsibility and explanation to the mother-in-law on the social worker without involving Mrs. A in this. Consequently a visit was made to the home and the mother-in-law was present at this visit. The mother-in-law was a young appearing person for her sixty years, seemed to have quite decided opinions, but spontaneously brought up the matters on her mind and was quite amenable to general discussion of these without becoming upset. This visit was perhaps therapeutic for Mrs. A in that she was able to see that presumed differences of opinion could be handled without creating further trouble for her. She had been extremely upset on the previous week at her clinic appointment because of the difficulties which she felt were ensuing between her and her mother-in-law. However two days following the home visit she was much more relaxed and able to see many positive things in her mother-in-law and spoke of how helpful she had been to her.

The pediatrician noted that the baby was premature but a healthy, vigorous one now weighing six pounds, twelve ounces, a remarkable weight gain; that the feeding schedule had been somewhat confused, which might have accounted for a recent bout of fussiness in the baby; that in general Mrs. A was doing quite well, asked sensible questions, and used well information which was given to her.

The social worker further stated that Mrs. A's mother-in-law had been invited to come into the clinic and it seemed as if this would be very helpful. The social worker raised the question as to how much further effort should be made in carrying out this plan and the psychiatrist felt that extending the invitation was probably the outside limit now, since if the issue were pressed Mrs. A might wonder about the motivation and become worried. This invitation had been extended by the pediatrician through Mrs. A to the mother-in-law and in person by the social worker.

The social worker noted that Mrs. A had brought out in

the home visit some guilt about having produced a premature baby, primarily discussing it in terms of diet and her own weight gain, and also her own slight frame and build as being contributory. This was the first of fifteen grandchildren of the mother-in-law to be a premature baby.

The nutritionist noted that Mrs. A did an excellent job in pregnancy in getting in her essentials, although occasionally she went off on binges and concentrated on certain things which were nonessential, and she herself did not see a correlation between the diet and prematurity.

The psychiatrist suggested that the social worker continue with this discussion of Mrs. A's feeling about having a premature baby at an early date. This might be handled by noting to her that women often feel that they are to blame for having a premature baby and the social worker might ask if Mrs. A may have had such thoughts. She could be told that mothers often feel that there is some danger or at least some extra concern in relation to premature babies and whether this is realistic or otherwise, they may develop a guilty feeling about it.

There was some discussion among the group as to causes of prematurity and the pediatrician expressed a feeling that it presents an uncomfortable situation for the social worker or anyone discussing this subject with a mother, to have no idea of how prematurity happens.

The psychiatrist felt that regardless of the real cause it was necessary to find out what Mrs. A herself thought. She should be allowed to talk and could be told definitely that most people do not know the answer, that the mystery makes mothers try to find an answer to it. The important thing for her was not to attach a false reason and feel so guilty that it would spoil the relationship between her and the child.

The pediatrician felt that Mrs. A was moving out of her fear of the vulnerability of a premature baby and would probably be able in a couple of more visits to think of giving care to a "normal" baby. In actuality the baby does not appear to be a premature from outward appearances and it was only by examination that this was in evidence. It was noted that Mr. A's reaction to handling the baby might also be due to the fact the baby was premature and less pleasing to a man to handle than a more sturdy, cuddly baby. It was decided that the pediatrician would speak to Mrs. A at her next visit, pointing out that it takes time in any event for fathers to become comfortable in handling babies.

The pediatrician noted that the baby is doing remarkably

well at breast feeding, better than some full-term babies at this age. The social worker brought up the fact that Mrs. A and her mother-in-law had been questioning the quality of the milk. The pediatrician said he had handled this indirectly so as not to create opportunities for differences between the two women. No mention was made of the quality of the milk but suggestions were made for addition of water and salt to Mrs. A's diet in the hot weather. It was thought that this indirect approach would help her to see that her nutrition was something separate from herself, and help her keep feelings about them separated.

The psychiatrist commented that things seemed to be going along quite well at this point.[4]

This account of a single piece of medical teamwork shows how each member of the team shares comfortably in the relationship and how they build on each other's contributions so as to evolve a broader understanding of the situation and a more comprehensive plan of action.[5] In the session presented above, particular attention is given to the social work contribution because of the social worker's recent home visit and further role in helping the patient with her feelings about the baby and the mother-in-law. The manner in which health teams discuss the knowledge and scientific theory relevant to a particular case is clearly shown in this conference, as is its pertinence to the worker's subsequent treatment focus. Following this conference the patient went through a difficult period when the baby was ill and she became so exhausted that she had her first quarrel with her husband. Thereafter, the situation improved and the record ends on a positive note when she told the social worker that she felt a second pregnancy would now be acceptable.

This comprehensive view of the care of a pregnant woman and her baby shows how effective teamwork in one conference is a part of an ongoing process involving literally hundreds of contacts made by the team members with the patient and with each other. The complex activity is integrated through a clear sense of purpose,

---

[4] Rice, *op. cit.,* pp. 8–10.
[5] *Ibid.,* p. 10.

a sharing of specialized knowledge, and the development by the particular group of teamwork skill through the experience of working together continuously over many months. Out of the analysis of such demonstrations we shall eventually come to understand the essentials of teamwork in multidiscipline practice.

SOCIAL WORK IN MULTIDISCIPLINE PRACTICE

We are now ready to consider social work's own approach and participation in multidiscipline practice in the health field. The preceding discussion of medical teamwork, which is multidiscipline practice in its clearest form, has enabled us to make a start in identifying some of the major characteristics of this practice. Until there is concerted effort to study it, social workers can best make progress by working to improve their own activity. While there is great interest in social work participation in this practice, only a beginning has been made in defining social work activities as they relate to working with members of other professions.

In searching for a base from which to start it would be well to review the aspects of social work knowledge, value, and technique applicable to all working relationships with other persons. These can be stated as: acceptance of and respect for the other person, understanding of the other person's background, sensitivity to his feelings and goals, assessment of his readiness to move toward change of attitude and behavior, skillful timing of activity, orderly patterns and arrangements for working together, a disciplined professional self (social worker), and knowledge of human behavior, culture, group process, administration. It can be perceived that these concepts apply equally well to the social worker's working relationships with patients and with members of other professions. They are applicable whether the social worker meets the members of the other professions singly or in regularly planned group conferences.

The next question to be asked is how, beyond these basic concepts, the working relationships with professional associates differ in important ways from those with patients. The distinction in goal, focus, and method is at once clear. In using the social casework method with the client or patient, the social worker focuses upon him and his concerns. It is a helping process, the goal of which is to enable the client to deal with his psychosocial problems in such a way as to relieve stress and to improve social functioning. In multidiscipline practice, however, the focus is not on the member of the other profession. Collaborating workers are not "treating" each other but are working together toward a common goal which is outside themselves and concerns individual and social welfare. The activity is in the nature of collaborative effort, in which communication and joint thinking are major techniques.[6]

In attempting to improve social work participation in multidiscipline groups there has been emphasis on better diagnostic thinking. It is suggested, however, that the problem goes deeper than that and starts in the knowledge base itself. As long as social workers regard their major contribution as that of casework skill, they are handicapped in multidiscipline conferences because a skill cannot be quickly and easily communicated through verbal channels. When social workers are clearer as to their own appropriate knowledge and values, and have readily at their command a body of concepts and generalizations as tools for analysis of the problems confronting them, they will have greater facility and confidence in taking responsibility for judgment and in conveying such judgments to their associates.

This approach requires a change in orientation from earlier practice, with emphasis on areas and activities not previously focused upon. There would be, first, more recognition and conscious use of social work knowledge and values, either advanced as general propositions or applied in specific instances and cases. In such situations the social worker must be able, if questioned, to

---

[6] Florence Stein, "Teamwork in the Medical Setting: A Skilled Process," in Dora Goldstine, ed., *Readings in the Theory and Practice of Medical Social Work* (Chicago: University of Chicago Press, 1954), pp. 286–298; Stein, "How Can the Professions Work Together in Service to Individuals?", *Medical Social Work*, Vol. 4, No. 4 (September 1955), pp. 160–171; Elaine C. Goldston, "The Medical Social Worker in a Clinic Team for the Occupational Evaluation of Cardiacs," *Medical Social Work*, Vol. 1, No. 2 (May 1952), pp. 1–8.

substantiate any specific statement from the theoretical base, referring either to recognized authorities, studies, or the observation and experience of social work. An illustration comes from a pilot study of medical social workers' interdisciplinary conferences.

> A worker and doctor were considering the possibility of transferring a veteran, at his request, from an acute-care hospital to a rehabilitation center, but were also wondering about his being discharged instead to the care of one of his married sisters. He was unmarried, had quiescent tuberculosis, seizures (quite well controlled on medication), no job to which to return, and a history of alcoholism. After some discussion, the doctor asked the social worker specifically what she thought of the idea of transfer. She replied simply that she thought it would be a good idea. While this opinion was given with considerable substantiating evidence, it was sought and accredited as a professional judgment of great importance in further plans for the patient. The worker's judgment was obviously based on considerable information about this patient's situation and attitudes (such as his vagueness about plans on leaving and his fear of drinking if left to his own devices) as well as upon her theoretical knowledge about alcoholism, and her prediction that a rehabilitation center would help him in his eventual adjustment to community life, whereas complete discharge now would leave him at loose ends. All these were put together in a configuration that provided a clear-cut, usable professional opinion.[7]

While this instance concerns a conference with one physician, the same principles regarding judgment based on conscious use of knowledge apply in working with a multidiscipline group.

In order to achieve this judgment, there needs to be more awareness of the systematic steps by which the social work contribution to the team is identified, formulated, and presented to the interprofessional group. This goes back to the two basic social work roles—the role with the patient and family and the role with the medical team. Social work has analyzed the role with the patient and

---

[7] *A Pilot Study of Medical Social Workers' Interdisciplinary Conferences* (New York: National Association of Social Workers, 1956), pp. 38–39.

family as social casework. The relative clarity with which it is perceived as a professional method gives security. Social work has also regarded the role with medicine and the other professions as important but has not gone far in analyzing and describing it. It is important to see how these two professional social work roles fit together and are interdependent.

The general goal of the clinical team is to make comprehensive care of the patient a reality. The social worker's contribution is to make sure that the psychosocial component actually is operative. Experience shows that even when there is recognition of the psychosocial aspects in a general sort of way, they are not likely to receive their due consideration by a multidiscipline health team unless they are clearly advanced by the social worker. Thus the social worker has a definite responsibility and opportunity not encompassed by any other profession. Social work participation in multidiscipline teamwork is a major channel for fulfilling this responsibility and for improving services to patients, families, and communities.

The steps for formulating and presenting the psychosocial component in comprehensive care to the multidiscipline team can be described as follows:

1. The social worker first applies relevant knowledge, concepts, and theory to analyze and assess the situation within the social work framework, which is embodied in the "constant elements" identified in Chapter IX. This is an assessment for social work purposes, covering all pertinent aspects of the medical social situation from a social work viewpoint.

2. Next there should be a conscious step of refocusing the analysis for presentation to the medical team. In doing this the social worker moves into another framework, that of medicine and health. What is relevant, important, and useful for this new approach is selected, related, and pointed up. It is not just a matter of presenting certain data. The worker must be ready to indicate the implications of the analysis in the form of a social work judgment. Social workers too often arrive at a decision by a fluid process of throwing together data and impressions and are hesitant to take a stand. Doctors expect each expert to make a definite

recommendation. The question is, what does social work *know* that enables the social worker to relate and focus the data so that its significance can be communicated, in nontechnical terms, to the multidiscipline group? What social work values stand out as important here? What is the social worker's judgment as to what can and should be done? Although medical social workers have learned to do this reorienting and focusing in preparing social summaries for medical records, they have not applied this skill so effectively in the verbal interchange of the interprofessional team. The importance of not only selecting ideas but also employing words and language without special social work connotations, that will be easily understood by the other professions, must be constantly kept in mind.

This process can be demonstrated through the case situation presented in Chapter IX, that of an adolescent youth who was suffering from gastrointestinal symptoms related to the stress and conflict he was undergoing because his father had deserted and his neurotic mother was holding him in a dependent relationship, yet expecting him to fill his father's place.

Within the social work orientation, the social worker would think about this youth's ambivalence over the conflicting roles imposed on him by his mother; his need to grow toward independence, yet guilt over going against her needs and wishes; and the even more serious possibility that he might fail to establish his own ego identity at this crucial point in the life cycle. The worker would consider how this particular individual might respond to such severe stress by developing chronic illness. She would further consider how she could help through offering him a supportive relationship (that of the "good parent") during the period of greatest stress and later a permissive relationship that would enable him, after his mother's death, to move toward greater self-direction and eventually independent social functioning with appropriate use of the community's resources.

Within the medical orientation, the social worker would present the situation of a youth under stress because of the desertion of his father and his mother's excessive dependence upon him through her neurotic need; then after her death the crucial problem of an adolescent left entirely alone and unprepared to function independently; and the hospital's responsibility to assist him in this situation. The social worker would indicate that she could help by working directly with the patient and using community resources for rehabilitation. Since teamwork with physician and psychiatrist would be necessary, there would also be interest in defining the social work role in this interprofessional process.

Note that the social worker would not be interpreting her method, but rather her knowledge and values. At present social workers are not sufficiently aware of how they use their knowledge in practice. In field instruction we talk a great deal about "application of theory in practice" but the actual use of theory—in the form of generalizations applicable to specific situations—is not clear or systematic. Social workers find abstract knowledge and values remote and feel more comfortable in emphasizing a sensitive relationship with a client. We must find ways to make social workers more aware of their knowledge base. Its use is a prerequisite to successful teamwork in the health field. There is no intent to push social work beyond its depth, as a learned discipline. We already have a larger store of knowledge and value than we are using and are in a position to keep adding to that store.

In applying relevant social work knowledge, examination of that knowledge suggests what the medical social worker currently has to offer in regard to understanding the patient in relation to his life situation and his illness. The successive steps in use of this knowledge should be noted. The medical social worker starts with a body of knowledge regarding health and disease and their psychosocial implications. This knowledge about the psychosocial aspects is at present unevenly developed but growing rapidly. In approaching any instance of illness or handicap, the social worker immediately sees it in terms of the problems and stresses it presents to patients and families. This manner of analyzing the illness is the social worker's equivalent for the doctor's diagnostic classification of disease. It provides an orderly framework for viewing any particular instance.

The second step in thinking comes when contact is made with

the individual patient. Now the social worker must try to understand the particular meaning of illness to the patient, how he defines it in terms of his own life situation. This is the step which is perceived most clearly at present. However, as the body of knowledge regarding the psychosocial aspects of health and illness grows and social workers have more security in using their knowledge, that phase of social work thinking will become more prominent. Social workers will be in a position, in multidiscipline conferences, to comment on those conditions and phases of treatment that are likely to be stressful to patients and families, the ways in which they are known to be stressful, the typical patterns of response, and the ways in which stressfulness can be minimized or lessened. Physicians do not always find it easy to follow social workers' comments about patients' motivation and about human behavior in general. They are more likely to respond to interpretation of the psychosocial aspects of illness, because this is within their own frame of reference. Even a brief pointing up of the implications of illness, through use of social work knowledge and theory in relation to individual patients or situations in program planning, will enhance the significance of the social worker's contribution. This contribution is important because it has potential for increasing the effectiveness of medical care, preventing regression and disability, and promoting recovery. To become operative in multidiscipline practice, however, it must be visualized by social workers themselves as theirs to give, clearly formulated, and convincingly communicated and demonstrated to the interprofessional team.

SOME ASPECTS OF MULTIDISCIPLINE PRACTICE IN PUBLIC HEALTH

Multidiscipline practice in public health is not so structured as in clinical practice in the hospital, where the physician is constantly the leader. In public health practice several professions have always worked together. While the health officer as administrator must be regularly consulted on important decisions and kept informed of action, he does not participate in all the activity of the public health staff. Social workers and other staff members function relatively independently in some phases of their work or may combine in temporary working pairs and teams according to the nature of the assignments. When their desks are close together in the same office, they have much opportunity for informal interchange. They may also travel regularly together to various local centers and communities within their region to offer direct or consultant services as a team.

In contrast with the clinical illustration presented earlier in the chapter, let us consider a situation in which responsibility is placed upon a public health staff, as a result of state legislation, to implement a new program for premature infants or for children with cerebral palsy. The members of such a staff, with whom the social worker will be associated, may be a public health officer, other physicians, a sanitary engineer, public health nurses, nutritionists, health educators, physical therapists, and speech therapists. In undertaking a new program, the group is likely to start working through general staff meetings to outline their general responsibilities and approach. Later, subcommittees may be appointed and finally assignments appropriate to each profession will be defined. The public health nurses may accept responsibility for casefinding. The physicians will take responsibility for defining medical standards and interpreting the program to the medical profession. The social workers may develop methods for identifying psychosocial problems related to illness and handicap in families coming to clinics and hospitals.

Sometimes social workers are the first to identify health problems with social implications. For example, a social worker engaged in evaluating services for crippled children discovered that patients were remaining in orthopedic wards much longer than was necessary, with unduly long separation from their families. Such a situation may lead in many directions. First, there is likely to be a demonstration of medical social "discharge planning" at its best, wherein the medical and psychosocial needs of child and family are fully evaluated and covered in the aftercare planning. In addition, new medical and social policies in regard to long-term patients may be defined. In some situations the result may be the establishment of new social service departments in certain hospitals, where it is evident that the social needs of the crippled children are not being met.

Another public health situation might be one in which a social worker on a health staff finds wide gaps in understanding between health and welfare agencies—perhaps between county health and welfare departments, or between community visiting nurses and a family welfare agency staff. The social worker then plays the integrating role described as characteristic of medical social work. The worker moves between the two groups, helping the members of the two agency staffs and of the various professions to understand each other and to work together more smoothly. This role is possible because medical social work speaks the language of both health and welfare.

As in the hospital, everything the social worker does in public health is within the framework of multidiscipline practice. The same general principles of separate professional identity combined with constant interprofessional collaboration apply here. In public health the scene is broader and the approach more positive. The public health social worker will, however, be required to maintain a constant focus on the psychosocial needs of individuals and families within the context of community health. The ability to see the individual with the problem always as a representative of many others with the same need, to individualize and yet to think in group and community terms is a major characteristic of the public health approach. Social workers share this approach with other team members.

SOCIAL WORK CONSULTATION IN THE HEALTH FIELD

Consultation, which is used by many professions as a way of enlarging the practitioner's knowledge and skill, has been extensively employed by medicine and public health over a long period. The various professions adapt consultation to their own purposes and requirements. It has been found particularly appropriate to any field of practice where there is a large body of technical knowledge and method, and where several professions work closely together. This discussion focuses on that form of consultation that is characteristic of the health field, namely, consultation with professional associates within the framework of multidiscipline practice.[8]

Consultation is already an activity of considerable importance in medical, psychiatric, and school social work and is growing rapidly. There is a small literature on the subject in medicine, psychiatry, public health, and social work. Other fields of social work seem less concerned with it, with the exception of public welfare, where a somewhat differently focused activity, administrative consultation, has been defined.

Medical social consultation was first recognized as a distinct professional activity in public health programs, where social workers found that direct service was often impractical because of the large numbers of individuals and families needing service. It is now probably the major activity of social workers in public health programs. Subsequently, social workers in hospitals realized that they had been using consultation in an informal manner in the care of individual patients. By deliberately using consultation—rather than being directly active themselves in so many situations—they found that they could influence change in many areas, such as policies and programs. Consultation is now occupying a large enough segment of medical social workers' time so that departments are attempting to identify and define it, and are experimenting with ways of recording and counting these activities.

Consultation offers valuable gains in extending the service and contribution of medical social workers. Once a professional associate has been helped through consultation, he is able to apply what he has learned in other instances in the future so that more people are benefited in the long run. Some persons tend to think of consultation as a substitute for casework but this is not a helpful

---

[8] Social casework consultation, offered to experienced social workers by casework supervisors and focused on individual cases, is a distinct activity with different purposes and methodology. It is not included in this discussion.

approach. Each has its own distinct place as a professional activity. When a public health nurse and public welfare worker are well established in practice in a small community, a medical social worker will often find that help is most effectively given to families by working through these local workers, particularly if the family with the medical social problem is already known to them. Social workers should learn to identify more clearly those situations in which consultation is the method of choice.

Like program planning, consultation in medical social work is an important and growing but still relatively undefined professional activity. There is a great deal of talk about it but fully recorded and carefully analyzed examples are still rare. There is uncertainty as to whether it should be considered a function or process, or both. It has not yet received recognition in the social work curriculum. Workers in positions described as "consultant" usually carry other functions, which may lead to confusion in roles.

No single satisfactory definition of consultation, useful and authoritative for social work purposes, has yet been formulated. Some of the major characteristics of the activity that are repeatedly mentioned in the various discussions can be restated here.

The general purpose of professional consultation is to help the consultee solve some problem in his own work. In the typical situation the consultee recognizes his need for advice and takes initiative in seeking consultation. The consultant must be an expert in the area in which consultation is sought and his knowledge in this area must be greater than that of the consultee. The authority of the consultant rests on his knowledge and experience. He is not in a supervisory relationship with the consultee and exercises no administrative authority in relation to him. Medical social consultation is based on general social work knowledge and special knowledge regarding the psychosocial aspects of health, illness, and medical care, together with the professional experience of social workers in the health field. The social worker must have more than average security in his own knowledge and practice to function as a consultant.

As Doris Siegel points out, consultation should be accepted by the health agency or hospital as an appropriate activity and as having a place in its program.[9] Administrative support is essential in order that consultation may find its proper place in the activities and working schedule of the social work staff.

Certain steps are important in preparing the way for each new instance of consultation. Administrative channels must be carefully followed by clearing with the appropriate executive and supervisory personnel, who must be kept informed of progress. No matter how skillful a consultation interview, it can create more problems than it solves if it awakens suspicion and insecurity in other persons in the consultee's agency. Often a request for social work consultation will come through a public health nursing supervisor; but when a nurse requests help directly, the social work consultant should make certain that the supervisor supports the request. When consulting with a member of another profession, the social worker must be informed regarding that other profession and the nature of the consultee's current practice. The social work consultant must also acquire the necessary information regarding the problem, some of which may be gained in advance, as through reading records.

In medical social work, consultation is most frequently given to other members of the health professions and to social welfare personnel. What the medical social worker offers in consultation is related to the background of the consultee. Consultation offered to members of the health professions builds on their knowledge of illness and thus focuses on the psychosocial component in health, illness, and medical care. Consultation to social welfare personnel usually emphasizes the meaning and implications of illness and medical care, with special concern for the interaction between medical and psychosocial factors.

In this discussion consultation is regarded as potentially covering all of the usual content of social work practice, including individual cases, social policy, program planning, teaching, and

---

[9] Doris Siegel, "Consultation: Some Guiding Principles for Medical Social Workers," in Eleanor Cockerill, ed., *Social Work Practice in the Field of Tuberculosis* (Pittsburgh: School of Social Work, University of Pittsburgh, 1954), p. 197.

research. The distinctive feature is not the content but the process.

Consultation is essentially a process of shared thinking that brings to the consultee enlarged insight and increased ability to deal with the problem, but leaves with him responsibility for decision and action.[10] The social work consultant works only through the consultee in relation to the problem and its solution. It is an essential part of the concept that the consultant take no direct action in relation to the treatment of the situation or the solution of the problem.[11] This is a point which seems difficult to grasp and much confusion arises over it in practice.

Consultation rests on mutual understanding of, and respect for, the contribution of consultant and consultee.[12] In medical social work—as in all social work activity—the social work contribution is seen as being given through the medium of the professional relationship and thus the significance of the relationship between consultant and consultee is recognized. It is emphasized that the consultant should start where the consultee is, give him acceptance and support in his approach to the problem, and recognize his strengths. This positive way of moving into consultation is important in order that the consultee may not feel forced to defend himself against a too aggressive or threatening approach and may not become discouraged over his limited capacity to deal with the problem.

Starting where the consultee is means encouraging him to tell in his own way about his work, his role in his agency, and the problem that is troubling him. Even though some of this information might have been previously acquired, it should be sought directly from the consultee. It is essential that the consultant acquire sufficient understanding of the consultee's way of thinking and feel-

---

[10] Harriett M. Bartlett, "Consultation regarding the Medical Social Program in a Hospital," in *Consultation* (Chicago: American Association of Medical Social Workers, 1942), p. 11.

[11] The social work consultant may at times make limited contact with the client or situation in order to obtain firsthand information regarding the problem but is careful not to become involved in treatment, if he wishes to maintain the consultant role.

[12] Siegel, *op. cit.,* p. 197.

ing to be able to focus on the problem as that of the consultee and to present knowledge in such a way that it can be used by the consultee toward solving the problem in his own way and within his competence. Usually the joint effort to clarify the problem, which comes logically as the first step, provides the basis for the desired positive relationship. In the early stages, the social worker's main activity may be that of listening, showing interest, and asking a few good questions. From this point, in ongoing consultation the goal is to assist the consultee toward greater understanding of the psychosocial aspects of the problem and toward perceiving how he can deal with these aspects more effectively within his own competence.[13]

The following two examples show common types of consultation in medical social work. The first has to do with consultation on an individual case.

> A county nursing supervisor asked help of a social work consultant in a state health department in regard to a family with whom she and the local public health nurse had been working. The local nurse was a warm, outgoing middle-aged woman, with a successful professional experience, who had shown marked insight into several difficult behavior problems. She had been greatly concerned that she was not able to reach this family, particularly the mother. She had known the family for years and was able to give a full description of the situation. The mother, a college graduate, married a man below her in education and social status, who was running a small filling station that brought in an irregular income. The four children were a problem in school. They were coming to class dirty and unkempt, and the two oldest were showing a tendency to withdraw from their classmates and from group activities. The nurse thought they were ashamed of their cluttered, dirty home and did not want to bring their friends there. While at the local well-mothers' clinic recently, the mother discussed recurrent thoughts of suicide, with a constant smile on her face while talking, but reacted violently against any suggestion of psychiatric examination.
>
> The social worker suggested that they discuss the positives in the situation, particularly the nurse's good relationship with

---

[13] Acknowledgement is made to Addie Thomas for assistance in identifying the major elements in medical social consultation.

the mother. The nurse thought that if this were so, the woman should have followed her suggestions about cleaning up the children, after the school complained about their being dirty. As they talked about people's feelings in response to direct orders, the nurse said spontaneously, "I guess I was pretty directive, but how do you help such people?" The social worker then led the discussion toward what motivates people and why this woman might behave as she did. The nurse said she had never tried to know her better or talk with her about herself. She knew that the woman felt inadequate and the townspeople had a pretty poor opinion of her. Maybe the woman was reacting to this situation by feeling depressed. As they talked, the nurse's interest and confidence in her ability to help the woman grew. She felt that with this increased understanding and awareness she could avoid some of the earlier pitfalls. As she continued to visit the family during the next few months, she did a remarkably good job. With the nurse's encouragement, the woman began to clean her home, sent the children to school in better shape, and eventually co-operated in a plan for attending a psychiatric clinic.

The manner in which the public health nurse takes hold of the social work consultation to involve herself and to develop self-awareness in regard to her own activity can be clearly seen in this example. The manner in which the social worker assists the nurse to work on the problem in her own way can also be seen.

The second example concerns consultation on agency program.

In a general hospital the members of the social service department had become increasingly concerned over the inadequacies of the admission system in the out-patient department. While the social service director considered the admitting function inappropriate for social workers, she did consider that the department had responsibility in relation to the impact of this activity upon the patients and families. It was arranged with the hospital director that the casework supervisor would offer weekly consultation to the admitting officers in connection with their problems in working with patients and families. As the discussion proceeded, various problems emerged, such as misunderstandings regarding the functions of the social service department and difficulties arising out of the feelings of one admitting officer toward certain groups of patients. As the project progressed, the relationships between the department and the admitting office steadily improved. Because of the success of this project, a similar plan was set up in relation to the ward admitting office.

In this instance it can be seen how the social work consultant assisted the admitting officers to function more effectively in their administrative role with patients. A by-product of the consultation was an improved relationship between two hospital departments—admitting and social service. While these results were helpful to individuals, this is not to be regarded as a casework activity, since it was not a part of the services offered to a particular patient but was a definitely planned series of conferences focused on the operation of a hospital department.

Some Special Problems of Consultation

One of the common problems in social work consultation is that the consultant, responding to inner anxiety, presses the member of the other profession to go beyond his own appropriate area of competence in dealing with the problem and to undertake what is actually a social work role. Such action, which grows out of the social worker's concern over lack of social work personnel and the extent of unmet needs, leads the consultee into inappropriate activity and to ultimate confusion of roles. Another problem is that the social work consultant finds it difficult to release the problem to the consultee. The social worker functioning as a consultant must have sufficient maturity to accept the limitations of the process.

Examination of present practice shows the need for the social worker to be more aware of what is involved when choosing between direct service and consultation, or when moving from one to the other. The alternatives need to be consciously considered, leading to a definite decision.[14] It appears that some social work activities, such as the informal contacts with physicians and other members of the health professions as a part of the daily job, are now carried on without awareness that this is a professional activity that has in it the seeds of consultation. In fact, these daily con-

---

[14] Harriett M. Bartlett, "Perspectives in Public Health Social Work," *Children,* Vol. 1, No. 1 (January-February 1954), pp. 21–25.

tacts with other health personnel may in the long run prove more significant in influencing health services to people than some of the direct casework services to which much time is given today. If consultation is to become a professional process in social work, it requires more recognition and control than it is currently receiving.[15]

Medical social workers operating within the health field and lacking the prestige of some of the associated professions, have found that their opportunities for offering consultation are limited by their environment. They feel that in their understanding of the social and emotional problems of illness and medical care they have something to offer which is not being sought. They have learned that they can themselves create favorable opportunities for consultation by making contacts with others within or without their agency, showing interest in their problems, and raising stimulating questions. As has been found in reaching out to patients, preliminary contacts not infrequently lead to requests for assistance. In her own teaching, the writer was accustomed to describe this approach as "consultation with initiative." This eagerness of the consultant to become active might seem to run counter to the nature of consultation, which emphasizes that the consultee must be the one to seek help. If handled in a sensitive manner, however, it can be appropriate and effective.

In the foregoing review it has been emphasized that the social work authority in offering consultation rests on professional knowledge and experience. Like all social work practice, the giving of consultation uses the essential social work knowledge, values, and skill, as has been shown in the discussion. Consultation is likely to become a major activity of medical social work in the future. Knowledge and skill have reached the point where the process can be taught through regular educational channels. The teaching which

---

[15] Dr. Gerald Caplan and his associates have attracted interest through their analysis of consultation in mental health. While differing somewhat from the focus presented here, their analysis should be examined because it offers many useful ideas and suggestions regarding consultation as a professional process. *See* Gerald Caplan, *Concepts of Mental Health and Consultation* (Washington, D. C.: United States Children's Bureau, 1959).

has been going on through supervision of individual social workers and through institutes can be formalized, through the co-operation of those schools and professional groups that have special interest in this professional activity.

RECORDING AS A TOOL OF MULTIDISCIPLINE PRACTICE

Recording of professional practice is recognized as a small but important tool in medicine and social work. While it has been used mainly in clinical practice, its use in other areas in the health field is being recognized. Social workers and members of the other professions in the health field have in recent years become increasingly aware of the contribution of recording in more effective interprofessional communication.

Because of the emphasis on recording in both medicine and social work, it has been given considerable attention throughout much of the history of medical social work. In fact, in one sense it has received more attention than it deserves. Too often groups have been formed to discuss problems at the level of recording, when what was really needed was an effort to identify basic knowledge, concepts, and skills. It was not recognized that there could hardly be good recording until the professional thinking itself attained a certain degree of clarification. Under such circumstances, attention devoted to recording can become an evasion of more fundamental professional tasks.

Professional recording in medicine is usually described as being undertaken for the following purposes: (1) for responsible care of the patient, for the use of the individual practitioner and other members of the team; (2) for education and professional development, for professional students and to further development of professional practitioners; and (3) for research. In medicine careful records are also necessary for medico-legal purposes. Emphasis on one or another purpose will affect the form and content of the record.

Medical social workers share these purposes of medicine in

relation to recording. In addition, they must record for two audiences, since some records are written for their own use as social workers and others for the use of the medical team.

Social records for social service files have ranged from brief cards to folder records of many pages. At the period when verbatim recording was favored, all caseworkers in any field of practice dictated long records. Because of the increasing questions regarding expense and value of such detailed recording, the trend turned toward condensed methods of recording. There is a considerable social work literature on recording, and experimentation has been undertaken to find the most effective way of showing the diagnostic and treatment essentials as clearly and concisely as possible. One aspect has perhaps not received as much attention as it should, namely, the distinction between *chronological* and *analytical* methods of presenting material. Both are needed to some degree. The former was emphasized in the past and the latter appears to be favored at present.

Recording for the medical audience has been a special concern of medical social work, shared only with one other field, psychiatric social work. The unit medical record, which developed in hospitals in the twenties and thirties, was soon recognized as an important tool for co-ordinating the practice of specialists, including various team members, such as nurses and social workers. The most common type of medical social recording was a social summary, usually on a colored sheet of paper, filed as a part of the medical record.

Since this recording is intended for another profession, special principles apply. Clarity and conciseness are stressed. The idiomatic language of social work is avoided. There is special effort to present the patient as an individual in his particular social situation. The psychosocial aspects, their relation to illness and their meaning to the patient, are emphasized. The degree of responsibility assumed by the social worker and action taken are indicated. The guiding principle for selection and discarding of content is its relevance to the medical situation. These criteria were set forth with illustrative instances in the report of a professional committee in 1945.[16] In spite of the interest in the subject, this appears to be the only authoritative statement in the literature of medical social work.

In general, it may be said that this recording on the medical record has been a successful tool. While not all physicians read it, many do. Some medical teachers stress its importance for their students. Medical social workers have developed considerable skill and discipline in presenting the individual aspects of each patient's situation within the limits of a concise statement. Certain problems persist, however. Physicians need the social data while they are actually working on the case in the ward or clinic, which requires prompt reporting by social workers. Furthermore, since these reports are on a separate sheet, they are not available at a strategic place in the record where they will be readily seen by the physician actively engaged in making some decision about the patient. As a result of these problems, social service departments are increasingly writing notes in the body of the record, at the point where the information is immediately relevant to the medical treatment. Some departments have also agreed to get a preliminary social statement regarding a new patient into the record within twenty-four hours after referral, so that the doctors may have the data when they most need them. In some hospitals physicians have used the regular consultation sheet to request a social service report and recommendation on a case.

More recording of noncasework activities is needed for the advancement of the field. It will not be possible to identify the characteristics of such activities as administration, program planning, and consultation until valid instances of practice are put into written form, so that they can be analyzed. Social workers trained in casework are able to record their direct service, their teaching of medical students, and their research interviews, but find it difficult to make the transition to recording other types of activity. Somehow they must be freed from the fears and inhibitions that block them from taking this next essential step.

---

[16] "Report of Sub-Committee on Recording Social Data on Medical Records," *American Association of Medical Social Workers Bulletin*, Vol. 18, No. 3 (July 1945), pp. 46–61.

PARTICIPATION IN TEACHING OF MEDICAL STUDENTS AND OTHERS

Teaching of medical students and other professional students in the health agency is another important phase of multidiscipline practice. While it is an educational activity, it can be considered as part of practice since it takes place there. Medical social workers have been participating in this teaching for nearly fifty years. This is a well-established area of activity, consistently studied and developed. Principles have been established and many references are available in the literature.[17] Its major importance within the context of this discussion is not in terms of methodology but as a channel for influencing health programs and professions. This teaching offered the first opportunity to work through some channel other than direct service. The great advantage of being part of a field that teaches its students through clinical practice and invites social workers to participate has been recognized from the beginning.

In the early days, clinical teachers sometimes took the first step to initiate this teaching by asking social workers to meet with a group of medical students and "tell us what you do." Social workers soon learned, however, the inappropriateness of teaching social work directly to members of another profession. They found that they must become familiar with the educational curriculum and methods of the other profession and then adapt the social work material to its needs. The social worker's teaching objectives were formulated as follows: "The primary objective is to help the member of the other profession to become a better practitioner through greater understanding of psychosocial problems as they relate to illness and maintenance of health and through learning to

---

[17] Harriett M. Bartlett, *The Participation of Medical Social Workers in the Teaching of Medical Students* (Washington, D. C.: American Association of Medical Social Workers, 1939); Joint Committee of the Association of American Medical Colleges and the American Association of Medical Social Workers, *Widening Horizons in Medical Education* (New York: The Commonwealth Fund, 1948); *Medical Social Workers Participate in Medical Education: A Case Book of Illustrative Material* (Washington, D. C.: American Association of Medical Social Workers, 1954).

deal with these problems within his own area of competence."[18] It was recognized that the instruction about social work as a method and resource would be included only as one small part of this broader teaching.

Because this instruction is carried on within the framework of multidiscipline practice and aims to help the student achieve integration of medical and psychosocial concepts, social workers do not undertake this teaching alone but in association with medical teachers. In the search for suitable learning experiences, various methods were tried. The lecture method was found to be relatively ineffective. The student's own cases and experiences have been found to be the best starting point, with informal discussion in small groups as the best method. The early projects were too isolated from the rest of the instruction, but increasingly the teaching is becoming related to the curriculum as a whole.

This participation in the teaching of medical students, which began in a small way so many years ago, has now become part of a major change in medical education. This change is described by a medical teacher as

> ... a return and strengthening of interest in the patient himself, his emotional, social and environmental characteristics and problems, their effect on him and his disease and its effect on them. It seeks to correct the imbalance resulting from the emphasis placed on the science of medicine and, without losing the value of the latter, to neutralize the mechanizing and depersonalizing effect of the increasingly greater emphasis on the science of medicine. It is hoped that it will aid the student better to appreciate the human aspects of his patients and their illnesses, the nature and principles of the doctor-patient relationship, its significance in practice, how to deal with his own feelings as well as those of the patient, and his responsibility in that situation.[19]

---

[18] "Social Work Practice in the Teaching Relationship within Educational Programs of Other Disciplines," in *Social Work Practice in the Medical and Psychiatric Setting*, Institute Proceedings (Pittsburgh, Pa.: School of Social Work, University of Pittsburgh, 1951), p. 97. (Mimeographed.)

[19] John B. Youmans, "New Approaches to Education for the Practice of Medicine in Modern Medicine," *Medical Social Work*, Vol. 2, No. 4 (October 1953), pp. 137–138.

To this statement on the clinical aspects should be added the growing concern for the family, the community, and the sociocultural forces in society.

A joint committee of medical and social work teachers engaged in a study of this teaching formulated the two fundamental assumptions as follows:

> 1. There are three major features of illness—physical, emotional and social. These are so intimately interwoven in the pattern of disease that they must be considered together, rather than as separate entities. All three must be included in the curriculum if medical education is to provide the student with the knowledge and skills necessary to fulfill the aims of medicine.
> 2. The medical student should learn to recognize and understand the social factors in every case, to evaluate them in relation to the medical problem, and to assume responsibility (himself or through others) for the relevant problems as a part of diagnosis and treatment.[20]

As a part of this new orientation one basic change in the medical curriculum—long recommended by social workers because of their experience with their own students—is being made so that students in many medical schools, who formerly had only relatively brief contacts with patients as they moved rapidly from one clinical clerkship to another in the second half of their four years, are now given the opportunity to meet patients and families early in their course and to maintain a sustained relationship with them. The first assignment is often a family containing a pregnant woman. The student follows the mother and her child over one or more years, with interest also in the family as a unit. Families in which there is a problem of chronic illness are assigned in the same way. Advanced students also are given the opportunity to function as physicians in clinics, under the close supervision of a medical preceptor and with consultation available from a team of specialists, including medical social workers.

Social workers are participating at many points all through these new programs. They assist in the selection of families for assign-

---

[20] *Widening Horizons in Medical Education, op. cit.*, p. 5. See also, "The Objectives of Undergraduate Medical Education," *Journal of Medical Education*, Vol. 28, No. 3 (March 1953), pp. 57–59.

ment to medical students. They assist medical preceptors in regular teaching sessions based on discussion of student cases. They are full-time members of the staff in clinics manned by medical students, where they operate mostly as consultants to students but also give direct service to patients when indicated. They are also doing a good deal of informal teaching by being available to medical students for unplanned discussion of their cases, above and beyond the formally planned assignments.[21]

Within the broader goals of this teaching a number of distinct but interdependent objectives can be identified. In co-operation with the medical instructor, the medical social worker endeavors to help the medical student to:

1. Become aware of the significance and accept the role of psychosocial factors in health, illness, and medical care.

2. Understand these factors in general and recognize them in his own cases.

3. Accept responsibility for psychosocial factors in his own practice, including them regularly in his assessment of his patient and plan for medical treatment.

4. Have some awareness of the manner in which his own attitudes may promote or interfere with his best care of his patients.

5. Recognize the importance of his own relationship with his patient as a part of treatment.

6. Understand the broader implications of psychosocial factors in the health field and accept the resultant responsibilities of the physician in relation to community programs.

As in all professional teaching, these objectives require the social worker to be concerned with the teaching of knowledge, skills, and attitudes. Several emphases are frequently covered within one teaching session. For example, a medical student assumed that he had no responsibility for the follow-up of one of his patients, saying, "If they really want to come in, they can arrange it." As the social worker drew him into further conference about this partic-

---

[21] Recently medical and psychiatric social workers have been working together through a joint committee under the auspices of the National Association of Social Workers to analyze and improve their teaching of medical students. See *Participation of Social Workers in Medical Education* (New York: National Association of Social Workers, 1961).

ular patient's past history and difficulties, the student became increasingly interested and concerned. Finally he remarked, "Now you've individualized this patient for me and I think I have a better understanding of him." He then proceeded to telephone the patient and arranged to meet him at the clinic. Awareness, motivation, and understanding were all achieved in this single conference.

In regard to teaching of knowledge, a social worker who participates regularly in such seminars finds that she is often called upon to discuss such topics as social growth and behavior, attitudes toward illness, cultural implications of illness, and community resources.[22] Students frequently need or ask for help with their own feelings in such directions as feeling uncomfortable during a home visit; dealing with their sense of rejection when their assigned family does not turn to them for aid in a crisis; learning not to impose their own standards of behavior on patients; or having sufficient security to discuss the death of a member with a family. Such problems and many similar ones come up repeatedly in the course of this teaching. Many medical teachers definitely look to the social worker to take the initiative in such areas of instruction.

Sometimes this teaching is formally structured, while in other instances it is left quite fluid. One chief of medicine said that he made it his job to individualize patients to his students, during the course of ward rounds. He had an understanding with the social worker on the ward that after he had stimulated a student to come to her on a case, she would not take over the problem but would make every effort to help the student to learn as much as possible and carry all appropriate responsibility himself in the particular situation. It is important to note that once the goals are clear, such informal methods may prove fully as effective as the more formal projects.

Schools of public health are using social workers, along with social scientists and psychologists, to teach the psychosocial and sociocultural aspects of health and illness.[28] Because of public

---

[22] Alice Ullmann, "The Role of the Social Worker in Teaching Fourth-Year Medical Students," *Journal of Medical Education,* Vol. 34, No. 3 (March 1959), p. 242.

[28] Elizabeth P. Rice, "Teaching of Social Aspects in Schools of Public Health," *Medical Social Work,* Vol. 2, No. 4 (October 1953), pp. 148–158.

health emphasis on the community, the more limited use of field work, and the fact that the students are fully trained and experienced members of their respective professions, the pattern of teaching differs from that in medical schools. In this situation the medical social worker does a considerable amount of formal class instruction and may teach alone as well as with a multidiscipline team. The fact that this is a multidiscipline teaching situation, as regards students as well as faculty, indicates that new insights in relation to multidiscipline thinking and practice may emerge from this experience.

In hospitals and health agencies social workers are also participating in the teaching of students of other professional groups. The instruction of nursing students in the social aspects of illness developed early as a responsibility and for a while medical social workers in a considerable number of teaching hospitals were giving full academic courses to large classes. As the nursing profession developed its own interest and competence in this area of its practice and education, members of nursing school faculties were increasingly able to take over this phase of instruction, a development welcomed by medical social workers as both appropriate and desirable. Social work continues to contribute through less formal teaching channels. The ward social worker may meet with the student group and nursing instructor on the ward to discuss the psychosocial implications of selected cases known to the students. Or a social worker may confer with a nursing student on the social aspects of a nursing case study which she is preparing for one of her classes.

Social workers are contributing to the curriculum for training of hospital administrators, according to a teaching plan developed in co-operation with the American College of Hospital Administrators. When a student administrator is assigned for a period to a social service department, as a part of his experience during his intern year, there is an opportunity for effective teaching and demonstration by the social workers in the department. There is also some social work participation in classroom teaching.

Social workers participate less formally, perhaps through an occasional discussion with a student group, in the teaching of such other professional students as hospital chaplains, nutritionists, occupational and physical therapists, speech therapists, and others. The principles regarding objectives and methods developed in relation to the teaching of medical students have been found equally sound and applicable in relation to the instruction of other professional groups.

This participation in the teaching of other professions makes heavy demands upon social workers in the health field, because of the numbers of students and professions involved. Increasingly, recognition through faculty appointments and salary is being given to social workers who carry such responsibilities. Much of the less formal teaching, however, must still be carried by departments as a part of the regular job. Finding personnel and placing this activity appropriately within the department's total program require careful administrative planning.

The requirements and qualifications for such teaching have been defined in the literature.[24] There must be well-established practice of medical social work in the teaching agency as a demonstration and source of teaching material. The medical social worker must not only be a competent and secure practitioner but must also have learned how to translate the knowledge and experience of social work into a form appropriate for the other profession.

PARTICIPATION IN MULTIDISCIPLINE RESEARCH

Participation of social workers in multidiscipline research in the health field assumed importance as a formal activity only recently. From time to time in the past individual physicians have invited social workers who were associated with them to take part in various types of clinical research projects. Some of the results were published in medical journals. Other situations, when social workers were asked to play a limited role—as in doing follow-up on a group of patients or in obtaining social data according to a routine outline—proved less satisfying as a type of interprofessional collaboration from the social work viewpoint.

---

[24] *Widening Horizons in Medical Education, op. cit.,* **Chapter VI.**

With increasing interest in psychosocial aspects of illness and availability of grants for multidiscipline studies, projects are being set up in which there is regular provision for a social worker on the study staff and social workers are given opportunity to participate in the planning from the beginning. Examples are:

A series of studies relating to the emotional and social adjustment of cancer patients, carried on at the Massachusetts General Hospital between 1948 and 1951 by a team consisting of surgeons, psychiatrists, and social workers.[25]

A family health study, involving a comprehensive program of service and research in relation to a group of pregnant women and their families, under the auspices of the Harvard School of Public Health. The study team included obstetricians, pediatricians, public health nurses, nutritionists, social workers, and a consulting psychiatrist.[26]

A comprehensive survey of social work in hospitals in the United States, carried on between 1954 and 1956 through the collaboration of the American Association of Medical Social Workers, the American Hospital Association, and the Division of Public Health Methods of the United States Public Health Service.[27]

It is of interest to note that while some of these studies can be regarded as pure research, others frequently combine the giving of service with the study process.

The extent of social work participation in medical and public health research is not known, since no general survey has been made. The discipline and competence required of the social worker are so demanding that only a relatively small number of individuals in the field is qualified to participate. The activity is of great significance to the future of medical social work.

---

[25] Harley C. Shands, Jacob E. Finesinger, Stanley Cobb, and Ruth D. Abrams, "Psychological Mechanisms in Patients with Cancer," *Cancer,* Vol. 4, No. 6 (November 1951), pp. 1159–1170.

[26] Florence E. Cyr and Shirley H. Wattenberg, "Social Work in a Preventive Program of Maternal and Child Health," *Social Work,* Vol. 2, No. 3 (July 1957), pp. 32–39.

[27] American Hospital Association, National Association of Social Workers, and United States Public Health Service, *Social Work in Hospitals* (Washington, D. C.: U. S. Public Health Service Publication No. 519, 1956).

implications for practice

11

implications and trends

The foregoing chapters have presented an analysis of social work in the health field. It remains to consider the implications of this analysis.

This monograph was undertaken because of the urgently felt need to obtain a comprehensive view of the practice of social work in the health field—to see all its components together and to grasp their relationships—so as to understand better what is needed for improving the effectiveness of that practice. The analysis involved using the three frames of reference proposed for analyzing social work practice in any particular field. The first provides for analysis of the essential elements in social work practice, the second provides for analysis of the general characteristics of the particular field (in this instance, the health field) as distinguished from the operations of the social worker in that field, and the third provides for the application of the essentials of social work practice in the particular field and the identification of the characteristics of the resulting social work practice. The approach emphasizes knowledge and values as the major elements influencing focus and growth of professional social work practice.

A working definition of social work practice, which is being developed by a committee representing social work as a whole, was used as the starting point. The essential elements in social work practice, as there identified, offer a frame of reference within which any piece, or subdivision, of practice can be described. The reader will have observed how all these elements—value, purpose, sanction, knowledge, and method—have appeared in medical social work. This practice encompasses individuals, families, groups, and communities. The major social work values are present, with the worth of the individual and the optimal functioning of individuals and groups placed squarely in the center. The identification of the medical social worker with those being served is constant and unquestioned. These social work activities clearly rest on basic knowledge of human behavior and social welfare policy and services. The social work methods are all applicable, though as yet unevenly employed. Social casework is the most widely used method. Social group work is developing fast. There is much activity in community planning but only a beginning in conscious application of community organization principles. The related methods of administration, teaching, and research are all being actively used. The professional relationship with other persons—whether clients or professional associates—is definitely recognized as the medium through which service is given. Observation, examination, and this preliminary analysis reveal that the essentials of social work practice are present, in varying degrees. More rigorous analysis through formal study is, of course, desirable.

Our primary interest is centered on the characteristics of the resulting social work practice when the essentials—as defined in the *Working Definition*—are applied in the health field. How were the characteristics identified? The health field was first analyzed separately so that its characteristics could be recognized and described in orderly form. This analysis covered: (1) the problem (condition) of central concern, (2) the system of organized services (programs, agencies, professions), (3) the body of knowledge, values, and method, (4) the sociocultural attitudes (in society), and (5) the characteristic responses and behavior of persons served. Social work practice and health practice were then brought together. Medical social work is the result of this integration. It was found that the over-all purposes and values of the health field are congenial to social work, so that sound integration can take place. Two principles that guide integration were constantly kept in mind. When functioning in a non-social work environment social work collaborates continuously with the other professions but must maintain its own identity. Social work becomes a part of the larger program. It continually influences, and is influenced by, the environment in which it operates.

The focus in studying practice is upon the operating social worker's activities, but with a long perspective that stresses potential as well as current contributions. The distinguishing characteristics must be demonstrated in the social work practice itself, not outside it in the setting. In working in a larger program one major social work aim is to make knowledge and appreciation of psychosocial factors operative in that program toward meeting people's needs more effectively. Thus first emphasis must logically be placed upon developing awareness, understanding, and acceptance of these factors and of the services related to them. Obviously social work will not be used unless there is such acceptance. The next step is actual rendering of the appropriate collaborative services and carrying through of related activities, either in direct contact with patients or in working through such indirect channels as consultation and participation in program planning. Social work must have a recognized and established place in the program. Its activities must be significant for the central purpose, not peripheral. It brings a substantive contribution of its own and should be in a position to deliver its services not only with and through the other professions but also through its own initiative and expertness.

CHARACTERISTIC ACTIVITIES OF SOCIAL WORKERS IN THE HEALTH FIELD

Through the analysis undertaken in this monograph much progress has been made in identifying the characteristics of social work practice in the health field. In order that they may be viewed together, the major characteristics are listed at this point. The basic knowledge of social work is assumed and only those features identified with practice in the particular field, the health field, are emphasized. The characteristics are formulated as activities and operations of professional social workers.

Placing Social Work in the Health Field

- Clarifying and demonstrating to professional associates and others the psychosocial aspects of health, illness, and medical care and their meaning to patients and families. The social worker is able to make this contribution through the particular insights offered by a helping relationship and constant identification with the patient, and through being a part of the health situation and viewing the problems from the patient's viewpoint.
- Identifying the components of a psychosocial focus in social work terms and the manner of its development and integration in a particular non-social work program, that of the health field.
- Clarifying the social work role and contribution in a complex, elaborately structured, authoritative, and scientific environment, where practice, education, and research are intimately interwoven.
- Maintaining social work identity and focus in the health setting, under various stresses and pressures peculiar to this environment.
- Managing potentially conflicting professional roles in concurrent identification with the patient and the medical team.
- Developing a comprehensive and balanced approach to social work activities and programs, working concurrently through two channels (in direct contact with patients or through collaboration with others), and keeping these various social work activities appropriately related. These activities are open to social workers because of their opportunities for participating in the major functions in health programs relating to patient care and program planning.

Applying the Social Work Essentials in the Health Field

- Dealing with the body of medical and public health knowledge, which is scientific and technical, distinct from social work knowledge, and not extensively used by other social workers; translating selected concepts into a social work frame of reference; keeping medical and social work concepts continuously related.
- Developing and testing generalizations regarding psychosocial aspects of health, illness, and medical care, on the basis of social

work knowledge and experience, with particular reference to regression, dependency, disability, and rehabilitation; incurable and terminal illness; the psychosocial aspects of specific medical conditions; the impact of health programs and medical care on individuals and families; health problems as related to the phases of the life cycle; and similar phenomena.
- Formulating social work knowledge, values, insights, and judgments in a form meaningful and useful for communication with the health professions.
- Working with physically ill and handicapped persons; meeting special problems such as deformity, mutilation, stigma, and social rejection associated with illness and handicap. This is done through application of social casework and social group work in helping individuals who may be regressed, isolated, limited in mobility, or otherwise affected by physical illness and handicap.
- Strengthening health programs and community resources for health care, with particular concern for their psychosocial aspects: through the use of principles and methods from administration and community organization, for the purpose of removing barriers that prevent the utilization and continuity of care, encouraging concern for the individual, increasing awareness of psychosocial stresses, and enlarging opportunities for prevention and rehabilitation.
- Identifying the special requirements of social work practice in the health field for mastery—through the practitioner's professional use of self—of intellectual and emotional responses to illness and handicap, to the subculture of the hospital and health program, and to multidiscipline practice.

Using Methods Characteristic of the Health Field

- Carrying on (and adapting, as indicated) all social work activities within the framework of multidiscipline practice; functioning as members of many types of health teams.
- Sharing patient (client) relationships with members of other professions in the health field.
- Communicating social work knowledge and judgments to other professions and sharing in planning, decision-making, and other

joint thinking, through both informal and formal channels of multi-discipline practice.
- Offering social work consultation to other members of the health team and to community agencies, as an increasingly important means of strengthening the social aspects of health services, in relation to patient care, programs, teaching, and research.
- Participating in the teaching of students from medicine, nursing, and other professions in the health field and in appropriate areas of medical research.
- Exploring and demonstrating ways of reaching out to individuals, families, and groups actually or potentially under stress, through being close to a large potential clientele; exploring methods of screening to determine social problems and social needs related to health, illness, and medical care.
- Exploring and developing ways of influencing medical care to become more responsive to the psychosocial needs of individuals, families, groups, and communities.
- Experimenting with, and contributing to, a preventive approach and emphasis in social work, using the well-developed philosophy, body of knowledge, and experience in public health relating to prevention, which is further advanced in this field than in most other fields of professional practice.

Awareness of Feelings and Assumptions

These professional social work activities can be regarded as roles, tasks, responsibilities, and opportunities associated with this particular field. Obviously, some are already well developed, while others are at an early stage—but still exceedingly important for social workers in this field to recognize and implement in the future. For such activities, disciplined self-awareness and professional use of self are essential. In every field social workers must come to terms with the special aspects of the practice which strike practitioners with disturbing emotional impact. In the health field the primary adjustment will be in relation to the upsetting, sometimes overwhelming, problems of physical helplessness, deformity and mutilation, incurable progressive illness, and death. The social worker must learn not to withdraw from and evade these problems and these patients because of his own reactions. The social worker must also come to terms with the special manifestations of authority as it appears in the health field and with the basic discipline of being able to share a large portion of one's professional activity with professional associates.

It is evident, however, that the competent social worker in the health field must develop more than awareness of feelings as stressed in current social work education and supervision. In this analysis, the following types of awareness have been found necessary for the competent practitioner. There must be awareness in relation to:

1. Emotional bias in working with patients, families and others.
2. Emotional responses to characteristic problems of illness, handicap, and medical care.
3. Cultural bias related to social class and ethnic group.
4. Professional and personal value assumptions.
5. Identification and use of knowledge (tested and untested generalizations) in practice.

The social worker who is practicing within a different frame of reference than his own, as in the health field, requires the clarity and security that come from all these types of awareness in combination. In a scientifically oriented field the last two, awareness of value assumptions and conscious use of social work knowledge, are particularly important. It may be that all these types of awareness will be found necessary in all fields of social work practice. Their specific content and the relative emphasis placed on each may differ between fields.

SIGNIFICANT VARIATIONS BETWEEN FIELDS

A next logical question is whether any of these characteristics of social work practice in the health field represent significant variations as compared with the rest of social work practice. This is not a question of "specialized" educational preparation within the basic professional curriculum but of the requirements for competent practice within the particular field. Since social work does not have any general practice against which to compare a particular field, these significant variations cannot be fully identified until all the fields have been authoritatively analyzed and described, with the use of sufficiently similar frames of reference so that comparison is possible and valid. A beginning can be made when one or two other fields have been analyzed for comparison. The unlike elements, or variations, must be found within the social work practice itself, not outside it in the setting. As a test of significance, it is suggested that there must be some recognizable difference in the social work knowledge, values, and methods, a difference which either in depth or comprehensiveness goes beyond what is needed elsewhere in practice. The knowledge must be formulated in generalizations, the values conceptualized, and the method elements demonstrated in transferable techniques, all appropriate to social work. A further way to identify the significance of these variations would be in the specific contribution they make to the social work profession and to the particular field. Value would be found in their potential for stimulating new questions and hypotheses to guide the further development of social work practice.

Clearly, then, identification of the significant variations between the health field and others must await further analysis of social work practice in the various fields and comparison of the results. At this point it is only possible to speculate regarding those characteristics of social work in the health field which seem to have potential for becoming significant variations when compared with social work practice in other fields. When eventually identified, such variations will indicate the distinctive responsibilities, problems, and opportunities that are to be found in the health field. They will eventually be formulated as criteria for competent practice in the field.

Definition of the requirements for competent practice in the various fields is urgently needed, in order to define the responsibilities of agencies, schools, and individual workers themselves for developing this competence in practitioners. It is evident that all the concepts and theory regarding the health field that have been presented in the course of this analysis could not be encompassed in the two-year curriculum, together with comparable concepts and theory regarding other fields. Furthermore, some of the learning demands a maturity which develops only with experience. It seems doubtful that all could be acquired through individual practice on the job. The considerable body of theory relating to the integration of social work in the health field and the psychosocial aspects of health, illness, and medical care appears to call for academic methods of teaching and learning, thus involving ongoing participation of schools as well as agencies.

Up to this point we have been considering the attainment of competence, which means practicing effectively in a particular field. Now it is important to note the distinction between competence and specialization. After developing competence in one field, such as the health field, the social worker who continues to practice in the field and to extend his mastery of knowledge, values, and skills in this setting eventually becomes a true specialist. It is not clear what criteria will later be employed to define specialization in social work, but it seems likely that some types will be related to advanced competence, including depth and breadth of knowledge, in particular fields of practice.

IMPLICATIONS FOR ONGOING PRACTICE

As has been shown, the principles and generalizations relating to comprehensive analysis of social work in the health field must be applied at the level of the operating worker, the social service department or unit, and the total group of workers in the field. The individual worker encompasses within his practice all the basic social work essentials, with the special emphases characteristic of the particular field. The social work unit builds its program through selection and balanced integration of the various appropriate functions. The total body of professional workers in the field carries responsibility for development of the practice as a whole, with special concern for producing expert personnel—practitioners, program planners, teachers, writers, researchers—and for expanding the body of knowledge.

Because this discussion has to do with social work in the health field, the focus is naturally upon the integration of social work in that area of practice. Before concluding this discussion, however, it is also important to give consideration to the relation of medical social work to its own profession, that is, to social work as a whole. Now that we have a basic concept of social work practice, this relationship can be more clearly defined than formerly, when such a framework was lacking.

Co-operation between social agencies is one area in which many problems exist. Since some of these problems arise from the differing orientations between social workers in different fields of practice, these problems should be identified and examined in the health field, with a view to improved interagency co-operation.

Social work agencies and departments have responsibility for supervision of workers and for staff development. Multidiscipline practice in the health field requires that the individual social worker be able to handle the job and make many decisions independently, without easy and constant access to supervision. This may have leavened some of the tendencies to oversupervision—currently a concern of the profession—but the problem is present in this field, as elsewhere.

The field instruction of social work students in the basic social work curriculum is another area of responsibility. Since the hospital has always been a center of clinical teaching, it offers a favorable milieu for such social work teaching. Public health agencies, also, are increasingly being used for field work. In medical social work an ongoing national professional committee on education has concerned itself regularly with methods and standards of fieldwork instruction and has undertaken some pioneer studies in this area. Although field instruction is recognized as a major educational method in social work, it still awaits authoritative analysis and evaluation by the profession. Problems related to its use in a non-social work setting, such as the hospital and public health agency, call for particular consideration.

The participation of medical social workers in multidiscipline research has been discussed. They also have responsibility to carry on their own research. Such studies have been undertaken under the auspices of the medical social work group as a whole, consistently throughout its history. But social workers who are closest to practice, in hospitals and health agencies, have not themselves taken responsibility to examine and report on their practice to the degree that might be expected, considering that they are in an environment where research is customary and welcomed. One might anticipate finding many social service departments and schools of social work, through their own initiative, in collaboration on such studies. What is the explanation for this lag? Have social workers' energies been too widely dissipated by the effort to meet the many demands of the stimulating multidiscipline environment, often with limited personnel? Have local practitioners been leaning too heavily on the activities of their national committees? Or have they left too much to medical leadership? Certainly the general situation now seems favorable for direct research in medical social work practice.

Social workers in the health field have responsibility for keeping open the channels of communication with leadership groups in the health professions. This means maintaining relations with the health professions at the national level. There needs to be consistent joint thinking where the interests and responsibilities of the professions converge. Medical teachers and medical schools are at the growing edge of medicine in relation to comprehensive care; hospital administrators are concerned with expanding hospital functions; and public health has its own responsive and creative leaders. Medical social work should be constantly engaged with some of these representatives of medicine and public health in serious thinking about long-range objectives.

Finally, social workers in each field of practice have responsibility for keeping up with the developments in their field, analyzing them, and conveying the results back to the social work profession, for use in practice and education. The social workers who will be able to make such a contribution are those who practice continuously in the health field and really master its content to the degree of expertness. There should thus be a constant flow of material from social workers in the health field to the profession as a whole, a flow which can be more rapid and efficient now that all social workers are within one organization. Regular channels for its accomplishment should be established. This is undoubtedly one of the major responsibilities of any field to the profession and a chief way in which the profession grows.

SEEKING NEW WAYS

This is an era of unprecedented movement and change in cultural and living conditions. In such a rapidly shifting social scene there are bound to be calls for new types of service and exploration of new ways of rendering service. Certain questions are useful in starting new directions of thinking. What, for instance, are the best points of intervention for giving effective service? In the past, the traditional method of intake in the hospital has been through referral of cases by physicians and others who perceived problems. Present knowledge suggests that help is more effective if given earlier, before problems develop, or at the very point of crisis when a relatively small amount of help may radically shift the situation toward the better. The identification of such situations requires sharpened diagnostic ability in recognition of incipient symptoms of stress and of vulnerable individuals who are at the point of readiness for help. The time and the place are important. Medical social workers are already experimenting in working in other places than the traditional clinic and ward. They do not always wait for referrals but reach out to find those to whom service can be given.

During the highest point of psychiatric emphasis in social casework the "intensive, long-term case" attained a superior status and those workers who had a high proportion of briefer cases were regarded as in some way inferior. Now there is increasing emphasis on the effectiveness of the brief piece of casework, with recognition that equal skill is required and that more persons can be helped through this channel. Evidence is growing that a small number of contacts—sometimes a single interview—when skillfully focused at the right time and place, can be of definite help. There are also promising possibilities in a single interview with the client combined with consultation offered to a member of another profession (such as physician or nurse) to help him recognize the social problem and deal with it himself. Telephone contacts are being studied and evaluated.

It is evident that there has been too much concentration on serving the individual client and that there must be movement toward working with families, groups, and communities. New bodies of knowledge, new diagnostic skills, new methods of bringing about change, are all implied. Some of these are suggested in this monograph and others will only be discovered in the course of actual experimentation.

We need to examine our frameworks of thinking, since these condition our activity. Certain concepts—the social component in illness and medical care, the social worker functioning in the medical setting and medical team, and the meaning of illness to the patient—have dominated our thinking in the past and will continue to be important. A fresh analysis of medical social work from new approaches, such as the life cycle continuum suggested by Cockerill and Gossett, will suggest ways of using knowledge and channels of service not as yet fully utilized.[1]

Health services are basic in our society and affect many millions of persons. Through being a part of such health programs, medical social work is related to large numbers of people. The opportunity for a single group of social workers to view their work so comprehensively is unusual in social work practice. When fully developed, this practice will encompass all of the social work essentials evenly applied and consciously used in relation to each other. The understanding of the meaning of illness to the patient derived from social casework with individual patients is used in teaching medical students. The knowledge of social stresses in community living derived from the experience of social workers in public health is used in influencing social policies and programs. It appears that medical social work has a special opportunity for such a comprehensive view and activity because care of patients, teaching, and

---

[1] Eleanor Cockerill and Helen Gossett, *The Medical Social Worker as Mental Health Worker* (New York: National Association of Social Workers, 1959).

research all commonly take place in hospitals and medical centers, and because social workers are employed both within institutions and also in broad health programs covering large populations.

New thinking and knowledge suggest ways of refocusing goals and activities. With limited personnel, there is still the persistent question of selection; but the decision is no longer limited to case selection and now relates to different ways of serving different groups of people or bringing about change in various aspects of programs. We have made gains in that we no longer feel we have to do it all ourselves and thus are freed from the old problem of "100 percent referrals" that kept mounting beyond the capacity of the social service staff to deal with them. We no longer feel that we must wait for others—for patients to come to the hospital or physicians to refer cases—but see ways of moving out to offer help through our own initiative. We are ready to move into new settings and new roles, if there is promise that what we have to bring will be helpful. There is room for courageous experimentation and demonstration, with built-in methods of evaluation so that assessment may be combined with service.

Greater proficiency in abstract thinking will be necessary for progress in concept construction and theory building. In the medical social work literature there is repetitive discussion of psychosocial problems of various illnesses and conditions without arrival at a consensus on core concepts. The tendency in casework thinking to emphasize unique differences rather than common characteristics appears in the health field as well as in others. The need for consistency and continuity in thinking is so great, in relation to investigating practice and formulating theory, that serious thought should be given to the possibility of developing one or more research centers where these needs of the field could be met through planned and cumulative effort.

A LONG VIEW

This analysis shows that if social work in the health field—or in any other field—is to make its appropriate contribution in future years, the following principles must apply:

- Social work activities must be seen as a whole and developed with a long-range view, which frees the individual social worker from involvement in temporary, inappropriate activities and permits emphasis on social goals, understanding of human needs, and effective professional service.
- The long-range responsibilities of social work involve an ongoing, substantive contribution in two directions: (1) to the particular field of practice (such as the health field), and (2) to the social work profession.
- The practice must incorporate the essentials of social work and be clearly established within the particular field.
- There must be balance in selection of, and emphasis upon, the various potential activities (such as doing casework or building social policy), based on understanding of the manner in which they interact to contribute to the total social work effort in the field.
- There must be motivation and flexibility for growth, which means keeping up with advancing knowledge, recognizing new needs and trends, and experimenting with new directions of thinking and rendering services.
- Continuous, progressive testing and validation of the application of social work knowledge, values, and methods in the particular field are essential.

Thus, as has been shown throughout this monograph, effective social work practice in any particular field depends upon a clearly defined relationship to its profession and to the field in which it operates. Until recently, conflicting influences made such definition difficult, if not impossible. It is doubtful if any single field could have solved its problems alone in the past. Now an integrated system of values and knowledge—of defined goals and generalizations based on social work practice—is emerging to provide the necessary foundation.

This comprehensive analysis of social work practice in the health field has proved fruitful and illuminating. Because the field of social work practice here analyzed involves extensive use of an additional body of scientific knowledge (health and disease) and practice within such strongly established major social institutions in our society (medicine and public health), the method and the findings of the analysis stand out with special clarity. While many problems remain unsolved, we can now perceive clearly how we arrived where we are and the important choices to be made in moving into the future. We have a consistent set of concepts within which to examine any particular phase of our practice. We need no longer fear division or overspecialization, because we see that what we share with other social workers is more important than our differences. We know that our practice rests on the social work essentials which are the same for all fields.

The philosopher Alfred North Whitehead points out that the practice of a profession cannot be separated from its theoretical understanding, and vice versa.[2] Social work has at last reached a stage of development where it has the motivation and the means to undertake comprehensive analysis of its practice. The analysis presented in this monograph indicates the evident need for such ongoing comprehensive analysis and clarification of social work practice in the health field, in other fields, and in the profession as a whole. Such an undertaking would be truly what Whitehead calls "an adventure of ideas," with promise of enabling the profession to move steadily toward recognition of its distinctive contribution in society and achievement of its full potential in service.

---

[2] Alfred North Whitehead, *Adventures of Ideas* (New York: The Macmillan Company, 1933), p. 72.

appendix

agencies in the health field

Below are listed the kinds of agencies in which medical social workers work.[1] The listing is in the approximate historical order in which medical social work has become a part of the agency service.

I. Private and Public Hospitals

    General hospitals
    Children's hospitals
    Special hospitals
        Chronic care
        Sanatoria
        Cancer
        Research
    Maternity homes
    Convalescent homes
    Domiciliaries

II. Clinics

    Outpatient departments

---

[1] This list is from the *Description of Medical Social Work Practice* (Appendix I, pp. 24–25), prepared by a subcommittee of the Medical Social Work Section, National Association of Social Workers, for the Council on Social Work Education, 1958. (Mimeographed.)

Special diagnostic clinics (for example, cardiac and orthopedic)
Community clinics
Regional offices (Veterans Administration)
Public health
  Prenatal clinics
  Well-baby clinics
  Crippled children's clinics
  Special diagnostic clinics such as tuberculosis, cardiac, cancer

III. Rehabilitation Units

Hospitals and outpatient departments
Clinics
Centers
Vocational rehabilitation
  As staff members in offices of vocational rehabilitation in relation to physical restoration and vocational rehabilitation

IV. Public Health and Preventive Medicine

Federal governmental programs
Public Health Service
  Divisions of Tuberculosis, Heart Disease, Chronic Disease
  Division of Hospitals
Children's Bureau
  Division of Health Services
  Crippled Children
  Maternal and Child Health
State health departments
Local health departments, city and county
Voluntary organizations such as the American Cancer Association, the American Heart Association, The National Foundation

V. Community Organizations

Health sections of community welfare federations and councils

Divisions of services to individuals of community welfare federations and councils

VI. Public Welfare

In federal, state, and local units, as consultants and/or in direct service to individuals with regard to health problems. (The latter service is more apt to be found in local welfare departments.)

VII. Professional Schools

Schools of social work
Medical schools
Schools of public health
Schools of nursing

In the latter three, medical social workers may be members of the faculty, full- or part-time, or may be engaged in clinical teaching

5M/61–66/M&H
1M/4/72

DATE DUE

BRODART Cat. No. 23-221